Thought leadership from world leading management academics, coupled with Ram Charan's unique ability to make dense and fairly complex content digestible for business leaders, *The Phoenix Encounter Method* is a must-read for HR and other leaders facing an incredibly difficult business terrain marked by COVID, social unrest, and economic downturn, and then use the method to navigate a new path forward.

> —JOHNNY C. TAYLOR, Jr., CEO, Society for Human Resource
> Management, and coauthor of *The Trouble with HR*

The need to find a burning platform to catalyze change has been well documented. What has received less attention is a way of preparing for and responding to this challenge. At DBS, we found that it paid to be paranoid, to anticipate competition from unlikely contenders, to try and master the new technologies to stay a step ahead. *The Phoenix Encounter Method* takes many of our learnings and packages them in a program (and in this book) that seems very impactful. It is a systematic way to prepare defense and launch offense, leveraging new work styles and technologies. A fantastic read for leaders seeking to survive and succeed in this dramatically changing world.

> —PIYUSH GUPTA, CEO and Director, DBS Group

Written by true experts in the field, *The Phoenix Encounter Method,* is a direct and clear-eyed approach to help leaders manage and survive potentially fatal disruptions to their businesses. As exogenous threats continue to make obsolete conventional thinking about managing uncertainty, the authors provide an invaluable and practical roadmap to help leaders successfully navigate an increasingly complex landscape. At stake is not just a methodology to help improve a business, but often an approach to save it.

> —PAUL MEEHAN, Senior Partner and former Regional
> Managing Partner, Bain & Company

Although disruptions and a rapidly changing environment present many risks to organizations, they also represent transformative opportunities. This well-researched book provides a practical and actionable approach for leaders in any sector or industry to face up to disruption and protect their business by helping them to find new responses and ways of thinking. A must-read.

> —PATRICK CESCAU, Chairman, InterContinental Hotels
> Group, and former CEO Unilever

Platforms and ecosystem-based business models are powering growth, innovation, and the future, fueled by massive technology shifts in big data, the Cloud, AI, and Edge computing. *The Phoenix Encounter Method* is vital reading for leaders and executives currently facing unprecedented challenges to drive innovation, growth, and resilience for a modern connected world.

—RALPH MUPITA, CEO, MTN Group Limited

The Phoenix Encounter Method is not only a powerful reframing of the importance of disruptive change in organizations, but it is also just as importantly a hands-on tool for the leaders who are responsible for invoking that change. *The Phoenix Encounter Method* stresses the necessity of swiftly and courageously breaking down systems that aren't working, but it equally provides future-facing blueprints for rebuilding from the ground up, encouraging readers (and leaders) to revisit their roles with radical debate and courageous flexibility".

—KEVIN RYAN, CEO and Founder Alleycorp; Founder, MongoDB Inc.

In this world of massive enterprise transformation, *The Phoenix Encounter Method* is a fresh approach for business to build your fortune and shape your differentiation using new strategic thinking tools developed by expert INSEAD faculty and Ram Charan. What makes this method so different, is that it can be used by leaders at any level, industry, or geography to create cut-through, actionable strategic options and moves, and is tested by more than 1,500 practitioners.

—RAJ VATTIKUTI, Founder and Chairman, Atimetrik Corporation, USA

Is it important for you that the spirit of renewal and innovation permeate your organization? If yes, you must read *The Phoenix Encounter Method*. This book showcases the exemplary thought leadership that you would expect from leading academics at INSEAD. The authors created the Phoenix Encounter Method to help leaders leverage the instruments of disruption to their advantage. COVID-19 increases the urgency for organizations to use this method to develop a bespoke script for their future.

—ILIAN MIHOV, Dean of INSEAD and the Rausing Chaired Professor of Economic and Business Transformation

The Phoenix Encounter is not for the faint-hearted. Experiencing it at INSEAD's Advanced Management Program led by Ian Woodward and seeing your course colleagues and faculty dismantle what you'd thought was a robust and defendable business with disarming ease was confronting. The real value was in the systems thinking around how to proactively plan to evolve and reshape your business to meet the emerging threats. The principles and processes learned through *The Phoenix Encounter* have been put to good use in our business in response to the COVID pandemic and the unstoppable forces it has unleashed.

—GLEN SOWRY, CEO Metlifecare, New Zealand

Leading a rapidly growing company in an uncertain and volatile industry requires diverse and opposing viewpoints during strategic debates. I was introduced to the Phoenix Encounter Method while attending an Advanced Management Program at INSEAD. It facilitated the radical thinking that is crucial for crafting our desired future while navigating previously unknown obstacles. I strongly recommend this book to any CEO or company executive involved in crafting business strategy. The book will be prescribed reading for my exco. It is a truly powerful method.

—ANDRIES VAN HEERDEN, CEO, Afrimat Limited

The Phoenix Encounter Method is relevant not only at the enterprise level, but also at functional or process levels. It can ask the question: How will we perform for our customers if we completely eliminate some function or process? This forces critical dialogue around waste, non-value-adding work, streamlining, and automation. The creativity and open mind thought process the Encounter method encourages has helped us redefine how work gets done, and in many cases to completely reinvent some functions, freeing up resources to further accelerate growth.

—STANLEY KOCON, CEO, Voith Hydro Inc. North America

Adaptive leadership is among the most important determinants of success for businesses today, and the team at INSEAD strike at the essence of that with the work they do. I have witnessed this firsthand through the programs they have led with our senior leadership group over a number of years. I credit that work as an important factor in the success and growth the business has been able to achieve.

—SCOTT CHARLTON, CEO, Transurban Group, Australia

Global leaders face unprecedented challenges and urgently need a very different kind of strategic debate. *The Phoenix Encounter Method* is a breakthrough process to help them do this. Switch attitudes and undertake the kind of "no-holds barred debates" that must shape future options to reinvent their future.

—PAULA CALIGIURI, D'Amore-McKim School of Business
Distinguished Professor, Northeastern University, and author of
Cultural Agility

The Phoenix Encounter Method is needed by everyone. And now more than ever I strongly recommend this book for business leaders who want to boldly and robustly innovate their businesses for the future.

—SERGUEI NETTESSINE, Dhirubhai Ambani Professor of
Innovation and Entrepreneurship, Wharton School of Business,
and coauthor of *The Risk-Driven Business Model*

I have used the Phoenix Encounter method in my consulting and executive education sessions, and the results are nothing short of amazing. Turning off the blinkers is hard, but the method allows leaders to break through this with unique tools and processes. The encounter method is based on deep insights from decades of academic and practice-based research. I strongly recommend this book".

—SHANTANU BHATTACHARYA, Deputy Dean, and Lee
Kong Chian Professor of Operations Management, Singapore
Management University

Before being Aldus Dumbledore's favorite bird in Harry Potter, the Phoenix was in Greek mythology the bird that cyclically regenerated itself from the ashes of its predecessor. *The Phoenix Encounter Method* is no mythology though. It is in fact a critical milestone in business strategy. It tackles one of the most difficult challenges any successful organization faces at some point: legacy, complacency, and the status quo. Read this book to become your own (best) enemy, adopt the Phoenix Attitude and reinvent your organization!

—THIBAUT MUNIER, Cofounder and Co-CEO, Numberly

The Phoenix Encounter Method presents a novel and engaging method for cultivating the mindset necessary to recognize the threats that even successful businesses face at this time of unprecedented change. It channels radical ideas and disruptive trends to bring a fresh perspective and guides leaders to rethink in detail how to remake their organization for the future. If you want to own the future in the post COVID-19 digital era, instead of being burnt by it, read this book.

—RAGU GURUMURTHY, Chief Innovation and Digital Officer,
Deloitte

Business transformation and disruption might have felt academic before 2020, but now it is a critical skill we all need. *The Phoenix Encounter Method* authors provide a straightforward map of how to not just survive, but how to thrive during these challenging times. This is a must-read for anyone leading or building a business today.

—KYLE NEL, EVP Uncommonn Partners Lab, Singularity
University, and coauthor of *Leading Transformation*

Credibility and relevance. Years of research and field practice makes *The Phoenix Encounter Method* one of the most important contributions to reshaping strategic thinking debates for organizational leaders as a core leadership capability. Loaded with vivid examples and action-oriented tools, this book is essential reading for any leaders of today and tomorrow wanting to deliver a reimagined future. Uniquely it is as relevant to any organization—for profit, nonprofit, and public sector.

—JUAN MIRANDA, former Managing Director-General,
Asian Development Bank

Engaging your talented people is crucial for organizational success and rebirth, especially in these volatile and uncertain times. Using *The Phoenix Encounter Method* exercises and tools is a tremendous way to stretch and test your talent. It gets people to shift their mindsets towards the future and think strategically in totally different ways. It can help your talent navigate the dramatically different path ahead.

—ELIZABETH A. MORE, AM, Professor, former Deputy
Vice Chancellor and Dean, Macquarie University, author of
Managing Changes: Exploring the State of the Art

THE PHOENIX ENCOUNTER METHOD

LEAD LIKE YOUR BUSINESS IS ON FIRE!

IAN C. WOODWARD
V. "PADDY" PADMANABHAN
SAMEER HASIJA
RAM CHARAN

New York Chicago San Francisco Athens London Madrid
Mexico City Milan New Delhi Singapore Sydney Toronto

1 2 3 4 5 6 7 8 9   LCR   25 24 23 22 21 20

ISBN   978-1-264-25763-8
MHID   1-264-25763-5

e-ISBN 978-1-264-25764-5
e-MHID   1-264-25764-3

Library of Congress Cataloging-in-Publication Data

Names: Woodward, Ian C., author.
Title: The phoenix encounter method : lead like your business is on fire! / Ian C. Woodward, [and 3 others].
Description: New York : McGraw Hill Education, [2021] | Includes bibliographical references and index.
Identifiers: LCCN 2020031771 (print) | LCCN 2020031772 (ebook) | ISBN 9781264257638 (hardback) | ISBN 9781264257645 (ebook)
Subjects: LCSH: Leadership. | Business planning. | Disruptive technologies.
Classification: LCC HD57.7 .W6645 2021 (print) | LCC HD57.7 (ebook) | DDC 658.4/092—dc23
LC record available at https://lccn.loc.gov/2020031771
LC ebook record available at https://lccn.loc.gov/2020031772

McGraw-Hill Education books are available at special quantity discounts to use as premiums and sales promotions or for use in corporate training programs. To contact a representative, please visit the Contact Us pages at www.mhprofessional.com.

The Phoenix Philosophy

All businesses sooner or later face the need to reconstruct their future. Businesses must innovate, or they will die. They will need to destroy part or all of the incumbent business model in order to build their breakthrough, future-ready organization.

This book takes you through a new method of leadership thinking —the Phoenix Encounter—relevant to all organizations in today's high-velocity digital era of firestorm disruptive change—dramatically accelerated by the COVID-19 pandemic.

The Phoenix Encounter method empowers leaders and instills the confident Phoenix Attitude required to imagine burning their business to the ground and then resurrecting it from the ashes.

This method forces leaders to create a much wider set of radical options for innovation and business model transformation through unconstrained strategic debate. It is a confronting battlefield of completely opposite perspectives to challenge the leader's status quo, confirmation-seeking, and legacy blinkers. Leaders can then revolutionize their organization with a future-facing blueprint to lead it to new heights.

The book contains the know-how and real examples for leaders to start their journey of dramatic change. Our method was developed and tested with more than 1,500 executives in INSEAD's Advanced Management Program and other senior leadership programs since 2016.

It works.

Contents

CONTENTS

PART III

PHOENIX RISING:
Encounter Breakthrough

ARE YOU ON FIRE?

Your bird—I couldn't do anything—he just caught fire.

—J. K. ROWLING in *Harry Potter and the Chamber of Secrets* as Harry describes encountering Professor Dumbledore's phoenix called Fawkes

If you're smelling smoke, there's a good reason. The business landscape is going up in flames around leaders everywhere. Forces of disturbance and change that sparked small fires in the twentieth century have turned into twenty-first-century wildfires—further inflamed by the COVID-19 pandemic. Unstoppable trends appear unexpectedly, and unpleasant surprises materialize out of nowhere. These are things that keep business leaders awake at night.

Leaders of legacy firms feel especially uneasy. Already working hard to keep their businesses running against increased competition, they now also have to figure out how to deal with new technologies, social media, platform-based business models, emerging markets, upstart entrants, demographic shifts, and new world orders—a veritable firestorm of changes. It's exhausting and it's terrifying.

WHAT SHOULD THEY DO?
WHERE SHOULD THEY TURN?

There are dozens of books that warn leaders about disruptive change like this and dozens more that tell them what they should do about it. *The Phoenix Encounter Method* is a different kind of book and method.

Yes, it surveys the many dangers and opportunities that are burning on the horizon, but it also does something more. It lays out a new, specific, step-by-step method that helps leaders throw themselves into firestorm change and turn it to their organization's advantage. The method cultivates a new leadership thinking—a new attitude and a new kind of strategic debate that seeks out fire and embraces it. The method helps leaders develop their own bespoke script for renewal and transformation. In the post-COVID-19 environment, this is an absolute imperative.

The method is challenging. It involves Radical Ideation, dramatic war-gaming, confrontation, and provocation. It unfolds in a series of what we call "Completely Opposite Viewpoints Debates"—structured exercises that require leaders to consider many radically different ideas before settling on a strategic agenda for their organization and its business model. This book is about how to have that debate and fundamentally switch leadership attitude, mindsets, and thinking.

The ideas unleashed by the Encounter method come from perspectives totally different from an organization's customary way of thinking. It is a very distinctive form of strategic encounter. These ideas may sometimes seem wild and crazy. At its soul, the method compels leaders to imagine fully destroying their current organization themselves with unconstrained firepower. It then takes them through the steps needed to generate a wider range of options to defend the organization, fortify the core business, and build the bespoke solutions for their business model with initiatives they need for renewal.

The Phoenix Encounter—a Very Different Approach

What makes the Phoenix Encounter method a very different approach to leadership thinking:

- A dramatic battlefield of strategic thinking exercises unfolding as a "burning down to rebirth process—groundwork, battlefield, breakthrough"—to build a sense of urgency.
- A deliberately structured and sequenced method to aid leaders to orchestrate strategic debate to identify a wider set of options

for renewal and transformation, using completely opposite viewpoints and diverse perspectives at every point (ideation, analysis,
decision, and execution).

- A process supported by specific tools and leadership habits such as
Proactive Scanning and Radical Ideation to personalize ideas to their
unique business context, increasing relevance and replicability.

- A method that forces leaders and teams to switch attitude and
mindsets and make stakeholder views (especially those of customers) central to strategic dialogue. It deliberately emphasizes
qualitative, nonblinkered thinking first, which is then subject to
quantitative and other analysis to help leaders break from biased
thinking and the status quo.

- The work of the Phoenix Encounter Extreme Attack, Horizon
Defense, and Future-Facing Blueprint that moves well beyond
traditional war-gaming and scenario planning, taking optionality
to the extreme. These options include disruptive and nondisruptive innovation to create value benefiting stakeholders while
fortifying the core business in tandem.

- A strategic leadership thinking method that leaders and their
teams can run and own themselves.

Our method requires the leader to adopt a new way of seeing, thinking, and acting. It cultivates a bold and farsighted talent that we call the Phoenix Attitude, a set of mindsets, habits, and behaviors that equips a leader to grasp firestorm disruption as a path to organizational renewal. At the heart of the method is a sense of urgency and a willingness to walk through fire. That's why we call it the Phoenix Encounter method.

The Phoenix Encounter uses specific exercises and language in very confronting ways in the method and throughout this book. Our method intentionally uses some aggressive military-like terms—this is done deliberately to bring urgency to the forefront of the opposites debate with the "do-or-die" nature of firestorm disruption. It is by no means a suggestion that aggressive leadership or tactics are the appropriate way for leadership engagement between people in a diverse and pro-collaborative modern world. Far from it, in fact, we believe that emotionally intelligent leadership is critical. It is the only way that a leader will be able to engage people inclusively in the kind of strategic debate we advocate.

You might react adversely to these depictions at first. If you do, please realize that this is a purposefully radical provocation to incite leaders to think and reflect differently and then take them forward in a measured and considered way toward decisions that encompass a wider set of strategic options. Our method might also feel too "alpha" at first, but the method is built on leveraging and involving as much diversity as possible.[1] In fact, the people who have the most difficulty with the Encounter exercises are the supremely confident alphas who dismiss outside views out of hand.

Since 2016, we have conducted Phoenix Encounters* with more than 1,500 senior executives, including the leaders of legacy companies, new entrants, entrepreneurial startups, family businesses, and nonprofit or government organizations. These leaders come from a broad range of industries and sectors in both developed and developing economies—everything from mining and manufacturing to fashion and finance. This is a very diverse group of women and men, and yet almost every one of them has left our programs with renewed confidence, new skills, and a specific, actionable plan to take their organizations forward. We are grateful to our program participants for their courage and feedback. Through them, we have come to believe that the ability to engage in the kind of strategic opposites debate we have developed for the Phoenix Encounter is now a mandatory skill for every twenty-first-century leader.

BECOMING A PHOENIX

In the twentieth century, many successful organizations and their leaders were a lot like crows. Crows are very smart birds; they are observant

---

*In the authors' programs and consulting work from 2016 to 2019, the method was called the "Strategic Encounter." The "Phoenix Encounter" method is entirely built from this. We have changed the titles of various elements to better reflect the "trial by fire" underpinnings of the research work that our method demonstrates.

and can both learn and play tricks. They can be fearless and will attack larger birds without hesitation (a flock of crows is called a "murder"). Both predators and scavengers, crows eat anything that will keep them alive, and they thrive in a variety of environments, from seacoasts to desert canyons. Highly resourceful, they are often overconfident.

In some places, they still dominate—but not everywhere. Consider the 'Alalā, species of crow native to the Hawaiian Islands. Unlike their cousin crows, these Hawaiian crows were unable to adapt to dramatic changes in the world around them, including new predators, diseases, deforestation, and competition for food. Their environment changed, but they didn't, and the bird is now critically endangered.

These days, many twenty-first-century businesses look a lot like the 'Alalās. Caught in a landscape of accelerating disruption, these organizations are very vulnerable. Their environments and habitats are changing fast, and they are unable to think clearly amidst the chaos and noise. In history, the dodo is perhaps the most famous example of symbolic extinction—it took less than a century to disappear.

For this book, we have our eye on a different kind of symbolic bird: the phoenix. The phoenix is a mythical, brightly colored, and long-lived creature that can regenerate itself, withstanding the flames of fire to rise from the ashes of its former self. For millennia, the phoenix has been a symbol of rebirth and new life.[2] Ancient Egyptians saw it as the companion of the sun god. Medieval monks saw it as a symbol of Christ's resurrection. In our mind, the phoenix is the kind of bird that leaders must become to survive the firestorm of disruption that marks our current century.

WHAT KIND OF BIRD ARE YOU?

Consider the story of a CEO we'll call James Menta.* In November 2016, James assured a colleague that his American fresh-food supply company was totally safe from harm. "We're the market leader, and we

---

*In deference to our Encounter participants' need for absolute commercial confidentiality, we have anonymized all examples in this book that arise directly from our work with global leaders in Phoenix Encounter exercises.

have our logistics and suppliers under full control," he boasted. "No one can replicate that."

A short time later, James took part in one of our Phoenix Encounter exercises, where his company was subjected to a series of simulated attacks.

The first attack exploited new technologies and introduced new regulatory frameworks that put James's company at a disadvantage. The second attack went after his key talent. In the third attack, the challengers built a digital platform that connected all James's suppliers (and new ones) to a larger ecosystem that better managed risk, created partnerships with technology providers with lower costs, and moved into neighboring markets. It was all a game, but James lost it decisively.

When the attack phase of the exercise was over, James was crestfallen. "We should be selling ostriches," he said as he surveyed the wreckage. "We have had our heads in the sand. Our current thinking is totally wrong. We need to look upward and rethink everything we do."[3]

We hear stories like James's all too often. That's why we wrote this book.

Throughout the book, we use vibrant examples to show how the Phoenix Encounter method helps leaders work toward transformational change. Many of these stories have never been told before. Most were shared with us by leaders who are convinced that their companies are where they are today because they took the initiative to conduct a Phoenix Encounter or otherwise applied much of the method. The experience has changed the way they lead and moved their organizations and business models forward, often against great odds.

How do they do it? They do it by changing their attitude and tackling firestorm disruption head-on in their business environment. They do it by engaging in extreme war-game-like Completely Opposite Viewpoints Debates. They do it by learning new leadership habits and formulating new blueprints for their organizations. They do it by walking straight into the fire and then returning to their organizations to carry out their plans and conduct Phoenix Encounters of their own. In this way, they kindle a shared vision of renewal within the organization, along with the skills to achieve it again and again.

They come into the Encounter as crows, and they go out as phoenixes.

The sheer importance of actually experiencing an Encounter yourself, and working your way through the book's entire content, was reinforced for us by a debriefing comment in 2019 from Daniella Silosa, the CFO of an Italian energy company:

> When I heard the lectures and read the setup materials for the Encounter exercises, I was intellectually curious but a little skeptical on where this would lead. After the radical debate was over, I could not believe just how massively transformative this was to my strategic thinking approach. It was the ultimate aha moment. Hearing and reading are not enough. You have to live through the frustration and discomfort of an Encounter to really believe—and then reap all its rewards.

WHO WE ARE AND HOW THE BOOK WORKS

The ideas for *The Phoenix Encounter Method* were developed by us, three professors at INSEAD, the Business School for the World, in collaboration with Ram Charan, the bestselling author of more than two dozen business books, for use in INSEAD's flagship Advanced Management Program, other strategic leadership development programs, and consulting work.[4] Our research includes field trials with more than 1,500 executive leaders and the compilation and analysis of a database of more than 5,000 articles, studies, reports, and books (both academic and business practice).[5] During the extraordinary situation of the COVID-19 health and economic crisis of 2020, we continued our research and practice work using the Encounter method—albeit virtually, with social distancing regimes in place. We found a heightened sense of urgency in the leadership teams and boards we worked with to use the Encounter method and tools to reimagine their post crisis future—and contemplate a much wider set of strategic options (including pilot exercises during the crisis period and projects in the post-lockdown phase).

As authors, we bring a broad range of expertise to the table. Our training and academic research cover fields from marketing to economics, leadership development to technology, strategy to management, business models to operations, leadership communication to organizational behavior. We have experience in the classroom, the boardroom, the executive suite, and government as well as across diverse economies and industries. We are a multidisciplinary team whose common link is intellectual curiosity. We also have a strong friendship supported by mutual respect—and a shared admiration for cricket—so we refer to each other by our first names in this book: Ian, Paddy, Sameer, and Ram.

As we have written this book, we have been guided by an overarching vision. While rigorously grounded in academic research, the method and book should be relevant, practical, and actionable. Leaders in any sector of any industry should be able to use it. It should offer a process for finding their own relevant solutions rather than dictating the solutions. In short, the book should empower leaders and their organizations to rejuvenate their own futures and create their own solutions based on their own unique circumstances, deep knowledge, and experience.[6]

Therefore, all the Encounter templates, case studies, and updated scans are online at www.phoenixencountermethod.com where anyone can use and share them. In this way, we hope to create an exchange platform for leaders to share their experiences and learning in working with the Phoenix Encounter method. Our belief is that this will encourage a crowdsourced force-multiplier effect that can carry leaders and organizations further forward than they might be able to go on their own.

The book is divided into three parts, each aligned with a distinct phase of the Phoenix Encounter method:

- **Part I, *Phoenix Seeking: Encounter Groundwork,*** discusses the "why" of firestorm disruption and the "what and how" of the Phoenix Encounter method in detail, outlines the "who" of the Phoenix Attitude for leadership, and teaches essential tools and habits for Completely Opposite Viewpoints Debates.

- **Part II,** *Phoenix Burning: Encounter Battlefield,* explores and scans the radical ideas and disruptive trends that can be used as firepower in the Phoenix Encounter to attack and defend incumbent or startup organizations or industries.

- **Part III,** *Phoenix Rising: Encounter Breakthrough,* shows leaders how to create Future-Facing Blueprints for their business models and innovation initiatives and embed the Phoenix Attitude and Breakthrough in their organizations.

Most chapters begin with "whiteboard notes" as a visual overview and finish with a checklist with summary thoughts and questions for reflection. At the end of the book, we've included extensive Notes, broken down by chapter, to help readers explore ideas, sources, references, and additional information on matters we raise. Finally, a separate *Facilitation Guide for the Phoenix Encounter Method* will be available to give a step-by-step practical guidance to leaders and facilitators on how to run Phoenix Encounter exercises in any organizational setting.

Accessing Phoenix Encounter Method Online Resources

Readers have access to our online Phoenix Encounter method resources at www.phoenixencountermethod.com. There are open resources and information for anyone at this site, and readers can register for additional content like newsletters.

A *Facilitation Guide for the Phoenix Encounter Method* is also going to be available as a companion to this main book.

We foresee a day when big dreams and radical new ideas come naturally to every leader and organization. And yet, we see scores of leaders each year still stuck with their heads in the sand—trapped in a kind of backward-looking, inside-out thinking that leads to complacency or, worse, helplessness. We believe these organizations can survive and prosper if their leaders step into a Phoenix Attitude and regularly engage in searing encounters that wrestle with big ideas and options for firestorm change. To become a Phoenix, leaders must undergo a trial by fire.

We invite you to take your first step into your Phoenix-like future.

PART I

PHOENIX SEEKING:

Encounter Groundwork

I PHOENIX or DODO?

it's an UNPRECEDENTED CHALLENGE...
...COMING from ANYWHERE!

the FIRESTORM DISRUPTION

IT'S YOUR RESPONSIBILITY to DEAL with IT!

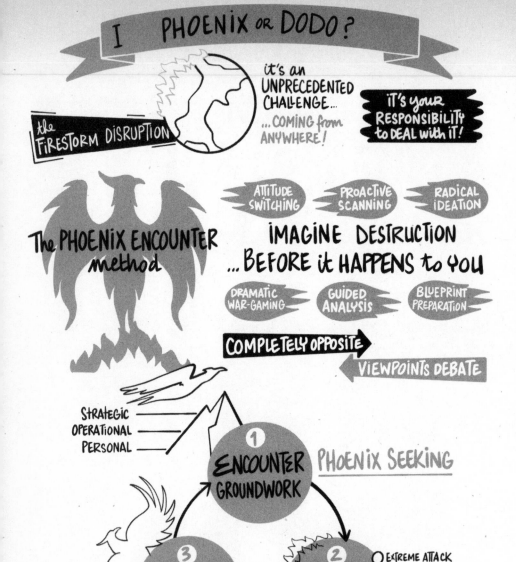

The PHOENIX ENCOUNTER method

ATTITUDE SWITCHING

PROACTIVE SCANNING

RADICAL IDEATION

IMAGINE DESTRUCTION
...BEFORE it HAPPENS to YOU

DRAMATIC WAR-GAMING

GUIDED ANALYSIS

BLUEPRINT PREPARATION

COMPLETELY OPPOSITE

VIEWPOINTS DEBATE

STRATEGIC
OPERATIONAL
PERSONAL

1 ENCOUNTER GROUNDWORK

PHOENIX SEEKING

3 ENCOUNTER BREAKTHROUGH

2 ENCOUNTER BATTLEFIELD

○ EXTREME ATTACK

○ HORIZON DEFENSE

PHOENIX RISING

PHOENIX BURNING

PHOENIX OR DODO?

*Sometimes you have to burn yourself to the ground
before you can rise like a phoenix from the ashes.*
—JENS LEKMAN, Swedish musician and songwriter[1]

In 2018, Sandra Johnstone was back in town after 20 years for her business school alumni reunion. She had recently accepted an offer from a private wealth management bank to become its CEO, which would require her to move to Europe from Canada, where she had lived and worked for a decade. As the night moved along, Sandra was gripped with nostalgia and delighted to reengage with fellow MBAs and old friends. At the end of the dinner, she found herself in deep conversation with her former classmate Michael, now the CEO of his family's consumer electronics manufacturing business.

Michael's company made essential components for one of the giants in the gaming console business. They were the exclusive supplier of these components and for years had enjoyed a steady and highly profitable flow of revenues. But things were changing fast—and much too unpredictably for Michael. "I came to this reunion weekend to get away from all work pressure," Michael confided. "I certainly didn't come to talk business, but I guess there may be a lesson to be learned from my story. I've been so clueless about the world outside my immediate reality. I had no idea that technologies like cloud computing and 5G would so quickly become a major threat to the gaming console business. I always thought gamers were die-hard fans of quality. I thought they'd be slow to adopt technologies with potential downsides such as slowness due to streaming, but I was so wrong. The technology is moving faster than I even imagined, and these new generation gamers are so willing to experiment. The technology giants are investing billions to create the Netflix of gaming. Soon, people like me are going to be dinosaurs in this industry. I just didn't see it coming."

Sandra listened to Michael's story with a mixture of uneasiness and excitement. She was soon to take the helm of another successful legacy firm, and she wondered whether she was ready. Private wealth management banks have historically relied on relationship managers to serve their wealthy clients, but perhaps the new age customer would be perfectly comfortable to have a well-programmed robot give them investment advice. Perhaps *more* comfortable.

During her return to Montreal, Sandra turned introspective. *Will we soon become a dinosaur in the private banking world?* she wondered. *Am I up to this challenge?* First thing on Monday morning, Sandra wrote an email to one of her former professors who had shifted his research from applied game theory to technology and business model disruption. To her surprise, she heard back from him in a matter of hours:

> Sandra, your timing couldn't be better . . . I just finished the first draft of a book coauthored with my colleagues that precisely talks about how leaders can corral the forces of disruption and give their organization a future. I am sending you the draft (please do not share yet). In fact, the book developed from the existential questions you are wrestling with. I think it has the method and tools that will help you find your answers. Of course, in return, please provide feedback on our thinking. The book is a result of our field research and teaching over the last few years, and we want to make sure it delivers value to leaders like yourself.

This was Sandra's first exposure to the Phoenix Encounter method and thinking, and since then, she has taken a monumental business and personal transformational journey using it.

FIRESTORM IS THE VISTA

There is a fire out there, and it is coming at you, ready or not. It is a wildfire—white-hot and unpredictable—firestorm disruption sparked by the emergence of new technologies, new markets, new actors, and new business models. It is driven by the winds of innovation, and it can burn down organizations big and small. And it is not only new actors; there are incumbents changing the rules of the game as well.[2] Many firestorm trends in technology and business models evident by the end of 2019 became turbo-charged in the COVID-19 world.

Maybe your organization will survive this firestorm, and we hope it does. But we do know that if your organization is to survive in the long term, you need to start thinking like a Phoenix leader. You need to embody the Phoenix instinct for renewal in every leadership decision you make. You need to constantly scan the horizon. You need to think in the future, not the past. You need to become willing to periodically set fire to your own organization so it can rise again.

The Phoenix Encounter method we describe in this book is built on a simple yet massively transformative idea: get leaders to think extremely seriously about how they would marshal the unconstrained forces of firestorm disruption to destroy their current organization, then generate a wider set of options to rebuild their future-ready organization and its business model. To do that, the method encourages leaders to engage in a series of Completely Opposite Viewpoints Debates—strategic conversations that require participants to look in every possible direction and give every opposing and radical idea due consideration. The method intentionally creates a roaring firestorm and then constructs a response.

Our method arises from the realization that business today can be a do-or-die proposition. Our research and fieldwork have persuaded us that only after you have launched a devastating attack on your own organization can you really understand how to defend it, fortify the core business, and generate that wider set of strategic initiatives that will propel the organization forward to a Phoenix Breakthrough. Though the experience is very challenging, leaders with the Phoenix Attitude will discover that *you are absolutely your own best enemy.* This is a virtuous cycle of renewal and transformation—an insurance policy against complacency and hubris. Unfortunately, leaders without the Phoenix Attitude become *their own worst enemy*, leading to a vicious cycle of stagnation, wholesale disruption—and where the firestorm is—devastation.

What the Firestorm Looks Like

In this book, we discuss dozens of examples in which disruptive firestorms have transformed or destroyed an established business. Some of those cases and leaders are well known; others will be new to most readers. We'll start with three noteworthy examples involving both disruptors and their victims.

First look at Sears, the once retail giant that filed for bankruptcy in 2018 and has shrunk even further during the COVID-19 pandemic.

> In the mid-1980s, Sears was the largest retailer in America. Today, the company is in the intensive care unit. The story of Sears's decline is a cautionary tale of what can happen when a business responds to warnings that the ship is sinking by simply rearranging the deckchairs. Instead of fending off the advance of big-box retailers and embracing online retailing, Sears clung to its outmoded local mall model, which is ironic considering Sears's signature mail-order catalog launched in 1893, was once as disruptive to local retailing as Amazon is today.
>
> The company dug itself into a deeper hole by overestimating the benefits of financial restructurings and underestimating the need for a value proposition built around assortment, shopping experience, and flawless service. In 2018, $5.6 billion* in debt, Sears relieved its CEO of his duties and filed for bankruptcy protection. Sears is hardly the only retailer to struggle with the disruption created by the new digital world—the roll call of store closures in the United States alone includes Brookstone, RadioShack, Payless Shoe-Source, The Limited, and K-Mart, Sears's luckless partner.[3]

---

*Where financial information is quoted in the book, our convention is for currency amounts with dollar signs ($) to be USD unless otherwise stated.

The second example involves Gillette and the Dollar Shave Club.

In 2011, Gillette's market share in the razor blade business was a dominant 71 percent. But lurking beneath that buoyant number was rising consumer resentment of the cozy oligopoly (Gillette, Schick, etc.) that pushed prices higher year after year as the firms rolled out increasingly complicated razors and cartridges. Enter a David who took on the Goliaths with a very different business model, "Shaving as a Service." In 2012, The Dollar Shave Club launched a subscription-based model that offered shaving cartridges priced as low as $1, home delivery, and a viral YouTube video featuring a punchy pitch: "Our Razors are F***ing Great."

Four years later, Dollar Shave Club had $160 million in sales, Gillette's market share had dropped to 58.5 percent, and Unilever shelled out $1 billion to buy the disruptive upstart. Meanwhile, Gillette announced that it was dropping prices on its products by as much as 20 percent, and an activist investor announced plans to get on the board of parent company Procter & Gamble to ensure they got the message about disruptive threats. The products introduced by Gillette in 2017 showed a striking reversal of its decades-long strategy: new technology for the Fusion product line with no increase in the retail price and lower-end options priced competitively to products available from Dollar Shave Club.[4]

The third example takes us to India, where a 50-year-old petrochemicals conglomerate, Reliance Industries, seized an unguarded market and created an entire digital ecosystem called Reliance Jio.

Reliance Jio invested $35 billion to blanket India with its first all-4G network in September 2016. Offering free calls and text messages, and data for pennies, it signed up 215 million 4G customers in 22 months, a world record. An innovative use of the Indian government's unique Aadhaar digital identity system, which greatly sped up the mobile subscriber identification module (SIM) activation process, meant Jio was carrying more mobile data traffic than Sprint, Verizon, and AT&T combined. Scale enabled Jio to create its own digital ecosystem of consumer apps—JioCinema, JioMusic, JioTV, JioMags, and JioCloud. In 2018, the average Jio customer engaged with Jio apps for nearly five hours a day.

When Reliance realized that many consumers could afford its digital services but not the 4G-enabled smartphones they ran on, it launched a line of midrange "feature phones" that could be had for a $23 security deposit. From the beginning, the Reliance team thought far beyond legacy borders, targeting Google, Netflix, Amazon, and Facebook as its competitors. While petrochemicals remain the parent company's biggest profit center, in the third quarter of 2018, its new digital, media, and retail businesses together brought in more revenue than the legacy side of the business.[5] The power of the Jio ecosystem is evident in the flurry of new investors who poured $20 billion into the platform in the second quarter of 2020, including Facebook, Mubadala, KKR, General Atlantic, Qualcomm, and Google.

As these examples and many researchers point out, disruption can come from any direction and at any time. It can come as a direct attack from a longtime competitor. It can sneak in at the bottom of your market with an inferior or niche product that seems barely worth your notice. It can come from the kid working in his garage next door, or it can come from overseas. It can come at you with a brand-new business model or innovative technology for your industry. Disruption needn't even be deliberate: your company could just be swept up in a firestorm created by an innovation in some distant sector, seemingly "out of nowhere."[6]

Today, the only thing certain is that firestorm change is coming. It is unstoppable, and firms can no longer rely on their experience and longstanding competencies to survive. Whatever you do, or fail to do, someone out there is hoping to eat your lunch.

Smart leaders know this. They understand that senior leadership is in the hot seat, fighting for the survival of their organizations. The words of Thomas Buberl, CEO of Axa,[7] the second largest insurer in the world, echo this theme: "The competitors of tomorrow will be Facebook, Google, or Apple . . . and not Lemonade or other small insurance companies," referring to the insurtech startups. We note that Buberl's list of future competitors does not include companies usually found in their insurance industry benchmarking studies. The advice that Meg Whitman (ex-president and CEO of Hewlett Packard and eBay) gave to CEOs struggling with different kinds of disruption—technological, cultural, or geopolitical—also stresses competition and survival: "Every big business needs to be thinking, 'Who's coming to kill me?' "[8] In other work, Ram quotes Jeff Bezos directing Steve Kessel (then head of its traditional media business—books/music/DVDs) to lead the Kindle digital media initiatives: "Your job is to kill your own business. I want you to proceed as if your goal is to put everyone selling physical books out of a job."[9]

Yet there can be significant psychological blockages in leaders considering burning down their own businesses, such as risk aversion, fear of failure, anxiety about the unknown or losing control, and mindset impediments that we discuss in Chapter 4. There can also be political factors or positions affecting leaders in private sectors, public sector organizations, and family businesses that stop even the debate around burning the business from happening at all.[10]

At the personal level, many experienced and successful leaders are now facing levels of professional anxiety and insecurity that are very high—and often paralyzing.[11] As one participant CEO said in a 2018 Phoenix Encounter session: "I've been putting on a brave face, but to be honest, what do I know about platforms, algorithms, artificial intelligence, sharing economies, and the like? I'm a chemical engineer trained 30 years ago. I don't even know what I don't know."

For many organizations, the time has gone way beyond disruption. It is not a bend in the road; it is the end of the road. The COVID-19 pandemic has made this starker. There is an urgent need to totally break from the old business path or model the company has had, whether you were an Atari (in the video game crash of 1983) or a Hertz (whose flawed business model of vehicle ownership drew them into bankruptcy in the COVID-19 collapse of the car rental market). This is far beyond disruption; it is the widespread firestorm destruction of the old order. As the Thracian slave Spartacus led the uprising against the heinous slave-owning masters of ancient Rome, his rallying call was, "Kill them. Kill them all."

Firestorm disruption like this is what keeps today's best business leaders in a state of perpetual anxiety, yet navigating firestorms has become the most important leadership capability of the twenty-first century. A leader's ability to recognize firestorm disruption, engage in strategic debate, and seize opportunities to ensure that the organization evolves is now a fundamental C-suite responsibility. Unfortunately, many leaders and organizations are unprepared to do this work. Many don't even see the urgency. They are dry tinder for that big fire on the horizon, and they need help.

In our strategic leadership sessions and consulting practices, leaders grappling with firestorm disruption typically ask us three things:

1. How can we generate a very wide set of strategic options for both our legacy business and innovation?

2. How can we fortify our core business against disruption while we chart a new future?

3. What can we do to create a shared vision of organizational renewal and transformation across the length and breadth of our organization?

In this book, we offer a new method to answer these questions. We propose a new leadership thinking attitude—the Phoenix Attitude—and a new strategic leadership thinking method—the Phoenix Encounter—that will help leaders walk their organizations into that big fire on the horizon and come out the other side, like the phoenix.

THE PHOENIX ENCOUNTER METHOD AT A GLANCE

The word "encounter" means distinctive things to different people. For some, an encounter is something to avoid; for others, it's something to look forward to. That's because an encounter can change things for the worse or for the better. A Phoenix Encounter can change things for the better by imagining the worst. It builds a devastating fire, and it rebuilds an organization.

We use the term "Phoenix Encounter" in two ways in this book: first to describe our overall method for helping leaders achieve a Phoenix Breakthrough, and second to describe the intense Battlefield exercise that is the centerpiece of that method.

The method combines attitude switching, Proactive Scanning, Radical Ideation, dramatic war-gaming, guided analysis, and blueprint preparation. It is powered by a new kind of strategic dialog we call the "Completely Opposite Viewpoints Debate." This debate is a deliberate engagement with diverse, opposing, and sometimes unwelcome viewpoints that force leaders to see differently, think differently, and act differently than they have in the past so they can draw up a blueprint for the future (see *What Is a Completely Opposite Viewpoints Debate?*).

Just as the phoenix renews itself in a cycle of immolation and rebirth, the Phoenix Encounter method unfolds in a cycle of three phases that take participants from groundwork preparation to battlefield debate and then to a breakthrough action plan. Figure 1.1 shows what the cycle looks like.

FIGURE 1.1 The Phoenix Encounter Method—Phases and Cycle

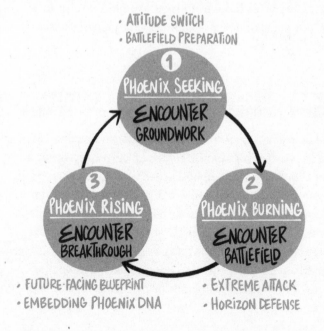

The three phases of this cycle are described briefly below and more fully in Chapter 3.

Phase One: Phoenix Seeking—Encounter Groundwork

Phase One lays the groundwork for a future Phoenix Breakthrough by confronting old mindsets and scanning for new threats and opportunities. It teaches the Phoenix Attitude and explains the Phoenix Encounter method, along with its habits and tools. It then prepares participants for the battle to come.

When we promote the Phoenix Attitude, we pay special attention to three altitudes of leadership thinking (50,000 feet–strategic, 50 feet–tactical, and 5 feet–personal—which we describe in Chapter 4) and highlight the need to fly across them seamlessly. When we teach the Phoenix Encounter method, we explore the power of Proactive Scanning, Radical Ideation, and the opposite viewpoints debate in brainstorming.

During this phase, participants also prepare several baseline reports and reflections detailing their perception of current strengths and weaknesses in their organizations. The goal of the groundwork phase is to help leaders break loose from legacy thinking; cultivate a constant, vibrant awareness of new possibilities; and prepare for the Battlefield exercise of Phase Two.

What Is a Completely Opposite Viewpoints Debate?

A Completely Opposite Viewpoints Debate (sometimes called an "opposites debate") is a form of strategic dialogue that deliberately engages people in totally opposing perspectives, each taken seriously and often provocatively. More than just spirited rebuttal or devil's advocacy, these debates are dialectical attempts to catapult discussion "totally out of the box" and "way beyond the status quo" to incorporate extreme thinking that busts through entrenched views.

In structured settings like the Phoenix Encounter, opposites debates foster Radical Ideation and help generate far-reaching option sets and ideas from the outset for innovation and business models. They do so by challenging participants' experience and preconceived ideas and by removing "real-world" constraints (like financial resources or technological capabilities) from strategy consideration at first.

Idea generation is specifically separated from deeper analysis and decision-making discussions to avoid the conflation problem that usually limits the range of ideas. In other words, the opposites debates have been specifically constructed to encourage participants to go wider on options rather then deeper on the most prospective ones.

In the same way that the phoenix instinctively poises life against death to achieve rebirth, Phoenix leaders use Completely Opposite Viewpoints Debates to up the ante and imagine the transformative power of self-destruction and unblinkered, outside-in thinking. We will follow the workings of well-constructed opposites debates throughout the book—and especially in the Phoenix Encounter Battlefield exercise stages of Extreme Attack and Horizon Defense.

Phase Two: Phoenix Burning—Encounter Battlefield

At the center of the Phoenix Encounter is an intense battlefield engagement that is waged over several days. Leaders work in teams organized for maximum diversity of thought and experience, with each team member taking a turn in the "hot seat." The engagement offers live practice for the Phoenix Attitude using the Completely Opposite Viewpoints Debate. Its goal is to both test the leader's thinking blind spots and generate a wider set of strategic options for the incumbent organization, including beyond out-of-the-box solutions suggested by Radical Ideation.

The Encounter Battlefield unfolds in two stages:

- **Extreme Attack.** After reviewing each organization's vulnerabilities and scanning the business landscape for firepower, the leader and team launch a massively destructive strike on the target organization. The attack typically uses contemporary weapons such as artificial intelligence, social media, platforms, and ecosystems to strike at the legacy operation; they might also ideate entirely new products, services, and business models to create value.

- **Horizon Defense.** Having attacked the target organization, the same team rushes to its defense. Using the Radical Ideation and opposites debate again, participants generate a comprehensive list of actions the organization could take to sidestep, confront, or leapfrog over the attack—first fortifying the core operation and then staging the other innovation options over multiple time horizons (immediate, short, medium, and long term). The list of actions typically includes both contemporary firepower (such as technology) and conventional firepower (such as well-known business practices like mergers and acquisitions, process optimization, or partnerships).

Phase Three: Phoenix Rising— Encounter Breakthrough

Phase Three builds on the ideas from the Battlefield exercises to chart a new course for the organization. The work includes analysis, planning, and execution, and it can take months and sometimes years to complete. The Phoenix Breakthrough itself begins at the point that the leader and organization commit to a renewal plan and begin implementing it.

Phase Three has two critical tasks. The first is to create a Future-Facing Blueprint, a kind of high-level flight plan for the renewed Phoenix organization. This part of the leader's Encounter Journal identifies new value propositions and key strategic initiatives and stages them over time horizons. It also identifies expected outcomes and likely pushback from stakeholders, as well as stress-testing analysis to be completed. The second task is to embed the Phoenix Attitude and the Phoenix Encounter method throughout the organization, engaging all players in the change journey ahead.

The goal of Phase Three is to transform the organization into its best future self and make the Phoenix Attitude a permanent and central talent that the organization can use to renew itself over and over again.

WHAT THE PHOENIX ENCOUNTER
METHOD CAN DO

As the use of military language suggests, Phoenix Encounters can be stressful events, and they frequently make leaders uncomfortable psychologically, emotionally, and intellectually. The Battlefield debates, for example, include no-holds-barred challenges that often expose vulnerabilities in the organization, including weaknesses in the leadership. It's tough love, designed to break the complacency of legacy thinking by envisaging extreme and worst-case scenarios. But it's also a redemptive kind of love, designed to instill personal and organizational confidence.

Our participants leave their Phoenix Encounters with a remarkable new capability: they can create a future-ready organization, and, like the phoenix, they can do it again and again. This is because the Phoenix Encounter method does not offer solutions; instead, it offers a methodology for leaders and teams to find their own solutions—solutions that are relevant to their particular situation, time, and place. As those circumstances change (as they almost certainly will), so will the solutions, but the method remains the same: ever adaptable, ever effective.

In academic circles, we call such processes "agnostic as to context." That means it is actionable in any sector or any industry. The method doesn't care whether your organization is selling fruit or splitting atoms or delivering humanitarian relief. It doesn't care whether you are organized as a family firm or multinational corporation or government agency. It doesn't care whether the challenge you face is a new technology, break in your supply chain, or pink unicorn. It cares only that the organization survives and prospers, and that you, the organization's leader, know how to make that happen.

We have run Encounters with leaders of a wide range of enterprises facing many different kinds of challenges, and the Phoenix Encounter method has proven quite versatile. We have found it to be especially effective in helping leaders find actionable insights and solutions to challenges like:

- How to transform attitudes and mindsets that are holding your organization back

- How to imagine a hostile attack on your organization and defend against it

- How to create an ecosystem for future growth and performance

- How to identify innovative value-creating new products and services

- How to use new digital technologies, social media, and platform-based business models to transform your organization

- How to evaluate the usefulness of targeted technologies like artificial intelligence and the Internet of Things (IoT)

- How to navigate emerging markets, sustainability, and government regulations

- How to assess gaps in your organization's resources, talent, and capabilities

- How to build an incessant learning culture throughout the organization

Given the current pandemic, it might also be prudent for leaders to ask how COVID-19 impacts the palette of the challenges highlighted above and what are their implications, including possible opportunities?

Whether you are looking to stress-test your current strategy or devise a new one, a Phoenix Encounter can uncover the hidden strengths and fault lines in your organization. Most important, it reveals to leaders that powerful essential truth we mentioned earlier: you are your own best enemy—and that's a very good thing.

MAGIC, NO—BUT A BULLET, YES

Our Phoenix Encounter method is not a substitute for the many contemporary analytic frames and strategic planning tools available to leaders; it is an essential complement. In fact, our method borrows freely from many of them, incorporating and extending ideas from war-gaming, SWOT exercises, design thinking, scenario analysis, and other well-known approaches to strategic thinking. By helping leaders adopt a new attitude and generate a wider set of options for future directions, the Phoenix Encounter method acts like a supercharger, making every strategic conversation, every framework, and every tool, more powerful. For example, we have found the Encounter method can both add ideas to and stress-test potential initiatives for value creation from innovation approaches such as *Blue Ocean Strategy*.[12]

The Phoenix Encounter is powerful, but it is not a magic bullet. We don't believe in magic. We believe in results, and we are encouraged by how many executives emerge from our Encounters with a heightened sense of urgency, a clearer sense of strategic priorities, and a healthier confidence to lead change in their organizations. They find they can now see firestorm disruption not just as inevitable but as a dynamic and exciting set of opportunities. The fire doesn't scare them anymore. It emboldens them. It forms the Phoenix Attitude in them.

We see this kind of leadership transformation time and time again when using the Encounter method. This debrief assessment from Szymon Nowak, the Polish deputy CEO of a multinational logistics firm currently implementing many of our Encounter ideas, sums it up nicely:

> I had never thought about disrupting my own business before I went into the Encounter. A reasonable person wouldn't normally start a strategic discussion by saying, "OK, what can I do to make a mess of my own business today?" You might think about what a competitor might do or what the worst-case scenario might be if something happened in one operation or another, but you wouldn't go so far as to plan to destroy your own business. To have that kind of discussion in a structured environment was an incredible experience. It totally changed my leadership thinking and opened my eyes to redrawing our business model.

Like the phoenix, leaders and organizations that undergo a Phoenix Encounter experience can be transformed into vigorous and ascendant future versions of themselves. Achieving this Phoenix Breakthrough will result in a major renewal of strategic, tactical, competitive, and opportunity-seeking positioning. It will fire-charge learning and curiosity. It will foster a fire-embracing culture in the organization and drive propulsive change. It can create a legacy that is not a trap but an achievement to be proud of.

CHAPTER **1** CHECKLIST

Summary Thoughts

1. There is a firestorm of disruptive change in today's business environment, and dealing with it is now a critical C-suite responsibility—even more so in attempting to reimagine the future of the organization post the COVID-19 crisis. Leaders who hope to steer their organizations through this firestorm must learn to act like a phoenix. They need to cultivate a Phoenix Attitude and practice the Phoenix Encounter method.

2. The Phoenix Encounter method compels leaders to imagine destroying their current organizations themselves using unconstrained forces of disruptive firepower. It helps leaders embrace the firestorm and turn it to their organizations' advantage. The Phoenix Encounter is "agnostic as to context." It is actionable in any sector of any industry. It does not tell leaders *what to do* but rather *how to develop the options for what to do* within their own context. It is a method, not a prescription.

3. The Phoenix Encounter method plays out over three phases: Phoenix Seeking—Encounter Groundwork, Phoenix Burning—Encounter Battlefield, and Phoenix Rising—Encounter Breakthrough. The final phase includes creating the blueprint for a future-ready organization and business model, as well as embedding the Phoenix Attitude in the organization.

Reflection

1. Is your organization prepared for firestorm disruptive change in its business? Are you prepared for firestorm disruptive change as a leader?

2. Are you, as a leader, willing to transform your attitude, mindsets, and habits to break against the status quo?

3. Can you imagine burning your business to the ground? Can you embrace firestorm disruption as an exciting opportunity for renewal? Therefore, can you imagine the opportunities that the COVID-19 disruption creates for you and your business, as opposed to just the challenges?

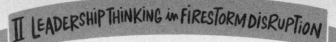

UNSTOPPABLE TRENDS
- DIGITAL & SOCIAL
- PLATFORMS & ECOSYSTEMS
- TECHNOLOGIES
- ALGORITHMS & ANALYTICS
- TALENT
- EMERGING MARKETS
- ACTIVISM
- REGULATION

"You don't know where the PUNCH in the FACE is going to come from."

TECHNOLOGIES ACCELERATE the FIRESTORM

* CREATE NEW PRODUCTS & SERVICES
* UNLOCK INFORMATION
* ACCELERATE the PACE of CHANGE
* TRANSFORM the WAY BUSINESS is ORGANIZED

ARE YOU and YOUR ORGANIZATION READY to DEAL with this?

PAST SUCCESSES can lead you to be...

COMPLACENT | ARROGANT | CAUTIOUS | OVERWHELMED

the LEGACY TRAP

the PHOENIX LEADER: DREAMER and DOER

SEE the FUTURE

LEADERSHIP THINKING IN FIRESTORM DISRUPTION

I wanted you to see what hubris looked like.
—EDWIN LAND, Polaroid founder, describing a warehouse
full of unsold Polavision cameras in 1977[1]

Disruptive changes are not new—we could look back to the printing press and the Industrial Revolution—but the firestorm that we witness now in the business world is different in terms of its scale, scope, and speed. There are reasons for this, and we will explore them in depth as we go along, but what is particularly striking about the current incarnation of firestorm disruption is that it is not a local phenomenon. It is happening within and across economies, sectors, organizations, continents, and peoples. It threatens all comers—legacy firms and startups, heavy industries and digital services—in every corner of the globe. It is this "everywhere-and-everything" nature of the firestorm that is so paralyzing for leaders because it doesn't look anything like business as usual. And it isn't.

This will be even more so in the post-COVID-19 era where the dramatic trends of change in technology, business models, work paradigms, regulation, and the like, have been given a velocity boost. An amusing social media meme circulated early in 2020 highlights this with a checklist list of who was responsible for accelerating digital transformation in the organization: CEO, CIO, or coronavirus?

FIRESTORM DISRUPTION

It's important to understand what firestorm disruption is and what it isn't. Increased competition, in and of itself, is not the disruption we worry about. There have always been intensely competitive industry sectors: commodities, consumer goods, telecommunication, and aviation, to name just four. Neither is this disruption about incremental innovation or consolidation among the key players in an industry—that's old hat.

What is different about firestorm disruption as we see it today is that it is redrawing the very boundaries of firms and industries. That's important because when the boundaries of firms and industries change, new players can stake leading positions right out of the gate, as Dollar Shave did by inventing the business model of providing low-cost shaving materials through the mail. Keen incumbents with a Phoenix Attitude can overturn the industry pecking order, as Reliance Jio did with their data-first model in the Indian telecommunications industry.

The e-commerce giant Alibaba did a similarly boundary-busting thing in 2013 when its payment affiliate, Ant Financial, aggregated all the small balances in its customers' accounts into a money market fund, allowing those customers to make a financial return on their surplus cash. By May 2018, that fund, called Yu'e Bao, which translates as "Leftover Treasures," was the biggest money market fund *in the world*, with $266 billion under management. Today, traditional banks in China and elsewhere worry more about these new entities and their clones than they do about their legacy competitors.[2] As Piyush Gupta, CEO of DBS Bank Singapore, remarked about firestorm disruption (in a play on a famous Mike Tyson quote), "You don't know where the punch in the face is going to come from."[3]

That's firestorm disruption of a particularly disturbing kind—what is sometimes called "big-bang disruption." The need to scan for it and mount an aggressive attack and defense against it is vital, as is the need to adopt growth mindsets, Radical Ideation, and extreme war-gaming to help leaders become more confident in making do-or-die decisions. Confronting this kind of firestorm disruption also requires leaders to understand the costs of inaction and to find ways to overcome risk aversion or legacy thinking. They first need to "rethink how they think" about firestorm disruption, as suggested by some of the finest strategic minds in the field of business research who have influenced our research on this.[4] Fundamentally, we believe the most important element is to switch your leadership thinking mode.

DIFFERENT KINDS OF LEADERS FACE THE FIRESTORM

Our most important sources of information about the effects of firestorm disruption in the modern business environment come from women and men in the live battlefield—the participants in Encounter sessions. These executives, who are mostly CEOs and other C-suite leaders, join Encounters from many countries and industries, and they arrive with a great variety of experiences and goals.

These are all great people. Many have successfully guided their organizations through major changes. All have potential. All have wrestled with serious management issues: maybe a hostile attack from a competitor or the arrival of a new market entrant, maybe rising costs or emerging markets or a tech disruptor. All want to become the best leaders they can be. But when it comes to dealing with the new order of firestorm disruption, many leaders admit they are struggling.

Our field research shows 80 percent of these executives fall into one or more of the following four types of strategic leadership thinking (they are not mutually exclusive).[5] You may even recognize yourself or people you know in this cast of characters:

- **The Complacent.** These leaders think disruption can't happen to them because they are in some sort of "exceptional" position. Perhaps they enjoy a monopoly or a favored nation status, or they have legacy government concessions. Perhaps their industry has shown limited volatility for many years and their company is very good at exploiting steady-state operations. Perhaps they just have blinders on. For whatever reason, these overconfident leaders are very fixed in their outlook and too comfortable in their place.[6]

- **The Arrogant.** These leaders believe they have all the answers and are dismissive of ideas different from their own. Older leaders in this category often exhibit excessive pride in an iconic brand, best-selling product, or solid previous financial performance, which leads to hubris throughout the organization. Deep pockets and current market leadership compound their illusion of invulnerability. Young leaders in this category are often the stars of in-house training programs—or an overhyped startup. Inveterate conference-goers or bloggers, they are up to date on the trade literature and super eager to share their own experiences, never suspecting that what they really need to do is *unlearn* much of what they think they know.

- **The Cautious.** These leaders mistake incremental improvements for dynamic progress. They think periodic introductions of "new and improved" products, an obsession with metrics, and tinkering with the organization chart will keep them safe. Real change in these organizations will be reactive, if it occurs at all, and usually comes far too late.

- **The Overwhelmed.** These leaders become paralyzed in the face of uncertainty. They schedule meetings, order reports, call in consultants, urge caution—but do not move forward. They mistake dithering for prudence. No one has ever schooled them in the organizational costs of inaction.[7] In these leaders, vulnerability is accompanied by intense frustration over their inability to understand the scale and velocity of change and their inability to manage it, survive it, or take advantage of it.

There are many problems here and it is easy to criticize, but there is also reason to sympathize. After all, many of the dysfunctional attitudes and behaviors we see in this list were encouraged or rewarded in organizations for generations. They are especially common now across the very senior ranks of legacy firms, but we also see them in some new entrants and entrepreneurial enterprises.

These leadership types find handling or imagining firestorm disruption incredibly difficult. That's why the leadership approach and attitude need to move to a Completely Opposite Viewpoints Debate.

This turns the strategic conversation around from confirmation seeking to contradiction seeking. When people can't do this, you can see the trouble coming right at them. Some of them see it, too, and many of them tell us they feel concerned. They are stuck—stuck in the kind of middle-vision, inside-out, backward-looking thinking that is very common in once-successful businesses. They are so caught up in their past successes or so invested in the status quo or their "grand idea" that they are unable to see what's coming.

In Their Own Words

Sometimes the Encounter participants say it best. Here is one leader who admitted he was in the ranks of the Arrogant.

To be frank, the mindset of my leadership team is a positive one, focused on getting results and supporting innovation in our business. Our challenge now is that we are just not fast enough in coming up with the breakthrough thinking we actually need, and we are full of ideas that are merely variants of our past successes. Our mindsets have little to do with the disrupting landscape or technologies ahead and everything to do with our past successes because we were really great with that.

—PEDRO SANTOS, CEO of a South American packaged consumer goods company

For leaders, we call this the "legacy trap," a focus on replicating past successes, improving the performance of existing components, and defending the existing space. Even when these firms see a small disruption in their market, they tend to ignore or dismiss it, arguing that the market segment is so small or of no strategic importance, or that a response to this disruption would cannibalize other parts of their business, or that there is limited capacity or ability in the organization to respond effectively. So many reasons to do nothing! Meanwhile, the firestorm disruptors gain market share; iteratively improve their technology, business model, and processes; and move in to attack multiple segments of the legacy firm's larger markets.[8]

Our experience is that these leaders too often look for strategic options "in the rearview mirror" as Ram says, "when they should be looking for bends in the road ahead."[9] They need to envision their *future* ecosystem (future customers, future competitors, future technology, future talent, and future partners), and they need to make *that* happen as soon as possible.[10]

The signs that stakeholders are becoming increasingly fixated on leaders capable of outside-in and future-back thinking are everywhere. Since 2010, a rising tide of once-bulletproof CEOs has been shown the door: Mark Fields at Ford, Jeff Immelt and John Flannery at GE, Ronald Boire at Barnes & Noble, John Flint at HSBC, and top executives at three of the six major Hollywood studios and three of the biggest luxury goods groups in the world. Investors and boards that once focused only on quarterly numbers are now looking for leaders who have real foresight, leaders who can make the kind of smart and fast bets needed to fend off disruptors and manage the execution of changes effectively. Mickey Drexler, the former CEO of J.Crew, summed it up well: "I have never seen the speed of change as it is today," he told the *Wall Street Journal* in 2017. "If I could go back ten years, I might have done some things earlier. We became a little too elitist in our attitude."[11] We note J.Crew filed for bankruptcy in May 2020.[12]

But the leaders we just described are not the only kinds of leaders we see. There is a fifth category, smaller at present but growing fast in numbers:

- **The Dreamers and Doers.**[13] These leaders are explorers and navigators who can both envision dramatic change and execute it. Neither overzealous imagineers nor obsessive micromanagers, they have their heads screwed on right. They are forward-thinking, they are on the ball, they connect the imagined big picture to the tasks at hand. They are willing to envision a future where change is a constant and they don't have all the answers. In fact, they find uncertainty stimulating and outside viewpoints exciting. These are Phoenix leaders in the making.

We think of one Encounter participant, Robert Cummins, who led a gene therapy research program at a leading Irish university. Robert saw the threat to his program that was presented by aggressive for-profit entities that moved fast and weren't afraid to take risks. With insights gained from the Encounter Battlefield and its follow-up discussions, Robert took stock of his program and devised a new blueprint business model for the work that he loved. He then took a sabbatical from academia and created his own private for-profit venture, an agile spin-off from his old department that exploited artificial intelligence and used faster computing technology for the gene treatments. There, as a new CEO, Robert maintained ties with the university but left the risk-averse foot-draggers behind.

SOME LEADERS KNOW TECHNOLOGY ACCELERATES THEIR FIRE

Embracing the velocity and acceleration of firestorm change is what Phoenix leaders must dream about and do. We talk a lot in this book about the role of new technologies in disrupting businesses models, as it is by far the most forceful source of firestorm fuel in the twenty-first century. Technology is that wild card that even the savviest, farsighted legacy leaders have trouble addressing in their strategic thinking, especially new technologies like cloud computing, platform-based ecosystems, algorithms, robotics, machine learning, and artificial intelligence. These are technical but not always in an observable, hands-on way, and the changes they could bring can be hard to foresee. So are the opportunities. Often, the promised rewards lie far beyond the frames of traditional business planning cycles. What is clear is that every firestorm opportunity that technology presents to one organization or industry presents a burn-down threat to another. Technological firestorm innovations divide the world into winners and losers—some thrive while some get burned.

New technologies put business leaders in a tough spot. They also serve as a litmus test for the different leadership thinking approaches.

Despite imminent technological innovations, complacent leaders continue to go about their business, thinking that what they don't know can't hurt them. Arrogant leaders double down on their company's indisputable core competencies. Cautious leaders undertake limited scope investigations and halfway measures, perhaps customizing some new technological solutions for a few existing business processes. Overwhelmed leaders become anxious and do—nothing. Only Dreamers and Doers think about stepping into the fire emdash they are "Phoenix-like".

Consider the early casualties of the digital revolution, including print newspapers, which were hit by a double whammy. On the production side, their daily and weekly news cycles were disrupted by on-the-spot Internet reporting; on the sales side, classified advertising was disrupted by Internet marketplaces like Craigslist. Other well-known casualties include government postal services across the world disrupted by email,[14] and independent book and music stores upended by Amazon and other Internet marketplaces. The roll call of organizations disrupted by tech-savvy upstarts at the end of the past century is long and familiar.

But not every legacy firm gets slammed. One of the early Dreamers and Doers we identify was Fujifilm. This photographic filmmaker avoided wholesale disruption in the late 1970s by embracing digital photography and redefining itself as an "image and information recording company." Kodak, by contrast, developed its own digital camera but buried it for years, fearing it would cannibalize the mainline business.[15] Fujifilm's reinvention of itself was neither tentative nor modest. It led to the development of high-priced hardware products not aligned with Fujifilm's legacy business model; it also required a major restructuring of the company, including the integration of its digital research and development (R&D) team with its mainstream R&D division.[16] It was the sort of wholesale, transformative response to a technological challenge that we would now characterize as a "Phoenix Breakthrough." And Phoenix-like Fujifilm (now 86 years old) continues to reinvent itself. In 2006, the company created a cosmetics line for its business portfolio by leveraging its experience with particular photographic film components and technologies, including collagen, antioxidants, light analysis, and nanotechnology, and applying them to skincare. In 2019, Fujifilm's healthcare and materials solution business accounted for 43 percent of revenues.[17]

Clearly, legacy firms can reinvent themselves Phoenix-like in the face of firestorm disruption. If they have the right leadership attitude, they can even use new technologies to do it. Conversely, once-dominant technology upstarts can also easily succumb to new players and new technologies: Blockbuster, undone by Netflix's streaming content platform; Polaroid, the imaging pioneer in the 1960s that got left behind by digital photography; Nokia, the king of mobile phones with a market cap in excess of $150 billion in its heyday, brought down to Earth in less than two years by Apple, a newcomer to the telecom business; Netscape, the biggest Internet name with a $2 billion IPO debut in 1995, beaten in the browser wars by Microsoft. Being tech savvy is no guarantee of success. Think of how 4G-enabled smartphones swept away the once-popular car-mounted GPS hardware systems made by TomTom and Garmin—a type of "big-bang" firestorm disruption where they were not even the intended targets but became collateral casualties of other battles.[18]

TWENTY-FIRST-CENTURY TECHNOLOGY IS A VERY DISTINCTIVE FIRESTORM

What is it about new technologies that makes them so powerful in firestorm disruption, even to disruptors? Why do innovations like platforms, social media, and big data analytics make even Dreamer and Doer Phoenix-like leaders so uneasy? It's not only because new technologies are creating new products and services. It is because they are fundamentally changing the way that business or industry is organized, rewriting the underlying business modes, and vastly expanding the size of competitive playing fields.

Firestorm disruption from these new technologies comes most directly from their ability to unlock information that was formerly guarded by middlemen, who for generations used it to create arbitrage rents for themselves. Think of travel agents in the business-to-consumer (B2C) markets and distributors/resellers in the business-to-business (B2B) world. Today, most of that once-exclusive information is freely available to businesses and consumers alike. As a result, many obsolete middleman operations are gone, and new enterprises like online travel agents (e.g., Expedia and Agoda) and platforms (e.g., Alibaba, GlobalSources.com, and IndiaMart.com) are taking the newly liberated information to the bank. And while the travel industry as a whole is undergoing arguably the toughest period in its history due to COVID-19, a consolidated group of digital-natives have a much higher chance of survival and post-crisis surge than traditional travel agencies. But they will require Phoenix-like thinking to do this!

Unlocking information flows radically reduces transaction costs across industries and geographies. This phenomenon takes us back to the work of Nobel Prize–winning economist Ronald Coase, who in the 1930s argued that the boundaries of twentieth-century businesses were largely dictated by the high price of three sets of transaction costs: the costs of search, the costs of coordination, and the costs of contracting.[19] Because the cost of satisfying these functions on the open market was high, companies often brought those functions in-house. Even in the United States, arguably one of the most informationally efficient markets in the world, two-thirds of all transactions in the twentieth century were conducted in-house.[20]

Those days are long gone. Today, digital mobility, information ubiquity, and connectivity have reduced, if not completely eliminated, many historical transaction costs that once burdened firms and turned them inward. New leaner and nimbler models have emerged in the spaces that the transaction costs once occupied, and they are challenging traditional legacy firms.

For examples, let's take a look at three newcomers. Notice the far-sighted vision of their founders, their disregard for accepted ways of doing things, and their enthusiasm for a new order. These are Phoenix-like organizations making their mark on the old world.

The first is BeingSattvaa, a yoga retreat and luxury wellness resort in Ubud, Bali.

> Founded in 2015 by a couple who had tired of the stresses
> of modern-day corporate life, BeingSattvaa had no corporate
> franchise, no brand recognition, no quality-control reports,

and no marketing apparatus to overcome the steep cost of getting its name in front of potential customers. In the analog world, the retreat would have languished, waiting for the stray yoga enthusiast to wander down its banana tree-lined path or read about it in a Lonely Planet guidebook. But this was the digital world, and it enabled social media. Today, almost all the information about BeingSattvaa is created by its customers on user-generated content sites like TripAdvisor and Expedia. Two years after launch, the retreat was among a handful of properties in Bali that had earned TripAdvisor's Certificate of Excellence and Expedia's Exceptional rating—credentials based entirely on user-generated reviews. New technologies had allowed BeingSattvaa to circumvent the once-prohibitive transaction costs associated with search.[21]

Next, look at Slack, a set of cloud-based communication tools that reduces coordination costs in the workplace.

Stewart Butterfield created Slack in 2013 to streamline team communications in his online gaming company, Tiny Speck. The gaming company folded, but Butterfield's toolkit worked so well that it quickly became one of the most popular workplace "chat" apps in the world. But Slack is more than just chat. It also allows teams to coordinate their work in real time using integrated spreadsheets, documents, and cloud storage. The resulting productivity gains are impressive. By 2018, companies with Slack collaboration tools in place report 23 percent fewer internal meetings, 32 percent fewer email messages, 23 percent faster time to market for development teams, a 13 percent reduction in overall sales cycle, and a 10 percent rise in employee satisfaction. Its IPO in June 2019 gave the company a $23 billion valuation.[22] And the power of Slack's technology became even more apparent when lockdowns forced organizations world over to overnight shift to accommodate almost exclusive remote work. It wasn't a surprise that they showed a 73 percent gain in share price during the first half of 2020.

A third example is Ujo Music, which has taken blockchain technology into the music industry to reduce contracting costs.

> One of the biggest problems for artists in the music industry is digital rights management: the ability to track and distribute payments across a very fragmented value chain of intermediaries including artists, publishers, and labels. Streaming sites like Spotify and iTunes provide this service, but they take a big cut of the royalties. In response to increasing complaints from artists that the prevailing arrangement denied them a fair share, Ujo Music proposed a blockchain solution. Working with musician Imogen Heap to release her track "Tiny Human," the company used Ethereum-based software to allow fans to buy licenses to Heap's music directly, while automatically splitting payments among Heap's collaborators. Ujo hopes to build a platform where artists can launch their own blockchain-based stores with payment gateways and "smart contracts" that specify the division of royalties, allowing artists to fully control the licensing and distribution of their music.[23]

All three of these enterprises—BeingSattvaa, Slack, and Ujo Music—have put emerging technologies at the center of their strategic business models, reducing or sidestepping transaction and other costs that once dictated how companies should organize, how business gets done, and how much that service would cost. In so doing, they radically redraw the boundaries of firms, and possibly whole industries, and they leave many legacy firms behind. Their leaders have Phoenix Dreamer and Doer instincts. Seeing opportunity in firestorm disruption, they cast off the old body of the traditional edifices and take flight as a Phoenix enterprise.

If a collection of yoga enthusiasts, online gamers, and struggling artists can do it, so can you. So, which type of leader for your organization will you be? The Phoenix Dreamer and Doer or something else? Are you curious about new technologies as an accelerator of change? Do you know how to harness these? Do you have potential firestorm disruption opportunities in your sights?

No? Not yet? Then you are like many leaders: interested but wary. Even some leaders we identify as Dreamers and Doers often struggle to commit to big technological or business model change. They want a Phoenix Breakthrough and they want to surge post crisis, but they don't know how to get there.

What they (and you) will need is a thorough attitude adjustment and a revolution in leadership thinking. That's why these matters are central to the Completely Opposite Viewpoints Debate and other processes of the Phoenix Encounter method.

CHAPTER **2** CHECKLIST

Summary Thoughts

1. The current firestorm of disruptive change is materializing at a speed, scale, and ferocity unprecedented in history. It is global in scope and cuts across every industry and sector. It includes unstoppable trends in technology, digital and social media, platforms and ecosystems, demographics, emerging markets, climate change, workplace expectations, and government regulation—to name just some. The COVID-19 crisis has increased the velocity of these firestorm trends.

2. Many once-successful firms are caught in a legacy trap, overly focused on replicating past success, improving the performance of existing components, and defending legacy obsolescence. Some firms struggle because their leaders are overconfident, complacent, cautious, or just overwhelmed. A handful of gifted leaders are able to see the future and act on it. They are curious and they embrace change. These Phoenix leaders are Dreamers and Doers. Some leaders display this talent naturally; others learn it in through the Phoenix Encounter method.

3. New technologies are unlocking information, radically reducing transaction costs, redefining business models, and redrawing the very boundaries of firms and industries.

Reflection

1. Are you prepared for the disruption from new technologies, digitization, platforms, and new entrants? Are you ready for demographic and social changes, changes in customer behavior, and changing regulations and public policy? Are you prepared for the acceleration of many of these trends due to COVID-19?

2. What type of leader are you today—the Complacent, the Cautious, the Arrogant, the Overwhelmed? How about your boss, your board, or your team? Do you want to become a Dreamer and Doer, if you aren't one already?

3. How are the disruptive forces changing your transaction costs (e.g., costs of search, coordination, and contracting)? How might this redraw the boundaries of doing business for you and your stakeholders? How might others take advantage of transaction cost changes to create value for their stakeholders?

1 PHOENIX SEEKING
ENCOUNTER GROUNDWORK

● ATTITUDE SWITCH   ● BATTLEFIELD PREPARATION

? MINDSETS
? VALUE PROPOSITIONS
? TRENDS
? PHOENIX ATTITUDE

WHY DO WE DO THINGS the WAY WE DO?

2 PHOENIX BURNING
ENCOUNTER BATTLEFIELD

● EXTREME ATTACK   ● HORIZON DEFENSE

DIGITAL · TECH · M&A

IMAGINE the MOST RADICAL ATTACK...
and LEAD your ORGANIZATION toward
a more FORMIDABLE FUTURE!

3 PHOENIX RISING
ENCOUNTER BREAKTHROUGH

● FUTURE-FACING BLUEPRINT   ● EMBEDDING PHOENIX DNA

IMMEDIATE
SHORT-TERM
MEDIUM-TERM
LONG-TERM

★ NEW VALUE PROPOSITIONS
★ NEW BUSINESS MODELS
★ NEW STRATEGIC PRIORITIES

CHAPTER 3

THE PHOENIX ENCOUNTER METHOD

We may encounter many defeats, but we must not be defeated.
—MAYA ANGELOU, American writer and author of *Still I Rise*[1]

Many leaders perceive the firestorm clearly (it is already scorching their feet) and they have some ideas, but many also don't know how to get to where they need to go. What these leaders want is a process to help them navigate the journey of firestorm discovery. The Phoenix Encounter method is exactly that. It is a set of rules, tasks, tools, and exercises that provide a structured process for ideation and detection that allows leaders to consider many different options and formulate a grounded Future-Facing Blueprint for their organizations.

This is crucial because we are all hardwired to "confirmation bias,"[2] that tendency to seek or interpret new evidence as endorsements of our existing beliefs and views. Looking for opposite thoughts and getting contradicted is not a natural desire for leaders. Yet seeking opposing views must become a habit for all organizational leaders. Why? All leaders will face firestorm disruption or destruction of some kind much more frequently than in the past. That's where the Phoenix Encounter method comes in. The Encounter bridges the gap between *perceiving threats and opportunities* and *developing a strategic blueprint to tackle them*—it forces leaders systematically to challenge their confirmation bias, individually and collectively.

The Phoenix Encounter's central Battlefield exercise provides the Completely Opposite Viewpoints Debate that leaders need for this. It is different from traditional business war games, in which participants typically assume the roles of known competitors seeking to win an identified battle created from a list of "what could be" scenarios.[3] Instead, the Phoenix Encounter builds several different Extreme Attack scenarios in which known, unknown, and even improbable adversaries can use a destructive and unconstrained arsenal against the incumbent's firm or sector or even the whole industry. Importantly, these Extreme Attacks are imagined without regard to such real-life constraints as time, money, or government regulation (because these constraints could change very quickly—and constraints restrict initial option generation). This extreme firestorm attack environment encourages boundary-breaking thinking, Radical Ideation, and unconstrained imagining of strategic options that are totally "outside the box."

By contrast, the Encounter's Battlefield defense exercise provides a complement to traditional scenario planning and competitive analysis by forcing participants to consider a very wide range of options for shielding and fortifying the core business, building a new business model and competencies, and creating breakthrough innovation initiatives. After the Encounter war game is over, the Phoenix method then guides the leader out of the "no-man's-land" by providing the tools needed for setting new strategic priorities and developing a future-facing blueprint of action plans to achieve them.

We overviewed the Phoenix Encounter method in Chapter 1, and now we explore it in detail.* In summary, the Phoenix Encounter cycle takes leaders and their teams through three phases: Groundwork, Battlefield, and Breakthrough (Figure 3.1).

---

*Resources for running a Phoenix Encounter, including templates, scripts, exercises, attack environment scenarios, and teaching tools, are available to readers and facilitators through our book website: www.phoenixencountermethod.com. There will also be a companion *Facilitation Guide for the Phoenix Encounter Method*.

FIGURE 3.1 The Phoenix Encounter Method—Phases and Cycle

To help readers understand the Phoenix Encounter method in practice, we share the story of Amy Kreutzer as she lives through all the phases of the Encounter method. Amy is the COO (and CEO designate) of a large British private hospital and retirement care business (Horcomp PLC) that had grown more than 30 percent during the previous five years.

Amy Enters Her Encounter

Amy walked into her Phoenix Encounter exercise with mixed feelings—some confidence and some trepidation. While a publicly listed business, Horcomp had three significant major shareholders owning around 55 percent of the company. Since joining Horcomp, much of her work had been focused on achieving efficiencies and modernizing corporate processes, as well as integrating some small acquisitions.

Amy had participated in Horcomp's off-site annual strategic planning just prior to joining the Phoenix Encounter as part of a senior leadership development program in early 2018. This program was to help her prepare for the CEO role later in the year. In her pre-program reflection, she wrote: "I have three big questions on my mind: What significant changes will be needed to ensure our business continues growing during the next decade? What risks are out there that we haven't thought about? What would I need to change in myself to be able to lead the team successfully in transforming our business?"

PHASE ONE: PHOENIX SEEKING— ENCOUNTER GROUNDWORK

The Encounter's Phase One lays the groundwork for the eventual Phoenix Breakthrough by confronting old mindsets and scanning for new threats and opportunities through two essential tasks:

- **Attitude Switch.** Participants identify their current mindsets, as well as those of others operating in their business environment, and consider how these might be blocking their organization's ability to deal with firestorm change. They learn about the Phoenix Attitude and make an inventory of the tools and habits of mind that will get them through the coming attack and defense. Then they link these learnings to their personal leadership development agenda.

- **Battlefield Preparation.** In their Encounter Journal, participants prepare a baseline report describing their organization's value proposition and evaluating its current strengths and weaknesses. This is the first of several strategic reflections they will create throughout the Encounter. Preparing for the Battlefield exercise, they scan new technologies, demographic changes, business model innovations, and other unstoppable trends of firestorm disruption.

The main challenge for facilitators at the Encounter's Groundwork phase is to instill a Phoenix Attitude and heighten participants' sense of urgency about firestorm disruption. We do this by exposing weaknesses in different styles of leadership thinking and by examining case studies of businesses that have been done in by wrong thinking or a failure to scan for unstoppable trends. After reviewing different leadership mindset problems, we explain the importance of diverse perspectives in strategic dialogue and the special power of using a Completely Opposite Viewpoints Debate. Another essential element at the outset is to help Encounter participants begin their strategic reflection through preparing their Encounter pre-work initial briefing report (see *Amy Starts Her Groundwork*).

Amy Starts Her Groundwork

Amy diligently prepared the pre-work initial briefing report on her business in her Encounter Journal. She described her business and market, with key facts about the sector and an overview of the kinds of clients they served in the two parts of the organization: hospitals and retirement care. She highlighted some strategic strengths, including geographic reach of the facilities across the country; their brand name in hospitals; the recent computer automation of care records for the retirement villages; the commitment of long-term staff in most facilities; a focus on two business streams (separately justified by core competency differences for each one); and a $10 billion market cap.

Her report showcased the core value proposition as "availability": hospital beds and retirement units where and when people needed them. She emphasized the stability of the business models for both segments and noted a couple of planned innovation projects that would improve procurement processes and maintenance services across the group. She listed the key strategic challenges and weaknesses: slowing growth; constantly changing government regulations; the tension between publicly and privately funded healthcare; difficult relationships with health insurers; largely manual systems for managing hospital clients; and a very risk-averse leadership team who had mostly been with the business more than two decades and "who know how to do what we do really well."

After pre-work is done, participants break out into their Encounter teams, called Phoenix Encounter Groups (PEGs) and the Encounter overview briefings take place. Ideally, a PEG team will have five to seven members—large enough to divide up tasks but small enough to develop esprit de corps. This is important because the same team will both attack and defend the incumbent organization. During this first meeting, PEG members share perspectives and questions about one another's initial briefing reports. The facilitator then explains the rules, language, and tools that will be used in the Battlefield exercise and encourages participants to start thinking about potential outcomes, including some that might be difficult (such as realizing their organization is not invulnerable).

The PEG teams are neither randomly chosen nor self-selected; they are carefully organized for maximum diversity of thinking and experience. When the Encounter takes place within programs that attract leaders from a range of public and private enterprises, we draw PEG members from different organizations (nondisclosure arrangements are in place). These are usually C-suite executives from different industries and geographies, representing organizations from the for-profit, nonprofit, and public sectors.

The more diversity there is on any PEG team, the better. Organizational affiliation matters less than attitude. CEOs sometimes balk at this arrangement, arguing that "outsiders" lack the expertise required to understand their industry or will bring misguided information to the table. This has not been our experience. Far from it, we have found outsiders to be *the most valuable* PEG members precisely *because* they don't know each other's business, especially when they are senior C-suite executives. They may not know how you do things, but they know how to run a business, they have information about other sectors, and their imaginations are freer to generate ideas. They are also less likely to defer to leadership authority in the war room.

Amy Joins Her Encounter Team Members

Amy paid a lot of attention as the Encounter facilitators described the process of scanning sessions and the Radical Ideation ahead to destroy one's own business and then rebuild it through a series of what they called Completely Opposite Viewpoints Debates with five other people from totally different industries and geographies. She told us later that at this point, she was not really certain "what value this might provide, especially with a bunch of people from different industries who could not possibly absorb the real details of my industry."

She shared her Encounter Journal initial briefing report with the members of her PEG team and received theirs as well. Her five other team members were: a German CFO in the automotive parts business; a French global marketing head of a beauty products company; the CEO of a family business in energy supply in Africa; the American COO of a digital travel services firm; and a New Zealand curator of an art museum.

At the initial PEG meeting, she was the first to describe her business and was completely surprised by the questions she was asked: "Your two business models are completely understandable—you provide base services consistent with your regulatory environment— but why don't you leverage service opportunities between both segments? Is your separate business line focus justified or are these really silo fiefdoms? Why are you not fully digitized in everything you do? With so many long-term leaders, are you worried that your 'gene pool' is too small? Is 'availability' really what your clients want?" Amy defended the status quo on all of these but found it quite discomforting that similar questions were asked for every different leader when they presented their business around the table in turn. She recalled the lectures on leadership attitude, mindsets, and bias from yesterday. And then she walked into three scanning sessions titled "Platform and Ecosystem Magic," "Firestorm Technology Drivers," and "The Workforce of the Future Is Already Here."

When the Encounter is conducted within a single enterprise, we strive for as much diversity as possible in the PEG teams across different departments, functions, skill sets, genders, cultures, and generations. Sometimes, when the target organization is small or especially insular, its leader invites outsiders to join the teams to give some external perspective (e.g., customers, partners).

In particular, we have found that including outsiders on the teams very often reveals just how stuck incumbent leaders are at a status quo confirmation level of thinking. Within the company, the CEO may be the most visionary person in the room, but in the war room, CEOs often have trouble with the question "Why in the world do you do things that way?" Moving the conversation from "how" to "why" is an important contribution from outside team members. Outsiders are often much better at spotting status quo or confirmation bias and other mindset problems than members of the incumbent's executive team. They are the catalysts and enforcers of the Completely Opposite Viewpoints Debate.

> The focus of the Groundwork phase is preparation; the methods are personal reflection and strategic conversation; the work includes switching attitude, preparing a status report, and preparing for battle; the tools include the Phoenix Attitude, the Encounter Journal reflections, and the habits and rituals of Extra Strategic Perception (see Chapter 5); the key words are *seek* and *study*.

PHASE TWO: PHOENIX BURNING— ENCOUNTER BATTLEFIELD

At the center of the Phoenix Encounter method is the Battlefield engagement that is usually waged over a couple of days. Each leader takes a turn in the "hot seat" as the PEG team first attacks with as much unconstrained and disruptive firepower options as possible. They will all later defend the target organization.

Throughout, team participants undertake a series of proactive scans, searching for disruptive firepower weapons. These weapons include both contemporary firepower (like new technologies and digital business models) and conventional firepower (like mergers and acquisitions and process or asset optimization). How the participants use these weapons—alone or in combination—is entirely up to their imaginations. The more inventive the thinking, the better, for the battle is waged in a series of Completely Opposite Viewpoints Debates designed to elicit radical ideas. Each participant leaves the exercise with a list of insights and options to think about. In the next phase, this list will be scrutinized, tested, and fine-tuned.

Let's look at the Battlefield exercise one stage at a time.

The Extreme Attack

Each stage of the Encounter is important, but the fire really erupts in the Extreme Attack, which pits a team of attackers against an incumbent organization. It is a guns-blazing, no-holds-barred firefight designed to be enormously destructive. This is the exciting, stressful, and truly revelatory core of the Encounter experience.

Participants begin by selecting one of many attack environment scenarios provided by the facilitator to create an overall extreme environments. All involve the disruption or destruction of some real part of the leader's incumbent organization—perhaps a business unit, the entire company, or even the entire industry. One attack environment scenario, for example, imagines that the incumbent CEO has been hired away to lead a new company intent on destroying the incumbent's business. Another imagines that a newly elected government decides to abolish the incumbent's departmental agency.

During the Extreme Attack stage, PEG team members dissect the target company's vulnerabilities, assemble the most disruptive weapons, and then advance different lines of attack to destroy the organization. When PEG team members come from outside organizations, they easily bring fundamentally opposite ideas to the table. When they come from the same organization, we ask each to assume the role of a different stakeholder (such as an entrepreneur, a big customer, a small customer, a supplier, a board member, an investor, or a regulator) and then build an attack from that set of interests. In all cases, team members contribute radical lines of attack to the Completely Opposite Viewpoints Debate. In the face of this opposition, incumbent leaders can easily become overwhelmed, so we suggest they also take a role in the attack, unshackling their thinking in their own list of attack ideas.

Once all the ideas are on the table, the PEG team goes to work debating them, arguing pros and cons, brainstorming new ideas, and then combining, editing, and finally consolidating the best options into the most destructive campaign they can collectively create. To make the Extreme Attack truly formidable, the rules of engagement remove all resource, funding, and technology constraints and usual market inhibitors from the plotting.

A well-constructed attack puts all the formidable firepower to use, especially contemporary weapons like new technologies, platform business models, demographic shifts, changing workplace behaviors, global market movements, social trends (such as sustainability, environmental activism, and climate change), and potential changes to government policy. In the Extreme Attack environment, where the game is unconstrained by legacy resources and paradigms, this arsenal can inflict a level of devastation seldom seen in ordinary strategic debate or even in traditional war-gaming (see *Amy Deploys Unlimited Firepower*).

Conventional weapons do have a place in the Extreme Attack, especially those like mergers and acquisitions that have the power to restructure the incumbent organization, not just tinker with it. But these weapons will play a bigger part in the Horizon Defense, when the work gets down to tactics.

Amy Deploys Unlimited Firepower

Amy was very uncomfortable with the Encounter Battlefield rule that as an attacker, she would have complete insider knowledge and totally unconstrained firepower—money, technology, and people. Equally difficult was the concept of separating idea generation from analysis in the Encounter discussions—generating a long list of radical ideas before diving into details.

Before the brainstorm for attack options, she prepared a short list of what she considered ambitious ideas for the attackers: hospitals and retirement villages where everything was digitized, with an internal data analytics team to help inform patient, elder care, and operational decision-making; hospitals building new facilities that could provide health services and care for different stages of people's lives; and a close alliance with three of the largest insurers to provide additional care services at lower costs.

She then listened to brainstormed attack ideas from her PEG team members. With unlimited funding and resources, their list had much bolder suggestions. The new company (called Newco) would not own facilities but create an integrated digital platform across the hospital, retirement, and other care services sectors. This would open the platform to any and all private hospitals, insurers, and retirement and care providers. Newco would build out the ecosystem to include lifestyle wellness care offerings (like massage, meditation, and nutrition counseling) and other services (such as a discrete social network for the retirees to connect with one another, their families, and friends)—all offered by other partners through the company's platform.

The new platform would promote users "being well for life." Newco would poach her best younger-generation talent. Operationally, it would engage a fully outsourced data analytics partnership to provide value-adding analysis for all the users. The platform would have a marketplace of partners in the arts and sports to create in-hospital and retirement village activities and would have an alliance with a digital travel provider. Artificial intelligence (AI) and robotic trials would be supported in hospitals via partnership with medical researchers. Drone-based delivery of prescription medications at the retirement homes could be coordinated through the platform. Post-procedure telemedicine counseling would be encouraged.

Newco and its partners would lobby government to remove restrictions on nonhospital services being collocated at care facilities. Another regulatory attack was to force companies with hospitals and retirement homes to divest one or the other to focus on reducing costs and increasing service value. One of the team's most radical ideas was Newco teaming up with an activist shareholder to force management change immediately in Horcomp and getting the major shareholders to support using their facilities as the starting partners for the new platform by getting them to swap out ownership in some of their facilities to a third party in exchange for cash, an operating agreement, and a major seed stake in the new platform.

Amy combined the most disruptive ideas from these suggestions into her Extreme Attack plan. The Extreme Attack debate led her to some startling conclusions she shared with us: "If this happened, the long-held business model of my firm and industry would be overthrown, facility ownership would become more like a utility, and the leaders of Newco would look nothing like my leadership team. Could anything like this really happen?"

In the aftermath of the Extreme Attack, an incumbent organization often finds that its boundaries have been breached or redrawn. Perhaps it has lost a market or a supply chain or longstanding partners. Perhaps its marketing strategy has been torpedoed by a hostile social media attack or activist campaign. Perhaps its core competency has been rendered obsolete. Perhaps key talent has been poached or new ecosystem alliances have been made. Sometimes a new regulatory environment arises, and sometimes an entire industry is reconfigured. From time to time, new product and services ideas emerge that the incumbent cannot exploit for one reason or another—but some other organization will.

The goal in the Extreme Attack is to take the highest, most strategic view of organizational firestorm change (i.e., the big picture 50,000-foot leadership altitude we describe in Chapter 4). The dreaming is now; the doing comes later.

The focus of the Extreme Attack is devastation; the methods are dramatic war-gaming with Radical Ideation; the work is Proactive Scanning, generating extreme, unconstrained options to devise a devastating attack; the weapons are contemporary and conventional firepower; tools include the Phoenix Attitude, the Completely Opposite Viewpoints Debate, and the habits and rituals of Extra Strategic Perception; the key words are *scan* and *strike*.

The Horizon Defense

The Horizon Defense stage answers the Extreme Attack on the Battlefield. Ideally, it does more than just keep the incumbent company alive by setting the perimeter. Like the best moves on a chessboard, a good Horizon Defense will lead the incumbent organization toward a more formidable future position.

Like the attack, the defense unfolds in a series of opposite debates, one for each team member. This time, each participant proposes one or more ways to repel the attackers, outflank them, or leapfrog over them. The ensuing Completely Opposite Viewpoints Debate begins with Radical Ideation and sometimes harrowing endgame scenarios, but it soon works toward more measured responses. The facilitators turn down the heat, and participants begin to descend to strategic and tactical reality. Real-world business context now becomes important, and there is more considered thinking. Three distinct missions come into view: (1) options to counter the immediate attack, (2) options to fortify the core business, and (3) options for business model changes, innovation, transformation, and dominance in the future.

Surrender is not a defense option, and we have seen many leaders struggle with the likelihood that some of their legacy business will succumb to the firestorm disruption presented by their attackers. One painful and not uncommon realization is that other leaders or entities might be better owners or operators of the organization under siege. In those cases, divestment, outsourcing, or termination of some activities or staff might be the best move, particularly if such a move would release resources for more promising ventures. Once this psychological hurdle is cleared, most leaders rise to the challenge of reinventing their organizations and business models.

The most effective defensive moves we've seen incorporate both strategic options and actions, as well as tactical options and moves. They find ways to transform the incumbent business into a more sustainable enterprise so it can power and release resources for the changes needed for renewal. They exploit hot technologies and socio-economic trends, if these are relevant, while also doubling down on conventional business levers, such as operations, finance, reputational trust, and intergenerational talent management. They look at the organization's business model with an eye to where they may have a future role in platforms/ecosystems. At the same time, they consider how traditional strategies like mergers and acquisitions, coproduction, and unbundling can help them. They shield the company from all levels and angles—high and low and far and wide—to create a comprehensive defense that helps manage growth, cost, and risk.

After the Horizon Defense debate, participants record their best prospective strategic options—a kind of "Hot List"—and sequence these across four time horizons for action: immediate, short term, medium term, and long term. We require them to do this because we know that effective long-term change requires intensive short-term actions, including deep analysis work, planning for pilot projects, and stakeholder engagement. At this stage, the ideas are still rough, but the first stirrings of the Phoenix Breakthrough are now evident in the energy, excitement, relief, and confidence that have entered the room.

Amy Mints a New Defense in Response to the Attack

For Amy's Horizon Defense debate, she had a few starting ideas to repel the attack. Her PEG team urged her to consider that while the devastating attack might not all happen tomorrow, if it did unfold over time, would patients and residents have more choices, more value, and a better range of services at lower cost? She admitted, "Yes, absolutely, but our owners and industry would never agree to this kind of wholesale change."

She and her PEG team members debated ideas all around, probing with questions: Why not? What if? If not you, who might do this? She told us later, "They continually challenged me with the opposite view to building all new initiatives ourselves, relentlessly suggesting partnerships and the staged development of an ecosystem for care. Two of the team members directly challenged my certainty on how much change our owners and sector could contemplate."

She then crafted her defense. She realized that the Encounter Battlefield opposites debate, together with intensive scanning sessions, must be undertaken with her team, board, and major owner representatives as soon as possible. This was one of her three immediate priorities. The other two were to create a complete stakeholder engagement plan and to start deep analysis of her possible short-, medium-, and long-term defense ideas, using additional outside talent.

For short to medium term, she concluded that the Horizon Defense would include creating a small team to focus on digital, technology, and medical knowledge sharing and partner identification in this space; developing a pilot project to talk directly with clients on possible value-added services and whether "availability" really was what they wanted; and identifying younger, high-potential employees to get their suggestions for engaging them more fully in the business.

In addition, the already-planned efficiency initiatives should be given a dedicated team to accelerate business optimization initiatives immediately. This could free up resources to use for stepwise reconfiguration of their business model to a hybrid physical and virtual operation in the medium to long term. She added investigation projects on facility ownership/acquisition options; evaluation of partners for in-home post-surgery care services and operational outsourcing possibilities; and assessment of some hospitals converting to focus on one medical area for scale and specialization advantages.

She concluded that a regulatory defense was needed to lobby government to restrict nonowners of facilities (such as platforms) from undertaking or coordinating hospital and retirement care activities. She also saw a big opportunity to leverage their brand and offer to demonstrate the personalization of care services—the digital platform is secondary to the trust and safety of health and life care. These are not transactions to click for but are essential moments in a person's life.

Her defense was not her attack. It was a much more considered combination of radical ideas to explore and realistic options to undertake.

In a surreal twist, she got a call from the board chair the final evening of the Encounter exercise to tell her an activist shareholder had visited him and the retiring CEO that afternoon suggesting a lot of changes, including selling the retirement villages. Her reply: "We need to talk. I've got a lot of ideas to share."

The goal of the Horizon Defense debate is to create an initial set of strategic options for deeper analysis, evaluation, and decision-making in the Encounter's final phase when it will be time for the leaders to roll up their sleeves and start to execute. In the Horizon Defense, as in the Extreme Attack, there is much to think about and little time to do it. Both stages promote a heightened sense of urgency. In that high-adrenaline, eyes-wide-open environment, options come fast and furious, both full blown and half-baked. It is the work of the third phase of the Phoenix Encounter to put these into order and action.

> The focus of the Horizon Defense is survival, fortification, and ascendancy. The methods are dramatic war-gaming and Radical Ideation; the work is Proactive Scanning for new ways of doing things, generating prospective "Hot List" options for later analysis, and sequencing prospective ideas across four time horizons; the weapons are contemporary and conventional firepower; tools include the Phoenix Attitude, the Completely Opposite Viewpoints Debate, and the habits and rituals of Extra Strategic Perception; the key words are *scan* and *shield*.

PHASE THREE: PHOENIX RISING— ENCOUNTER BREAKTHROUGH[4]

Phase Three builds directly on the ideas that emerge in the Battlefield to chart a new course for the organization—to turn ideas into action. It can take a long time, often months and sometimes years, to work through the two tasks:

- **Future-Facing Blueprint.** Soon after the Battlefield exercise, participants collect and synthesize all the most promising ideas that bubbled up into a new high-level plan for their organization, using the Encounter Journal's template for a Future-Facing Blueprint. "Looking back from the future," this Blueprint can define potential new value propositions for stakeholders, identify new strategic priorities and business model transformation, or reprioritize or adjust existing initiatives.

Strengths are recalibrated to those needed for the future. Participants determine actions to be taken to realize the new strategic shifts and to fortify their core—to play out as "flight plans" over four time horizons: immediate, short term, medium term, and long term.

- **Embedding Phoenix DNA.** Participants take their Future-Facing Blueprint back to their organizations to test (including deeper rigorous analysis), revise, and implement the best initiatives identified. At the same time, they work to embed the Phoenix Attitude, tools and habits, the Battlefield exercise, and other elements of the Phoenix Encounter method into each of their organizations so it can transform itself again and again.

Early work on the Future-Facing Blueprint requires one last opposites debate with the PEG team. In this debate, the team works together to sort, select, prioritize, and stress-test the long list of options generated in the Horizon Defense, winnowing the options down to the top candidates and suggesting how each might be evaluated through deeper analysis, investigation, or experimentation (e.g., through pilot tests). The team must consider the likely gaps in the organization's resources, capabilities, talent, and culture, and they must provide unflinching feedback on the leader's own ability to lead the proposed change. After hearing all the opposing viewpoints, the leader decides which actions to include in the blueprint.

Immediate and short-term actions might include actions for engaging stakeholders (e.g., partners and boards) and setting up deep-dive analysis or pilot projects. Medium- and long-term actions might include acquiring new competencies and talents, monitoring and evaluating progress points, and embedding a culture of renewal while the business model transforms.

Once the Future-Facing Blueprint is ready in draft form, we encourage leaders to apply different strategic and analytical frameworks to their new ideas in their context for yet other perspectives and stress-testing. Helpful frameworks include various forms of quantitative analysis; Blue Ocean Strategy; scenario analysis; and Red Teaming.[5] Leaders can also consider other outside business advice they think might be relevant. Seeing now through the eyes of the phoenix, they should quickly discern which prescriptions are likely to be useful and which are not.

Amy's Blueprint for Breakthrough

Amy went back to her Encounter Journal and fleshed out her Future-Facing Blueprint based on attack and defense ideas. She imagined a transformed physical/digital business model over time with a "whole of life care" vision. She told us in the debrief: "I can now see a completely new way to achieve growth and manage cost and risk into the future. We must reinforce the current core business and bring forward some of our 'out-in-the-future' ideas. We must stop some activities (such as self-provision of many ancillary services), replace them with a series of new partnership providers, and create an AI-charged system to connect our retired residents with other services (like massage and games afternoons) and make social connections with their families and friends seamless. We should assess our talent against future requirements, not our past. As a leader, I want to light a fire under our business from next week."

Amy organized an Encounter debate back at Horcomp, with the retiring CEO agreeing not to be part of it. She then took up the reins as CEO and began embedding some transformative changes. In the first year, her leadership team was revitalized and adopted a "whole of life care" vision. They recruited talent to spearhead the technology and digital revolution work. They sought out a core partner (with funding and technical resources) who would work with them to create a future ecosystem of care support across a person's life cycle—integrated with physical care, and where the hospital surgery was part of the bigger health-life journey. The team entered into an ongoing dialogue with government and insurers to advocate policy changes, as well, including protecting the current industry on safety, trust, and compliance grounds.

In the Future-Facing Blueprint, and in the ongoing embedding work to come, a very important task for leaders is to regularly review their personal leadership development agendas, assessing areas of strength and weakness that have been revealed in the Encounter process and getting the kinds of support necessary to make themselves the best Phoenix leaders they can be.

The focus of the Breakthrough phase is the future of the organization and business model; the work includes action planning, stakeholder engagement, and embedding; methods include reflection, depth analysis, stress-testing, decision-making, game-planning, and implementation; tools include the Phoenix Attitude, the Completely Opposite Viewpoints Debate, and the Future-Facing Blueprint; the key words are *secure* and *surge*.

TAKING IT HOME

In some cases, the vision of the future company that emerges from the Phoenix Encounter Battlefield exercise is so compelling, and the leader is so decisive, that the Phoenix Breakthrough happens right there in the war room. Watching from the sidelines, we have little doubt that the new strategic priorities will race like wildfire through the incumbent organization.

In most cases, the Phoenix Breakthrough happens more slowly, through the hard work of refining and executing the Battlefield insights; engaging with stakeholders; revisiting the organization's mission and vision with the top leadership or board; and teaching the Phoenix Attitude and the Encounter method to other team leaders to conduct smaller-scale Encounter exercises in-house (see *Conducting a Phoenix Encounter in Your Own Organization*).

Conducting a Phoenix Encounter in Your Own Organization

The Phoenix Encounter method can be a centerpiece of strategic leadership development programs. But the method can be used in many different organizational settings. It can be executed anywhere, at any time, either as a planned strategic review exercise or as a kind of on-the-spot intervention when the organization is facing some unexpected challenge. We have seen it used successfully to address all these organizational tasks and challenges:

- Strategy and business model reviews
- Option building, priority setting, brainstorming, and box busting
- Consideration of strategic choices through debating opposite perspectives
- Reimagining strategic directions for recovery and opportunity after a crisis situation
- Stress-testing of entrepreneurial business plans and new value creation projects
- Needs and resources assessment and reconfiguration
- Talent spotting in leadership development
- Culture building
- Crisis management alternatives
- Stakeholder engagement

Guidance on conducting a Phoenix Encounter in your own organization is also in the separate *Facilitation Guide for the Phoenix Encounter Method*. Other relevant information is available at www.phoenixencountermethod.com.

We have found that even if an Encounter exercise does little to transform an organization immediately (e.g., it merely confirms existing strategies or reprioritizes planned actions), embedding the process and using it at least once a year can reveal the need for change later. In that sense, embedding the process is an anticomplacency therapy. It trains people to think differently, continually question orthodoxy, and generate new insights, not once but over and over again.

Embedding the principles of the Encounter method into the DNA of an organization installs an engine of propulsive change, one that fuels new capabilities and game plans. It instills an instinct for continual renewal of strategic, tactical, and competitive positioning. It allows the organization to investigate every new firestorm that comes at it and know exactly what to do.

Amy and Her Team Continue Their Phoenix Journey

Amy's Encounter discussions generated a lot of ways to fortify the core options that led to a 10 percent cost reduction with service improvement within 12 months, such as centralizing systems across more than 60 hospital sites while digitizing their procurement processes. Other stakeholders (e.g., doctors and nurses) were taken through Encounter thinking to find novel ways to reduce patient waiting times and ensure an efficient yet more personalized health and care experience. These have led to a series of small pilot projects—successful ones are intended for group rollout. Amy told us, "The board and executives are energized to develop a lean and learning culture that is service-oriented and sees our business in a future ecosystem that might change the ways healthcare will be funded and delivered—on a holistic basis rather than an ever-upward cost for services basis."

Speaking with her a year into the job, she told us, "When I'd finished my Encounter at the program and the ones we did back in the business, I built three things into my leadership habits: scan and do an Opposite Viewpoints Debate regularly and on every major proposal we consider; get outside-in perspectives as a matter of course; and lift the altitude of thinking high in the discussions in all our leadership meetings while holding a full-scale Encounter at least once a year."

Amy and her Horcomp team remain on their Phoenix journey. So much so, that in thinking about their post-crisis future, Amy and her team ran a special Encounter session in April 2020, which confirmed the tremendous value of their digital/data pilots in operating their health facilities in the COVID-19 world and intensified their client and medical stakeholder engagement. With its partner, Amy's company decided to accelerate the "health-life" ecosystem rollout.

Amy's experience showed that the foundation of becoming Phoenix-like is to confront and then switch your leadership thinking. This means seriously reviewing your leadership mindsets, habits, and behaviors. This is where we focus next.

CHAPTER **3** CHECKLIST

Summary Thoughts

1. The Phoenix Encounter method proceeds through three phases, each with its own imperative:

- ***Encounter Groundwork:*** Participants switch to a Phoenix Attitude and study the method, rules, tools, and habits they will need as preparation for a Completely Opposite Viewpoints Debate that seeks the phoenix—burning to rebirth

- ***Encounter Battlefield:*** Proactive Scanning and Radical Ideation construct the strike of an Extreme Attack and an actionable, prospective Horizon Defense that shields against it

- ***Encounter Breakthrough:*** The core organization and business model is reimagined and a Future-Facing Blueprint of immediate, short-term, medium-term, and long-term actions are shaped to secure the renewed organization and ensure it surges forward

2. Phoenix Encounter Groups are teams carefully chosen to include as much diversity of thinking and experience as possible. All team participants practice using their Phoenix Attitude and different leadership thinking altitudes (strategic, operational, and personal) throughout every phase of the Encounter and its activities. The Radical Ideation and multiple perspectives sustain a series of provocative strategic conversations that use opposing viewpoints in debate to generate a very wide set of options for the organization.

3. A Phoenix Encounter is a very challenging event. It can be stressful or even deeply unpleasant, but it can also be powerfully uplifting. The rewards come in the renewal of the organization's strategic agenda and in the conversion of a person's leadership thinking.

Reflection

1. Does your organization currently engage in Completely Opposite Viewpoints Debates in its strategic conversations? Does your organization understand its vulnerabilities and recognize the internal and external forces that can destroy it?

2. Does your organization have the imagination to articulate a defense against any attack, including hostile attacks bent on destruction? Are the people in your organization diverse enough in their thinking, backgrounds, and experiences to generate the widest set of strategic options for the future? Does your organization currently have a strategic and panoramic view that identifies immediate, short-term, medium-term, and long-term priorities for Phoenix-like change and renewal?

3. What scares you the most about undertaking a Phoenix Encounter? What gives you the most hope? What might you need to change in yourself to lead the Phoenix-like actions you'd like to undertake?

IV. the PHOENIX ATTITUDE
SEE, THINK, ACT DIFFERENTLY

SEE the WORLD and OPERATE SIMULTANEOUSLY at 3 LEADERSHIP ALTITUDES

50,000 ft
STRATEGIC Level
SCANNING with CURIOSITY & CONSIDERING OPPOSITE VIEWPOINTS

50 ft
TACTICAL Level
CONTINUALLY TESTING & LEARNING while EXECUTING

5 ft
SELF-AWARENESS Level
SELF-DEVELOPMENT & HONING PHOENIX ATTITUDE SKILLS

BEWARE of ALTITUDE SICKNESS

- HEAD in the CLOUDS
- MANY IDEAS, NO IMPLEMENTATION

- Too "HANDS ON"
- TRAPPED in the REARVIEW MIRROR

- MICROMANAGEMENT
- NARCISSISM

MINDSETS
- DREAMER & DOER
- ACROSS ALTITUDE THINKING
- FUTURE-FACING WORLD VIEW, GROWTH, & LEARNING
- DECISIVENESS with AGILITY

HABITS
- OPPOSITE VIEWPOINTS DEBATE
- PROACTIVE SCANNING
- In STAKEHOLDER SHOES
- HIGHLY FOCUSED PRIORITIZATION

BEHAVIORS
- SELF-AWARE LEARNER with HUMILITY
- OVERCOME FEARS
- BUSTS through BIAS, BLOCKERS, & BUREAUCRACY
- ROLE MODELS PURPOSE, MASTERY, & AUTONOMY

CHAPTER 4

THE PHOENIX ATTITUDE

Football is football and talent is talent.
But the mindset of your team makes all the difference.
—ROBERT GRIFFIN III, American football quarterback
and 2011 Heisman Trophy winner.

We met Simon Draper in 2017 when he was the new CEO of an Asian bottle-gas distribution business operating in a region with a growing economy and local preference for gas cooking. Simon felt fairly sure he had the "right stuff" for success: a low-cost supply relationship with one of the world's biggest oil majors, countrywide logistics, and recent improvements in margins and returns thanks to cost-cutting initiatives. Going into his Encounter, Simon felt he had little need to do anything different. His attitude was perhaps overconfident.

That attitude took a hit in the Encounter as Simon realized there was nothing stopping his suppliers (or others) from servicing his customers via a digital platform and on-demand third-party freight service providers for the last-mile delivery. Simon went back to his firm with a long to-do list. Since then, the company has digitized the business and built a mobile-enabled platform to connect with customers, suppliers, and new partners.

Simon's most important insight: "We just need a very, very different attitude. That begins with me."

In business, as in life, everything starts with your attitude. It can also end with your attitude, and if that attitude is flawed, it will probably end badly.[1]

One classic illustration of the danger of a flawed attitude in business was published in 1960 in the *Harvard Business Review*.[2] Written by Theodore Levitt, the article described the response of railroad companies to the threats from other forms of transportation, which was, unfortunately for the railroads, no response at all. That's because the attitude of railroad leadership was stuck in the nineteenth century. It focused entirely on trains and not on transportation, while other minds in that sector were turning their twentieth-century perspectives to cars, trucks, and airplanes. Worse, railroad attitudes were focused on the operational level—in this case, literally keeping the trains running on time. The railroad executives' attitude lacked foresight and self-awareness. And it killed them.

Levitt's case study is still taught today because its lesson is still relevant today. In fact, it's even more relevant than it was in 1960. In today's world of firestorm disruption, leaders can ill afford to spend too much time trying to keep the trains running on time. They can't spend all their time up in the clouds daydreaming or down in the mailroom micromanaging. Leaders cannot afford to get stuck at any one level of perspective, but many do. In fact, Ian's research suggests that more than 70 percent of senior business executives find themselves trapped at one level of leadership thinking (or what we call "altitude") for a disproportionate and detrimental length of time.[3]

We also know this because executives tell us about it during their Phoenix Encounter experiences. They have also been telling us this during the COVID-19 crisis. They feel their leadership is neither nimble nor expansive enough to lead the change. These are serious shortcomings, especially in times of firestorm change. In cases like these, we have come to see, the best medicine is preventative. It's a switch in leadership attitude—to a Phoenix Attitude.

What is a Phoenix Attitude? In essence, it is a set of personal attributes—mindsets, habits, and behaviors—that allows a leader to embrace firestorm disruption as the essential pathway to organizational renewal. It is the mental embodiment of Phoenix DNA. Leaders with a Phoenix Attitude see very differently, think very differently, and act very differently from leaders of the past. They continually scan the outside world for new trends. They have the foresight and imagination to recognize future-facing opportunities. They question the status quo and confront their confirmation bias through Completely Opposite Viewpoints Debates. Their minds are constantly working, thinking fast and thinking slow, flying across different leadership altitudes (height and depth), generating wider sets of options for consideration, and then moving decisively to action.[4] Leaders with a Phoenix Attitude embody dreaming and doing. Optimistic imagineers, they see a world bursting with possibilities and opportunities yet connect this to the realities of engineering the implementation. When they feel the heat of the coming fire, their pulse quickens. And they step right into it.

In mid-2018, one Encounter participant, the CEO of a major hospital in Asia-Pacific, had an epidemic (like Ebola) in his Extreme Attack situation that would critically change the healthcare capacity of his institution. As part of the Horizon Defense, he developed a series of pilot projects using robotic services together with supply chain reconfiguration and a major push in data analytics. These were rolled out and have helped enormously in managing during the COVID-19 situation. This leader took his Phoenix Attitude back to his organization; and the benefits are now obvious to everyone.

ATTRIBUTES OF THE PHOENIX LEADER

We don't expect any one leader to hold every attribute of the Phoenix Attitude, but every leader with a Phoenix Attitude will hold an intense desire for renewal and change. This is the difference between Jeff Bezos, who founded Amazon with a radically new business model in 1996, and the leadership of Walmart, which tacked an e-commerce project onto their legacy business a full four years later. Bezos has a Phoenix Attitude. So does Mukesh Ambani (Reliance), Aliko Dangote (Dangote), Piyush Gupta (DBS), Robert Iger (Disney), Jack Ma (Alibaba), Satya Nadella (Microsoft), and Indra Nooyi (Pepsico). All have imagined and reimagined their organizations and primed them for rebirth and growth.

Table 4.1 presents some of the key attributes of the Phoenix Attitude as we have seen it embodied in Phoenix-like leaders such as these and in the aspiring Phoenixes who come to Encounter exercises—attributes such as mindsets, habits, and leadership behaviors. Though not exhaustive, the table presents an idealized list to serve as an exemplar; real leaders exhibit their own unique combination of these attributes that is directly pertinent to themselves and their organizational context. This list builds on well-known vital leadership attributes that still remain relevant. However, four underlying characteristics are the enablers of all the Phoenix Attitude attributes identified in this list: emotional intelligence, business acumen, talent development capabilities, and effective communication. The attribute list, emphasizing strategic leadership and thinking dimensions, is even more relevant during the challenges of leading in a firestorm crisis, which has been the experience of almost everyone in 2020.

TABLE 4.1 Key Attributes of a Leader with Phoenix Attitude[5]

THE PHOENIX ATTITUDE LEADER *Underlying Enablers: Emotional Intelligence, Business Acumen, Talent Development Capabilities, Effective Communication*		
Where It Lives	**What It Looks Like**	**How It Manifests in the Leader**
Mindsets	• Decisive future-facing growth thinking, learning, and action across the three different leadership altitudes—strategic, tactical, and personal	• Dreamer and Doer • Across altitude thinking and dialogue • Future-facing worldview with a growth and learning mindset • Decisiveness with agility
Habits	• Prioritized renewal-seeking practices built on scanning, stakeholder-centricity, and embracing Completely Opposite Viewpoints Debates as a necessity	• Completely Opposite Viewpoints Debate • Proactive Scanning • In the shoes of stakeholders • Highly focused prioritization
Leadership Behaviors	• Future-facing leadership development and capabilities with self-awareness and humility	• Self-aware learner with humility • Confidence to overcome fears and unleash change drivers • Courage to bust through bias, blockers, and bureaucracy • Role model to motivate future-facing purpose, autonomy, and mastery orientations

The leadership mindsets, habits, and behaviors of the Phoenix Attitude leader are to continually seek renewal and new perspectives by enthusiastically engaging in the Completely Opposite Viewpoints Debates and Radical Ideation of the Encounter method. Such a leader practices imagining a fundamentally different future informed by the destruction of his or her current organization, the future needs of stakeholders, and an intense desire for rebirth. This leader explores and navigates altitudes (discussed below), continually scanning the horizon to seek knowledge beyond the boundaries of the organization, sector, and geography and into the future. The Phoenix leader engages deeply with stakeholders (such as customers and investors) to discern value-creating opportunities from their perspectives. He or she sets clear, crucial priorities and focuses personal leadership energy on the three most important priorities for action at any point in time.

Leaders with the Phoenix Attitude also hold profound self-awareness, humility, and resilience. They have clear purpose and vision. They relentlessly communicate and engage their team, promoting a psychologically safe working environment. They are opportunistic and excited, not defensive and agitated. They search for knowledge with intellectual honesty. They seek people and ideas outside their own organization, expertise, and experience. Learning is a key performance indicator (KPI) for them. They have the confidence and courage to blow up the echo chamber around them and are eager to overcome fears and blockers to unleash the positive drivers of change in self and organization.[6]

Phoenix leaders think outside-in, relentlessly questioning assumptions and searching for new ideas, options, and perspectives. They act decisively, take risks, and learn from failure. Theirs is a growth, not a fixed mindset. Uncertainty, ambiguity, and opposite viewpoints are stimulating; these are, as Ram says, "friends, not enemies." These leaders want to generate big and wide option sets first and then rigorously stress-test these using multiple lenses and stringent analysis. They are wary of confirming evidence to their prepossessed views.

With a bias to action and incessant curiosity, Phoenix leaders see, think, and act at three leadership altitude levels: strategic, tactical, and personal self-awareness. They connect these together and are not trapped at any one level. As they think about the future, they will ask themselves "what if" and "what might be," not "what is" and "what can't be." They are data fanatics. They develop future-facing leadership talent and capabilities (people and organizational), dump legacy strengths that are future liabilities, and constantly hone their own talents through learning and development. They have the confidence to hire people better than themselves—and empower them with autonomy. They seek renewed purpose and mastery of what will matter in the future. They respect the past but do not dwell there.

We know the list of Phoenix leadership attributes is daunting. In fact, when our Encounter participants discuss them, they often express a fear of obsolescence, both personal and organizational. They worry that the skills and leadership abilities that once brought them success will not take them successfully into the future.[7] The good news is that the Phoenix Attitude is buildable. It can be cultivated. By using the Phoenix Encounter method as well as the tools we present in Chapter 5, these leaders can reinvent themselves as Phoenix Attitude leaders in very concrete ways.

Consider the example of Janet Freeman, the regional leader of a major oil and gas company operating in Africa. Janet came to our Encounter program with an open mind and a clear-eyed view of the company's current position. Notice the strengths and weaknesses she listed for her firm in a SWOT analysis she undertook in the groundwork preparation for the Phoenix Encounter (Table 4.2).

TABLE 4.2 Janet's Pre-Encounter

EXTRACT FROM THE SWOT ANALYSIS FOR HER FIRM	
Strengths	**Weaknesses**
• Brand and reputation • Experience and market-leading position • Technical expertise in traditional production methods • Access to capital	• Captive to expiring government concessions and strained partner relationships • Field declines and need for new acreage • Very limited understanding and deployment of new technologies in this business unit • Limited HQ buy-in to changing strategy with very slow decision-making

These strengths, by the way, are pretty typical of the assets that legacy firms bring to the Phoenix Encounters. The technology challenge is also common. During the Encounter Battlefield exercise, Janet was both an eager participant and a quick study. When it came time to make her future-facing SWOT inventory after the exercise, she gave a rather different assessment (Table 4.3). Notice how some of the former "Strengths" have moved to the "Weaknesses" column. The Future-Facing SWOT is part of the new blueprint and recorded in her Encounter Journal after the Battlefield exercise. It treats strengths as those that must be required to succeed in making the future breakthrough changes. These are also assessed for how they contribute to managing future growth, cost, or risks. It defines weaknesses as current situations that would stand in the way of successful change.

TABLE 4.3 Janet's Post-Encounter

FUTURE-FACING SWOT ANALYSIS—CONTRIBUTION TO MANAGING GROWTH, COST, AND RISK	
Future Strengths That Will Be Needed	**Current Weaknesses (or Obstacles or Gaps)**
• Exceptional government and partner stakeholder relationship management *(Risk)* • Deploying capital for cross-border transactions to create value for her firm with their local partners *(Growth)* • Agile decision-making with HQ buy-in *(Growth, Cost)* • Data mining to achieve productivity increase in hydrocarbon output with capacity to deploy new artificial intelligence (AI) and robotic technologies *(Growth, Cost, Risk)*	• Brand and reputation legacy (in this situation is now negative) • The previous stakeholder experiences and perceptions (including with government) and so-called market-leading position • Local management's inability to persuade HQ of the urgent need for change in approach • Capital is parent company only—not in partnerships

Clearly, Janet's attitude has changed. She now sees some of her company's legacy strengths as traps, and she imagines new directions that weren't even on the table before. She's changing her perspective and attacking blind spots. She's thinking about technology. She's thinking about redrawing the boundaries of the firm. She's thinking about building consensus for a bold move forward, and her thinking is specific. The Phoenix Encounter has galvanized her.

Janet also looked at her personal leadership development agenda. She asked, "What will I need to change in order to spearhead these breakthroughs for the company?" and identified two personal goals: to build her emotional resilience and to develop her persuasive skills. She also resolved to engage the decision-makers in her home office by taking them through their own Phoenix Encounter.

A PHOENIX FLIES ACROSS DISTINCTIVE LEADERSHIP ALTITUDES

Ram and Ian have both spoken and written widely about "leadership altitudes," arguing that leaders must learn to see their world from three very different perspectives: 50,000 feet, 50 feet, and 5 feet.[8] These altitudes correspond, respectively, to strategic, operational, and personal levels of leadership engagement. They suggest that visualizing these three altitudes discretely can dramatically focus leadership minds in a simple yet profound way, one that yields invaluable insights. They go on to argue that the most effective leaders are those who can operate *simultaneously* at all three leadership altitudes.

In this book, we take Ram and Ian's thinking a step further, arguing that the ability to move seamlessly through the leadership altitudes is a signature attribute of the Phoenix Attitude talent. A leader with a Phoenix Attitude will have the right mindset and habits at each altitude. More important, that leader will know how to integrate all three leadership altitudes on the fly for a view of the big and small pictures in every moment.

Everyone who has flown in an airplane knows that different altitudes reveal different aspects of the world. For leadership, synthesis is key. First, let's take the altitudes one by one:

- **The 50,000-foot leadership altitude.** The 50,000-foot view lets us see what's coming across a wide horizon. In the context of the external landscape, it can reveal the sweeping changes of unstoppable trends in the outside world, from technological advances to demographic shifts. Its big-picture vantage point promotes Proactive Scanning and Radical Ideation. Ram and Ian call this "outside-in" and "future-back" thinking and describe its payoff as "perceptual acuity." It's the kind of thinking that emboldened Elon Musk to build electric vehicles, Jeff Bezos to envision the Blue Origin spaceflight venture, and Steve Jobs to launch what became in August 2018 the world's first trillion-dollar company.[9]

The view from the 50,000-foot altitude is strategic; its insights come from the habit of scanning with curiosity and considering completely opposite viewpoints.

- **The 50-foot leadership altitude.** While thinking at 50,000 feet can inspire a grand and sweeping vision, making that vision real requires an understanding of tactical and operational matters best viewed from 50 feet. This is, after all, where things happen most of the time. It's where day-to-day and month-to-month actions are executed and where quarterly results get reported. The 50-foot level is where former Honeywell CEO Larry Bossidy famously connected his vision to his discipline for getting things done, a practice that he described in detail in *Execution*, coauthored with Ram.[10] Here, agility and acumen connect to big-picture future purpose to build the execution and talent capacities of the organization.

The view from the 50-foot altitude is tactical; its insights come from the habit of continuously testing and learning while executing plans.

- **The 5-foot leadership altitude.** This is the level of self-awareness. Only when leaders understand who they are and why they do what they do can they govern themselves and engage others, and this is also the essential message of Ian's book on leadership blockers and drivers.[11] The organizational importance of self-awareness became clear to Google in 2006, when an engineer at the company named Chade-Meng Tan created the

"Search Inside Yourself" course on emotional intelligence and mindfulness. The course soon became one of Google's most popular training offerings. In 2013, Google took the concept to a higher level, launching a Search Inside Yourself Leadership Institute and making the program available to all.[12] Another highly self-aware leader, often mentioned as a role model by Encounter participants, is Sheryl Sandberg, the COO of Facebook, whose best-selling book *Lean In: Women, Work, and the Will to Lead* connects self-awareness to leadership that promotes diversity.[13]

The view at the 5-foot altitude is self-aware; its insights come from the habit of self-development and honing the Phoenix Attitude habits and behaviors.

Thinking Across the Altitudes

Ideas formulated at 50,000 feet can transform industries, not just organizations, and a major mistake here can be catastrophic—for instance, Pets.com's legendary dot.com disaster in 2000, when it used sock puppets as spokespeople and recklessly overexpanded its facilities, taking the company from e-commerce poster child to bankruptcy in less than a year, or the 2017 closure of Silicon Valley startup Juicero.[14] Leaders often fear big failures like this and so avoid high-altitude thinking altogether. Yet avoiding the 50,000-foot view is very problematic. Consider the litany of traditional retail firm failures because they did not adapt quickly enough to the power of digital platforms and e-commerce opportunities.

For this reason, leaders must spend some time each week at 50,000 feet, scanning the horizon of the outside world, assessing its possibilities, its changes, and its trends, and considering how what they see might affect their organization. Almost every leader today recognizes that this kind of high-altitude strategic and visionary work is a C-suite responsibility. Most embrace it, though not all are good at it, and many fail to encourage high-altitude thinking at other levels of the organization where it is equally important.

We find that many leaders are much more comfortable working at the 50-foot level, where things are visible, tangible, familiar, and literally manageable. This is the altitude with the closest view of the playing field, the place where trains can be made to run on time, where current business strengths and weaknesses are readily spotted, and where incremental change is doable, if sometimes painful. Mistakes made here can usually be corrected. The tactical focus of this leadership altitude can have strategic rewards if the leader is diligent about learning continuously and seeking insights from the day-to-day work in every corner of their operation.

Phoenix leaders must spend time at the 5-foot level, making an effort to reflect on who they are, what they are doing, why they are doing it, and how they might challenge themselves to be the best Phoenix-like leader that they can be. This work includes making time for contemplation, seeking feedback, directing one's own learning process, and overcoming personal blockers to transformation.[15] We are very aware that introspection does not come naturally to many executive leaders, but it must come in whatever way it can. It is essential to the Phoenix self-renewal they need to embrace and bring into their companies.

We use all three of these altitude skills sets in the Phoenix Encounter, sometimes separately and sometimes together. For example, 50,000-foot altitude skills use the Extreme Attack and Horizon Defense stages to generate as profoundly wide an option set as possible. Fifty-foot altitude skills are brought into the Encounter preparation work, and especially later work, to design, execute, and embed the future-facing blueprint of the organization. Five-foot altitude skills are central to the Encounter participants' personal leadership development agenda plan, which is updated throughout the Encounter process.

As Dreamers and Doers, Phoenix leaders move seamlessly across leadership altitude levels, a skill we call "flying the altitudes." Leaders who can move with agility across these altitudes can also learn to synthesize information from different and even contradictory viewpoints and handle them productively in the strategic debate. They think radically and multidimensionally, and they can encourage their teams to do likewise—a skill that is essential to executing strategic renewal and embedding the Phoenix Attitude throughout the organization.

Avoiding Altitude Sickness

Flying the altitudes is an uncommon ability, and it is justly sought after and praised. But while some leaders soar, most suffer from what Ian calls "Altitude Sickness"—feeling trapped at one of the three altitudes for a disproportionate length of time and spending virtually no time at the other altitudes.[16] A concerning majority of our Encounter participants tell us that they are all too familiar with this affliction. We worry that these people can be a hindrance, even a danger, to themselves, their teams, and their organizations. The reasons for concern are set out in Table 4.4.

These three "trapped altitude mindsets" are different but equally limiting; each feeds a narrow, fixated way of thinking that makes it difficult to achieve a Phoenix Attitude. Leaders can overcome their Altitude Sickness and learn to combine insights gained at every leadership level, but they must be honest about their starting point. Further resources and information on the Phoenix Attitude and the concept of leadership altitudes can be found at our online site: www.phoenixencountermethod.com.

TABLE 4.4 Recognizing Altitude Sickness

TRAPPED AT 50,000 FEET
• These leaders with Altitude Sickness have their heads in the clouds. They focus too much on the long term and chase after too many opportunities, leaving the present in shambles.
• These leaders have lots of ideas. They announce a new vision or initiative every other week and never execute effectively to deliver results. They offer visionary words but nothing gets done.
• Typically uninterested in implementation, these over-dreamers often try to hand off the Blueprint work in our Phoenix Encounters, leaving analysis, prioritization, and execution to underlings. They are so overconfident in their ideas that they are often unaware that they are the wrong leader to take the company in a new direction.

TRAPPED AT 50 FEET
• The largest group of leaders with Altitude Sickness are trapped at 50 feet, in the tactical zone where their businesses have been very successful in the past.
• These leaders have often come up through the ranks, where they have been well trained and rewarded for their specialized knowledge and skills sets.
• Leaders stuck at the 50-foot level know their stuff. They are operations- and execution-oriented. They deliver on performance metrics and are very good at repetitive and predictable actions.
• Trapped in the "rearview mirror" of past performance and complacency, these leaders can be "clubby" and resistant to change. They see radical ideas as nonsense. They focus on incremental improvements and short-term gains rather than on firestorm innovation or disruptive change.
• These leaders often say they are "too hands-on" to do the 50,000-foot work of Radical Ideation and "too busy" to find their 5-foot personal leadership compass. This narrow view of their own leadership value makes the confronting work of the Phoenix Encounter especially challenging for them.

TRAPPED AT 5 FEET
• This relatively small group of leaders can be trapped unhealthily inside themselves. The group includes some self-indulgent idealists as well as some obsessive micromanagers, super egoists, rampant narcissists, and scheming self-promoters.
• Among the egoists and narcissists, true self-awareness is a foreign concept; they will dodge (or manipulate) any attempt at leadership development, reflection, and personal transformation unless orchestrated for their own self-interest. These people get in everybody's way.
• While 5 feet is the positive self-awareness and actualization zone for the Phoenix leader, being trapped here impairs the capacity to engage other people, appreciate multiple perspectives, and leverage diversity. In our experience, these leaders might discover a Phoenix Breakthrough idea but not take their people with them to achieve it.

In Their Own Words

Participants in our Encounter programs learn to recognize Altitude Sickness. Here are some comments in their own rueful words:

"I thought I was a strategic thinker but I'm flying at 10,000 feet, not 50,000."

—ELSA NILSSON, COO, Swedish manufacturing firm

"My team and I are not trapped at 50 feet. We are so blindingly tactical; it is more like 17 feet."

—YOSHI TANEKA, regional GM, Japanese heavy machinery manufacturer

"I wasn't connecting my own leadership style to the challenges changing other people's thinking. I needed to shift my own 5-foot awareness first."

—FRANCOIS CLESTER, CEO, Belgian FMCG supply business

"The realization now is how tactical my thinking has been. It's a little embarrassing. I thought I was pretty hip because of the nature of my work, being in the digital transformation space, but I had a very narrow focus."

—RAKESH KATAL, VP Digital Transformation, US tech company

ATTITUDE AND MINDSET AWARENESS IS EVERYTHING

Our attitude and its mindsets influence what we think about the work we do; they also influence the decisions we make. They shape our assumptions first and then our priorities. They influence what we see as interesting or important, as threatening or promising. They limit or expand our range of options and ideas. They encourage habits of mind—for good or bad.

Mindsets are notoriously subject to bias, and those biases are often difficult to overcome. For this reason, leaders in disruptive environments must be especially aware not only of their own mindsets but also of other legacy mindsets operating in their organization and their sector. There are some mindsets they will want to instill and others they will want to challenge and unlearn.

That's important because attitude awareness helps an organization seize opportunity when disruption threatens. This critical C-suite obligation is the subject of much modern scholarship, but it has a long pedigree, appearing at least as early as the writings of the ancient Chinese military strategist Sun Tzu, who pointed out 2,500 years ago that while wars are fought on the battlefield, they are often won or lost in our minds.[17]

This means that leaders have to come to terms with contemplating totally opposite views: *Everything should be on the table to destroy or cannibalise, any or all. If we do not, someone else will.* Think of Sears, Nokia, and the others we have already talked about.

Consider some mindsets that have been identified by psychologists and sociologists as having important consequences for business environments and leadership attitudes. First, consider fixed or growth mindsets. These mindsets, described by Stanford University psychologist Carol Dweck, arise from different views about the nature of intelligence and talent. People holding a fixed mindset believe intelligence and talent to be innate and static; those with a growth mindset believe them to be dynamic and developable.[18]

From this single insight unspools a cavalcade of differences that profoundly affect people's attitude for success and achievement. People with fixed mindsets have a deterministic view of their own abilities; they tend to avoid challenges, feel a need to prove themselves, and yet view learning effort as futile. People with growth mindsets, on the other hand, have a freewill view of their own achievements; they seek out learning opportunities, embrace challenges, take feedback, and show persistence.

Gary Klein, another psychologist, builds on Dweck's work to relate fixed and growth mindsets to workplace orientations. Klein tells us that fixed mindsets often lead to a preoccupation with errors and to the mistaken belief that the only way to improve performance is by reducing errors. Conversely, growth mindsets encourage interest in making new discoveries to help propel performance.[19] This is Phoenix thinking.

Once leaders become aware of fixed and growth mindsets, they tend to see them everywhere. They learn to identify which kinds of thinking are propelling their company forward and which are holding it back. They can then use that knowledge to imagine change in the company. For example, Jackson Townsend, a COO in an Australian agrichemical firm and one of our program participants, began using some Encounter exercises in his annual goal-setting exercise with his direct reports, seeking to instill the growth-minded habit of constantly looking for opportunities for change. Within six months, Jackson told us, this effort produced new product and service initiatives and the creation of the firm's first artificial intelligence (AI) analytics project.

The most important views on mindsets come from Nobel Prize winner Daniel Kahneman. In his book, *Thinking Fast and Slow*, he draws a distinction between two ways of thinking. The first is unconscious, fast, and frequently emotional; the second is deliberate, slow, and logical.[20] Both ways of thinking are useful to the Phoenix Attitude, but each can also introduce bias into judgment and decision-making. "Thinking fast" is especially problematic, as it can lead to such well-documented problems as framing or anchoring bias, overconfidence bias, groupthink, confirmation bias, and status quo bias—problems we also see in business leaders trapped at the 50-foot altitude. These biases are rampant in the business world, but it is possible to overcome them, as Kahneman, Richard Thaler, Cass Sunstein, Iris Bohnet, and others have shown.[21] At INSEAD, our colleagues Anil Gaba, Spyros Makridakis, Ziv Carmon, and Klaus Wertenbroch have written extensively about processes that can be used to arrive at sound decisions about future direction—an endeavor central to the work of the Phoenix Encounter—especially in pushing through status quo and confirmation biases.[22]

A final note about mindsets: like everything in the firestorm environment, they must be fluid. In our executive program work, we have found that leaders facing technological transformations want their companies to be "learning organizations." That's exactly what they should be, but we also know that some of the most important lessons will involve *unlearning*, a mental process that involves stepping outside one mental model in order to choose a different one.[23] Unlearning is often much harder than learning. It requires a willingness to let go of an existing frame that is no longer relevant, the ability to create a new model, and the ability to ingrain new mental habits into the organization. It requires sharing the Phoenix Attitude far and wide.

Mindsets and the Phoenix Attitude

The Phoenix Attitude is not a single mindset but a set of sightlines that synthesize and integrate many different mindsets and ways of thinking, changing altitude at will as it generates new insights. It then translates those insights into action. It is a kind of meta-mindset for the disruptive leader who is both a Dreamer and a Doer.

Practitioners of the Phoenix Attitude have a wizard-like ability to be in many places at once: at different altitudes; in past, present, and future; thinking fast and thinking slow; and working from the head and heart at the same time.[24] Distinguished authors and thought leaders Dan and Chip Heath describe a Phoenix-like mindset in their book *Switch: How to Change Things When Change Is Hard,* in which they use the well-known analogy of the rider and elephant to represent the rational and emotional sides of thought. Riding an elephant is hard, they point out; the human and the animal must work together. The same is true of organizational change. The leader must direct the rider, motivate the elephant, and shape the path.[25]

We think the Phoenix Attitude is both a will and a way. It is the ability to see, think, and act differently. It is a willingness to embrace firestorm disruption and a way of walking through it. The Phoenix Attitude comes naturally to only a handful of leaders, but it can be learned and practiced using the Phoenix Encounter method. So, in the next chapter, we cultivate the Phoenix Attitude through a set of tools, habits, and practices that we call Extra Strategic Perception. These are all used in Encounters to enable the kind of thinking that leads to a Phoenix Breakthrough and the transformation that turns the crows into the firebirds they need to be.

CHAPTER **4** CHECKLIST

Summary Thoughts

1. A Phoenix Attitude it is a set of mindsets, habits, and leadership behaviors that allows a leader to embrace disruptive change as a path to organizational renewal. It is the mental embodiment of Phoenix DNA.

2. Leaders with a Phoenix Attitude *see differently*, *think differently*, and *act differently* from leaders of the past. Their mental attributes include curiosity, foresight, imagination, Radical Ideation, and decisiveness. Their habits include embracing the opposites debate and searching, scanning, questioning, and adopting multiple perspectives as an imagineer, with focused prioritization. Their leadership behaviors include role-modeling the opposites debate, future-talent building, emotional resilience, humility, and self-awareness. These leaders have mental agility to operate at three leadership altitudes simultaneously.

3. The three leadership altitudes are 50,000 feet (the strategic level), 50 feet (the operations or tactical level), and 5 feet (the self-awareness level). The characteristic practice at 50,000 feet is *scanning with curiosity and considering opposite viewpoints*. The characteristic practice at 50 feet is *continually testing and learning while executing*. The characteristic practice at 5 feet is *self-development and honing Phoenix Attitude skills*. Being stuck at any one leadership altitude is Altitude Sickness—dangerous to leaders, their teams, and their organizations. Altitude Sickness at 50,000 feet is over-dreaming; at 50 feet, it's change resistance; at 5 feet, it's micro-obsession and navel-gazing.

Reflection

1. In what ways does your leadership attitude resemble a Phoenix Attitude? In what ways is it different? Can you describe the attitude and mindsets of your three nearest colleagues? Of your boss or your board chair?

2. Do you have Altitude Sickness? Which level are you trapped at? What altitude are you most comfortable at? Which one are you least comfortable with? What changes would you have to make to begin flying across the altitudes?

3. Are you and your people trapped in the thinking and practices of the past? Are you subject to internal groupthink, confirmation bias, or status quo bias? What are you doing to build and lead a culture of disruptive thinking in your organization? What might be holding you back?

PROACTIVE SCANNING

- BEYOND INDUSTRY & GEOGRAPHY
- OUTSIDE-IN THINKING
- FUTURE-BACK THINKING
- PERCEPTIVE QUESTIONING

DEBATE RITUALS

RADICAL IDEATION

The SEPARATION IMPERATIVE:

SYNTHESIS ▸ ANALYSIS ▸ DECISION-MAKING

ENCOUNTER JOURNAL

OPTIONS INSIGHTS ACTIONS

* EXTRA STRATEGIC PERCEPTION

can be developed through PRACTICE

PHOENIX TOOLS AND HABITS: EXTRA STRATEGIC PERCEPTION

Perception is strong and sight weak. In strategy it is important to see distant things as if they were close and to take a distanced view of close things.

—MIYAMOTO MUSASHI, Japanese soldier, strategist, writer, and philosopher[1]

The Phoenix Attitude and Breakthrough transformation doesn't happen by itself, not even in leaders and organizations eager to change their old ways.

One Encounter participant, Damian Higgins, the CEO of an Asian-Pacific equipment manufacturer, summed up this dilemma:

> You know, I thought I was a strategic thinker. But I now know I was probably thinking at 37.5 feet, as opposed to what I really need to do at the 50,000-foot level, which is to say: look, go across the altitudes, and think much, much higher. The Encounter process and tools were key to making this happen for me and my team.

Overcoming old attitudes and mindsets is hard. Switching attitudes is even harder. And while there is robust research on the pressures that block the adoption of growth mindsets, there is little by way of guidance on how to enable them—to make them a habit.[2] Tellingly, a common observation from participants after the Encounter Battlefield is how using Encounter tools in their attack and defense debates helped them switch their attitude. Damian's quote exemplifies this. So, in this chapter we highlight three critical tools and habits of mind that leaders should practice to help build their Phoenix Attitude.

Debate and ideation are central to the Phoenix Encounter method. Not just the polite kind of "your-turn-my-turn" debate familiar to debate clubs everywhere, but a much wider ranging, roll-up-your-sleeves kind of strategic dialogue conducted in a Completely Opposite Viewpoints Debate that we have emphasized since this book's introduction. In the Encounter debates, new ideas and extreme options come hard and fast, and they may not be fully fleshed out—that is, they may appear without thorough examination for analysis and refinement (which will come later). In the debate, there is a lot of brainstorming, some crazy talk, and much devil's advocacy. Outside-the-box thinking gets bonus points as do direct challenges to the status quo. The point of the debate is to stretch the thinking, diversify the points of view, disconfirm legacy beliefs, and generate as many ideas and options as possible for the attack and the defense.

The Phoenix tools are a mixed bag of techniques, as we've alluded to throughout the previous chapters. Some are new ways of seeing; some are new ways of thinking; all are about generating options and documenting insights and solutions. All help develop skills at the 50,000-foot leadership altitude Ram first talked about in 2007, where leaders are typically least comfortable.[3] The three tools and habits help create what we call Extra Strategic Perception (ESP), an intuitive embrace for the Phoenix leader with the kind of farsighted, agile-thinking, and purposeful conversations that enable a constant, vibrating sensing of new possibilities. These tools fight against the confirmation bias of blinkered thinking.

The Three Senses of Extra Strategic Perception

There are three Extra Strategic Perception tools and habits of mind that should be learned and practiced to develop a leader's Phoenix Attitude:

1. **Proactive Scanning** that supports the "seeing" sense for the Phoenix leader. Develop the habit of continual "scanning" for insights, trends, ideas, and dangers while learning to think and inquire in new ways to better recognize future threats and opportunities. This combines scanning with perceptual acuity and strategic inquiry.

2. **Debate Rituals** that support the "speaking and listening" sense for the Phoenix leader. A Completely Opposite Viewpoints Debate requires a psychologically safe and collaborative environment to discuss far-reaching, different, and opposing perspectives. Two fundamental rules enable the team to create the farsighted discussion that enables discovery of a diversity of perspectives on attack and defense, namely:

    a. *Radical Ideation*: Embracing unconstrained thinking to generate as wide an option set as possible.

    b. *The Separation Imperative*: Focusing debate and discussion separately on ideation, synthesis, analysis, and decision-making and appreciating them as distinct and discrete phases of strategic dialogue.

3. **Encounter Journal** that supports the "writing" sense for the Phoenix leader. It documents and tracks ideas, analysis, and actions throughout the entire Phoenix Encounter to ultimately generate the Future-Facing Blueprint for the organization and its breakthrough changes.

Does this sound like hocus-pocus to you? It often does to businesspeople, especially those pragmatic, linear-thinking leaders who are trapped at the 50-foot leadership altitude. But building Phoenix ESP does not require either a crystal ball or a Zen master. Neither does it require genius. What it requires is restless curiosity, a tolerance for ambiguity, and a hair-on-fire desire to scan, debate, and document possibilities to escape extinction and create new opportunities. Leaders and their teams need to practice these tools as a mental gymnastics workout to stretch their mind and build the muscles of foresight and change. Phoenix Attitude leaders don't just manage firestorm disruption, they go one step further and create change on their own terms. They put their Extra Strategic Perception to work.

PROACTIVE SCANNING

We believe you cannot have a Phoenix Attitude without practicing scanning unceasingly. We think of it as an intense and anticipatory curiosity that can help overcome Altitude Sickness, increase attitude awareness, improve forward thinking, make sense of new knowledge, and help translate possibilities into actionable ideas.

The idea of scanning is not new. Nearly 40 years ago, Donald Hambrick, the seminal thinker on strategic leadership, noted that although environmental scanning is crucial for leaders and a key step in the process of organizational adaptation and performance, leaders often do not scan widely enough outside their organizations to create or inform their organizations' strategies.[4] The heightened velocity of change in today's world makes Proactive Scanning a compulsory habit. For example, how can any leader today seriously debate strategic options for business models or innovation without scanning about the accelerating possibilities of digitization and technology?

Proactive Scanning should be systematic, wide-ranging, and continuous. It is a prerequisite for disruptive strategic thinking and extreme option generation. As a technique, it does more than just look ahead; it involves gathering, analyzing, and disseminating information combining both objective (data and examples) and perspective viewpoints from different people and sources.

For example, in almost all Phoenix Encounter sessions we run, we undertake a broad scan of current and emergent trends (e.g., technology, data analytics, artificial intelligence [AI], robotics, social media, platforms, digital ecosystems, and the like). We illustrate the firestorm disruptions created by these forces on businesses and organizations with many examples in Part II of this book. The intent of Proactive Scanning is to familiarize and even overwhelm the leaders with ideas that could change the course of their businesses through generating plans to destroy them, jump-starting concepts for new pursuits, and developing solutions for fortifying their cores.

Proactive Scanning is not the same as routine business intelligence gathering, which is typically conducted as a targeted grab of existing data or insider information for use in a competitive analysis. Proactive Scanning casts a wider net and makes a deliberate approach to look at different industries and geographies. It makes a special effort to seek information outside the intense echo chamber of the inward-looking organization. In Phoenix leadership practice, Proactive Scanning becomes institutionalized as a formal system with associated strategic activities and outputs, organized by a cadre of information managers.[5] But it can start with a leader, alone in the office, in a car, or on the Internet, thinking about interesting stuff he or she has seen, heard, or maybe just imagined, wondering what is new, what it might mean, and what if.

It's important to remember that disruption opportunities don't come only from outside forces like technology changes and business model innovations; they can also appear in an organization's internal operations and ongoing business relationships. For this reason, leaders must scan both inside and out. Some risk-management experts rate potential disruptions by two criteria: the likelihood of occurrence and the magnitude of the impact. Leaders should too. Quick detection, one of the potential benefits of continual scanning, can mitigate the impacts of many disruptions and also amplify the opportunities. MIT professor Yossi Sheffi highlighted the use of external and internal data sources, such as those described in the next example, to quickly spot potential disruptions and opportunities.[6]

> One Encounter participant, Mbungwa Didoso, the business sales head of an African equipment provider, used his scanning, external and internal, to realize a huge opportunity in durable goods for construction, where the vast majority of equipment tools are underutilized. Building a sharing marketplace could not only improve utilization—it could also improve profitability. The initial external trend scan had highlighted "products as a service" and "platform ecosystems" as big ideas. Their internal data scan showed the real-world value unlocked by optimizing equipment use. An equipment-sharing platform has now been launched as a breakthrough initiative in the company.

Leaders with the Phoenix Attitude have an instinct for scanning. In his book *The Attacker's Advantage*, Ram describes a talent he calls "perceptual acuity." It is a kind of psychological and mental preparedness to "see around the bends in the road ahead," an alertness that allows leaders to spot potentially significant anomalies and contradictions in the external landscape well ahead of others. Ram compares it to a kind of human radar that lets you see through the fog. The acuity talent supports a core outlook that sees opportunity in disruption—that sees uncertainty as an invitation to go on the attack.[7] Someone with a Phoenix Attitude has this because they constantly scan and imagine, allowing their perceptual acuity to grow as a habit of mind inquiry and curiosity, including:

- **Outside-In Thinking.** Scanning the unfamiliar external environment, rather than tactically looking to the familiar.

- **Future-Back Thinking.** Using the scanning insights to imagine an opportunity, change, disruption, or goal and then stepping backward to generate insights about actions and resources that you'll need to meet it.

- **Big to Small and Back Again.** Scanning the big issues and trends for their relevance to your situation and then coming back to the big implications for change. This process can also connect short-term and long-term options.

- **Perceptive Questioning.** While scanning, using open-ended questions for strategic conversation and inquiry; valuing asking more highly than telling, and putting questions and options before answers and decisions.

In Encounter debriefings participants tell us that developing Proactive Scanning habits is one of the most important and productive changes they have made as leaders. For example:

Peter Horvat, the Croatian global marketing head in a consumer beauty products firm, has instituted a weekly practice with his team: each person is assigned in rotation to share a TED talk or online video or online link related to a new technology. After the scan, each team member completes an online survey answering the question "what if" for the organization. Each month, the team debriefs the new knowledge. In addition, every month one other team member shares information on a technology or change story happening in one of their main customers or partners in their supply chain. He told us, "Our team has already seen innovation projects creating new personalized beauty products to connect IoT technology and digitally enabled personal customer design."

During the COVID-19 crisis, the importance of Proactive Scanning was accentuated. "Necessity is the mother of invention," and through the pandemic we saw astonishing technology acceleration. For example, with social distancing and lockdowns, it was amazing to watch real estate agents adopt virtual reality property tours and AI-driven e-closings.[8] During the pandemic, leaders who were looking outside their industry and geography had a distinct advantage based on knowledge, ideas, and options.

Proactive Scanning stimulates thinking about ideas from the customer's perspective to imagine new products and services that no one yet provides: nondestructive innovation.[9] When leaders and their teams undertake Proactive Scanning and take insights into the Completely Opposite Viewpoints Debate, they unleash the kind of futuristic thinking needed to anticipate the impossible and impractical. Old-timers will appreciate the exercise. After all, readers of the 1946 *Dick Tracy* comic strip saw Dick's interactive wristwatch as science fiction, while fans of the original *Star Trek* saw holographic communication play out 150 years in the future. And yet today, the Apple Watch and Cisco's holographic telepresence video conferencing are both possible and practical.

DEBATE RITUALS

The Completely Opposite Viewpoints Debate that Proactive Scanning fuels is the central Phoenix Encounter tool and habit. Debates also have ritual rules of engagement to create a safe atmosphere. The environment for the Encounter method debates must be psychologically safe, so Encounter group members believe they can positively engage in unconstrained exploration without fear, and there is mutual, respectful, and constructive devil's advocacy.[10]

This kind of brainstorming debate is dialogue enabled by fair processes, supported by clear and agreed protocols for open involvement. Dialogue and idea generation must include diverse perspectives. This is an energetic discussion to create, consider, and communicate multiple options for innovation. The teams often use visualization techniques in the war room to engage people around screens or boards to see ideas (built on design thinking) quickly. In all, the Encounter's debate approach is designed to provide multiple ideas from multiple sources, informed by Proactive Scanning to generate the much wider options set the Phoenix leader needs. Two specific rituals are absolutely essential for this kind of debate: Radical Ideation and the Separation Imperative.[11]

Radical Ideation[12]

A Phoenix Attitude is extreme. Like the counterculturists who style themselves as "attitude dudes," leaders with a Phoenix Attitude confront, challenge, and rise above incrementalism and the status quo. Similarly, Radical Ideation pushes beyond the barriers of the leader's traditional options set because the Phoenix leader embraces the extreme in everything he or she thinks. Control is placed only on the decisions and actions, never on the ideation.

Radical Ideation is deliberately unconstrained by legacy resources or other restrictions. It is way beyond the norms of doing what we're doing now, but faster and cheaper. The ideas are progressive and include the improbable as well as the possible. They are extreme because many radical ideas would not appear on face value to be doable or desirable to the orthodox leader. Yet when outsiders look at these ideas, they often don't see them as at all radical. The problem is that radical ideas often do not fit the inward-looking worldview of leaders in legacy organizations. For example, the traditional hoteliers would never have thought a sharing platform like Airbnb for renting out rooms or homes to tourists would ever make sense.

Extreme events, even hypothetical ones, can promote both high-level engagement and dramatic thinking. For example, in November 1983, the ABC television network broadcast an apocalyptic movie about a nuclear attack called *The Day After*. The broadcast achieved the highest viewing numbers ever for a TV movie on a US network, and the extreme consequences depicted—devastation, radiation poisoning, looting, a military crackdown—prompted a very active public debate.[13] We borrow that dynamic in our use of Radical Ideation in the Phoenix Encounter because when the status quo is challenged in an extreme way, powerful insights and ideas emerge.

Radical Ideation is used in both the Extreme Attack and Horizon Defense debates of the Phoenix Encounter. It shows up as the unconstrained use of weapons in the leader's plan to destroy an organization from the outside by throwing as much firepower as the leader can imagine. It shows up as unconstrained option generation in the Horizon Defense phase as leaders imagine every possible escape route and road to ascendency. Radical Ideation is a "head game" and "mindset converter." Its most important function is shifting participants' focus from simply challenging the status quo to destroying it. When Radical Ideation happens, the phoenix has entered the room.

Because the Phoenix Encounter deploys Radical Ideation in the war-game environment, it can be an uncomfortable experience both intellectually and emotionally. We see that often, and we sympathize, but we believe that leaders and their teams need to challenge their mindsets in as dramatic and profound a way as possible. Radical Ideation gives the Completely Opposite Viewpoints Debate airtime and life.[14] Leaders would do well to remember that Radical Ideation is already part of the attitude of entrepreneurs disrupting traditional industries. Thinking about destruction provides leaders and their organizations with an insurance policy against experiencing it.

The Separation Imperative[15]

When Radical Ideation occurs in the Encounter Battlefield debate, two phrases are totally banned: "The problem with that is . . ." and "That does not make sense." This ban is part of another crucial debate ritual: the Separation Imperative.

The Separation Imperative is a practice that uses fair yet dynamic discussion protocols to enforce the understanding that ideation, synthesis, analysis, and decision-making should be distinct and separate phases of strategic dialogue. It prevents leaders from conflating these phases and rushing to judgment in the war room. By insisting that analysis and decision-making be held in abeyance while future options are being generated, the Separation Imperative ensures that the widest and most radical option set will emerge for later conscious consideration. Once those radical ideas have surfaced, then reality testing can begin in earnest. In this way, the Separation Imperative supports the notion of being bold in thought first, and then being cautious in the deeds undertaken.[16]

The Separation Imperative helps Encounter participants avoid the common traps of brainstorming that confuse and conjoin ideation and analysis. It confers the same benefit in the real-world strategic conversations that often follow Phoenix Encounters. It can also be developed as a habit of mind that leaders can use to review all new information as it is received. Applied this way, the Separation Imperative enables the open-minded curiosity of the Phoenix Attitude to sift information and ideas and confront the confirmation bias of status quo thinking.[17]

> Susanna Schmidt, the Austrian COO of a global insurance company, summed up the importance of the debate rituals in her Encounter experience. "I could never imagine that five other people from totally different industries could come up with a set of attack options that were both destructive and terrifyingly realistic that I hadn't thought about before—and had never surfaced in our leadership team's strategy sessions. At first, they seemed so far-fetched, and I had to hold myself back from killing the ideas straight away during the discussion to explain why they would never work. Having the Radical Idea generation separated from analysis was the key for me to see a very different future for my industry. It is a future already starting to play out."

THE ENCOUNTER JOURNAL

In a different age, C. S. Lewis wrote in his novel *That Hideous Strength,* "There are a dozen views about everything until you know the answer. Then there's never more than one." When working toward a new strategic business model agenda, the imperative of the Phoenix leader is to hold all those dozen views close until a new way forward is decided and then to revisit them periodically, even as change is embedded in the leader's organization and a dozen more views open up. This is a tall order.

The Encounter Journal is an organizing and documenting tool to ensure the Phoenix leader retains all insights and ultimately creates a Future-Facing Blueprint for the Phoenix Breakthrough. It distills the collective wisdom generated along the way—the insights, options, and actions before, during, and after the Encounter Battlefield exercise—and provides a common language to execute the Completely Opposite Viewpoints Debate. Its most important section is called a blueprint because it leads to a future-facing road map of prospective Breakthrough initiatives (organizational, business model, and personal). The Encounter Journal work requires some mental gymnastics, especially as it moves the leader through the altitudes and from qualitative thinking to critical thought and on to in-depth analysis, quantitative examination, and tactical deployment (Figure 5.1, next page). The Encounter Journal is also discussed in our book's online site: www.phoenixencountermethod.com.

The main Encounter Journal sections are:

1. **Encounter Groundwork**
   a. **Encounter Method Overview.** A brief summary of the key activities the leader will undertake during all the Encounter phases and stages ahead.
   b. **Initial Status Reflection and Briefing Report.** A panoramic taking-stock of the leader's organization from the perspective of different stakeholders on its:
      i. Current vision, mission, and strategic priorities; value propositions, strengths, and challenges (incorporating a standard SWOT).

FIGURE 5.1 Encounter Journal: Essential Sections and Elements

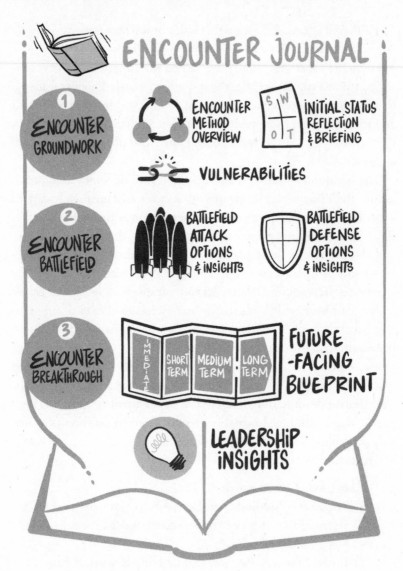

    ii. The business model for value creation and capture. Because this briefing section is ultimately shared with other Phoenix Encounter Group members, we add relevant baseline data and information to help them understand the target organization and industry.

  c. **Vulnerabilities.** A short section for the leader to capture insights from the first discussion meeting with the Encounter group on possible vulnerabilities to exploit in attack and watch out for in defense.

2. **Encounter Battlefield**

  a. **Battlefield Attack Options and Insights.** A section to outline and capture the destruction scenario and options from the Proactive Scanning and Radical Ideation in the Extreme Attack debate.

  b. **Battlefield Defense Options and Insights.** A section to outline and capture the high-level draft of promising Horizon Defense ideas from the Proactive Scanning and Radical Ideation in the Battlefield Defense debate, from the immediate and short term toward medium and long term.

3. **Encounter Breakthrough**

  a. **Future-Facing Blueprint.** An extensive section that reexamines the panorama of the organization—outside and within—by completely revisiting the strategic priorities, value propositions, and needed strengths (including a future-facing SWOT) from different stakeholder perspectives Essentially, it takes the insights from the Battlefield into a renewed future view of the business model. It highlights the most prospective initiatives for immediate, short-term, medium-term, and long-term action—both transformation and core fortification. It reflects on where these achieve goals around growth, cost, and risk, as well as potential innovation outcomes. This blueprint is the high-level plan for action.

  b. **Leadership Insights.** An optional section, for the leader to document key insights and implications in relation to their agenda for strategic leadership priorities, as well as their own personal leadership development. These are leadership insights arising from their intention to pursue the Phoenix actions in the blueprint.

Informed by the qualitative ideas from the attack and defense debates, the Encounter Journal focuses on the most prospective ideas in the organization's Future-Facing Blueprint. This determines priorities for deeper analysis work and other initiatives (such as pilot experiments) that are immediate, short term, medium term, or long term.

One question Encounter participants often ask is why we separate qualitative ideation in the Encounter Battlefield from quantitative analysis in the Encounter Journal. In our complex, diverse, and volatile world, it is difficult (if not impossible) to represent an innovative business model quantitatively right at the conceptual stage. Often the organizational data bank is entirely drawn from the legacy business, and far too many questionable assumptions need to be made to extrapolate the Future-Facing Blueprint. In many instances, it will take resources and time to generate the needed data from nontraditional sources (e.g., social media).

We believe that a more pragmatic and fruitful way of going forward with breakthrough ideas is the "Fail Fast" philosophy,[18] one that accepts that it will never be possible to access all the relevant data before launching a project. Relying on a comprehensive quantitative analysis is a recipe for falling into the incremental thinking trap: making bets only on ideas that have a well-quantified return on investment, plus robust assumptions and data. The real world is characterized by incomplete data and fragile assumptions. In such environments, "test-learn-test-learn" approaches enable agile experimentation guided by sturdy qualitative hypotheses.

By qualitative, we do not mean, "I don't know why, but I have an intuition that this will work." Instead, we're talking about qualitative hypotheses buttressed by completely opposite perspectives and unconstrained thinking. The test-learn-test-learn cycle will quickly confirm, disconfirm, adjust, or generate completely new ideas.

As each Journal section iterates, it provides a thought-conserving mechanism for articulating the progressive insights, ideas, and options the Encounter method generates. This lets leaders and teams work through successive versions of their blueprint before "going live" with an agenda for change. There are often false starts and detours, and some ideas are thrown out along the way. A telling moment arises when leaders or teams review the very first iteration of their strategic priorities, strengths, and weaknesses—the one they made on the first day of the Encounter, when they captured the baseline briefing snapshot of their current organizations—and compares this to their Future-Facing Blueprint. Leaders and teams see that they have already come a long way in their Phoenix thinking and are inspired to finish the work and get to Breakthrough. Ultimately, as leaders consider the future, they also reflect upon themselves. Frequently leaders add key insights about implications for their own strategic leadership priorities, as well as their agenda for personal leadership development and growth at the end of their Journal.

PHOENIX LEADERS EXERCISING THEIR ESP MATTERS

The Phoenix Encounter method with the tools and habits of mind that make up Phoenix ESP are there for the taking; they can be practiced and honed. Leaders can use some of them or they can use all of them. But the more comfortable leaders are using them, the sooner and more effectively they will adopt the Phoenix Attitude to transform their companies. These tools and habits are the "how" of the Phoenix Encounter, and they are a joy to learn because they open whole new ways of seeing, thinking, discussing, and leading.

The "why" is more urgent. It's the story of Yekutiel Sherman, a young Israeli entrepreneur, who designed a smartphone case that unfolds into a selfie stick. Within a week of his posting the idea on Kickstarter, it had been copied and put up for sale on the Chinese site AliExpress at a fraction of the price he'd anticipated charging. Sherman never saw it coming—not the copycat, not the abuse of Kickstarter, not the manufacturing capability, not the fury of his investors—none of it.[19]

The *why* is the winds of change, which are blowing harder every year—and they aren't buffeting only young entrepreneurs. Legacy companies have the most to lose in the firestorm environment, and too many are behaving like dodos. This is true even among some of the first- and second-wave multinational technology firms, which are having a hard time seeing themselves as anything less than innovative. They once were, but compared to nimble startups, they now appear to be overengineering perfectionists or innovation laggards. Too often we see firms like these failing to take any new ideas to market and instead becoming reactive to challengers. Use your Phoenix Attitude and ESP!

Smart companies can move fast and in unexpected directions. For example, Google formed a major partnership with Walmart, perhaps to outflank Amazon—which, like Google, knows what consumers are interested in but, unlike Google, also knows what consumers actually buy. The information could give Amazon a powerful competitive edge over Google. Remember, it was Oracle that created cloud capacity, but is was Amazon Web Services that took a market-leading position. All of that is real, and it's been happening. Who will win? It's hard to say, and it may not matter for very long because in these firestorm times, today's winners may be tomorrow's losers.

In Part II, we enter the Phoenix Encounter Battlefield in search of a new blueprint and breakthroughs. We proactively scan and radically ideate toward the Phoenix future we'll outline in the book's final part.

 # CHAPTER 5 CHECKLIST

Summary Thoughts

1. To facilitate the Completely Opposite Viewpoints Debate and build a Phoenix Attitude, three Extra Strategic Perception (ESP) tools and habits of mind are: Proactive Scanning, debate rituals, and using an Encounter Journal. ESP comes naturally to a very few leaders, but its tools and habits of mind can be taught and then developed through practice.

2. Proactive Scanning uses a kind of wide-angle, future-directed curiosity to continually monitor both inside and (especially) outside the organization, industry, and geography for new developments that can signal a

danger or opportunity ahead. It helps the leader ask: What is new? What might it mean? What if?

3. Debate rituals are tools to support a psychologically safe yet robust strategic dialogue where opposite viewpoints are surfaced and considered. Radical Ideation generates extreme thinking about ideas and options. The Separation Imperative ensures the debate remains focused on the discrete stages of ideation, synthesis, analysis, and decision-making—avoiding the usual conflation problems (such as closing off options too early) in brainstorming. The Encounter Journal helps leaders work through every activity in the Phoenix Encounter method by documenting options, insights, and actions, including their Future-Facing Blueprint.

Reflection

1. Have you ever met a leader who seems to have an intuitive grasp of coming change and an instinct for strategic decision-making? If yes, what strikes you about the quality of his or her thinking and leadership style? Do you see any of the ESP practices and habits of mind at work in this leader?

2. Do you currently undertake any kind of regular scanning of external and internal forces of disruption to inform you on how to lead your company? How is it the same or different from elements of Proactive Scanning?

3. Are you using any form of Radical Ideation in challenging the status quo of your business today? Are you ensuring separation in the brainstorming discussions of ideation from analysis and decision-making (the Separation Imperative)? Are you mapping the implications of scanning, ideation, and insights into a Future-Facing Blueprint for your organization?

PART II

PHOENIX BURNING:

Encounter Battlefield

SCANNING FIREPOWER FOR EXTREME ATTACK AND HORIZON DEFENSE

The battlefield is a scene of constant chaos. The winner will be the one who controls that chaos, both his own and the enemies.
—NAPOLEON BONAPARTE, French statesman and military leader

Throughout Part I, we discussed the Phoenix leader's need for opposite debates and Proactive Scanning to seek firestorm ideas. In Part II, in the Encounter Battlefield phase, we take leaders through a range of scans, debates, and ideation—first wide, then deep. This is essential for generating a wide range of radical ideas—the firepower of Extreme Attack and Horizon Defense. In this sense, Chapters 6–12 will have a different tone and purpose for the reader than Part I. These chapters focus on the outside world, with a 50,000-foot altitude view connecting to 50-foot actions, across industries and geographies, to help leaders sense the panorama of firestorm disruption opportunities and threats.

We want leaders to look carefully at the external environment of firestorm disruptive trends, from technology to demographics; from digital and social platforms to emerging markets; from talent, sustainability, and activism to reimagining traditional business levers. Leading strategy scholars such as Rita McGrath highlight the special significance of scanning across sources of contemporary firepower as "key to the discovery of inflection points which have the power to change the very assumptions on which organizations were founded."[1]

SOURCES OF FIREPOWER

Proactive Scanning allows leaders to identify "firepower" for Extreme Attack (destroying or creating) and Horizon Defense (fortifying and transforming). The firepower sources are the arsenals to deploy for future organizational success or change, and they shape businesses, industries, and markets. In the Encounter method, we describe two different types of firepower:

- Contemporary firepower of the new world (the modern arsenals such as emerging technologies, platform business models, and shifting demographics)

- Conventional firepower of the old world (the traditional arsenals, such as business strategy, leadership, marketing, operations, finance, and human resources)

We provide a checklist of contemporary and conventional firepower in Figure 6.1. This is a partial inventory of the contemporary and conventional arsenal available for consideration in the Encounter debates. We recognize that the boundaries between these columns are very fluid. Contemporary and conventional firepower can be joined in combinatorial innovation, which we discuss in Chapter 12. We also note that the velocity of technological change, virtual adaptation and innovations during the COVID-19 pandemic is significant. As Satya Nadella, Microsoft CEO, said in April 2020, "Microsoft has seen two years' worth of digital transformation in just two months."[2]

FIGURE 6.1 Examples of Firepower for Extreme Attack and Horizon Defense—Contemporary, Conventional, and Combinatorial

CONTEMPORARY FIREPOWER

TECHNOLOGY DRIVERS

- DIGITIZATION
- NEW TECHNOLOGIES
- EMERGING TECHNOLOGIES
- ALGORITHMS & ANALYTICS

BUSINESS MODEL TRANSFORMATION

- CUSTOMER POWER
- PLATFORMS & ECOSYSTEMS
- REDEFINING FIRM/INSTRUMENT BOUNDARIES
- NEW ENTRANTS & PARTNERS
- NEW PRODUCTS, SEGMENTS, & MARKETS
- NEW CAPITAL SOURCES

DYNAMIC INNOVATION

- EXPERIMENTATION
- DISRUPTIVE INNOVATION
- NONDISRUPTIVE INNOVATION
- FUTURE-FACING LEADERSHIP
- ACCELERATED LEARNING

MACRO LEVERS

- INTERGENERATIONAL & DIVERSITY TALENT
- SUSTAINABILITY
- ACTIVISM
- REGULATION & POLICY ADVOCACY
- GEOPOLITICAL & ECONOMIC FORCES

CONVENTIONAL FIREPOWER

COMPETITIVE POSITIONING

- VISION & STRATEGY
- MERGERS, ACQUISITIONS, & DIVESTMENTS
- CAPITAL INVESTMENTS & RESTRUCTURING
- REPUTATION & TRUST
- BRAND, MARKETING, & SALES
- INCREMENTAL INNOVATION
- INTELLECTUAL PROPERTY

OPERATIONAL STRATEGY

- BUSINESS, PRODUCT, SERVICE DEVELOPMENT
- FINANCE
- PARTNERSHIPS
- ASSET & RESOURCE OPTIMIZATION
- SYSTEMS & PROCESS EFFICIENCY
- ANALYSIS, PLANNING, & PROJECT MANAGEMENT

ORGANIZATIONAL CULTURE

- GOVERNANCE & VALUES
- HUMAN RESOURCE MANAGEMENT & DEVELOPMENT
- LEADERSHIP CAPABILITIES
- PERFORMANCE ALIGNMENT

MACRO LEVERS

- REGULATION & POLICY MANAGEMENT
- CORPORATE SOCIAL RESPONSIBILITY
- MARKET FORCES

COMBINATORIAL FIREPOWER = CONVENTIONAL + CONTEMPORARY

To assist readers and Encounter participants, we have divided some of the contemporary and conventional firepower sources into four categories that can assist people during their Completely Opposite Viewpoints debates and Radical Ideation work to ensure a holistic view of option generation.

Options for contemporary firepower that are often less familiar to leaders in the legacy world can include:

- *Technology drivers* such as digitization, algorithms and analytics; new technologies such as artificial intelligence (AI) and cloud computing; and emerging technologies such as robotics and Internet of Things (IoT)

- *Business model transformation* built on empowered customers, creating platforms, and ecosystems; developing new partners, products, segments, and markets

- *Dynamic innovation* using experimental research, development, and pilot projects; seeking out disruptive innovation options; creating nondisruptive innovation and value creation initiatives or products; developing Phoenix-like future-facing leaders; and promoting accelerated learning as a continuous priority

- *Macro levers* allowing firms to understand and take advantage of unstoppable future trends in talent diversity (gender, cultures, and intergenerational); demographic shifts; sustainability imperatives; activism (both social and investor); proactive regulatory and policy advocacy; and the forces of geopolitical and economic power tilts

Options for *Conventional Firepower* that are very familiar to leaders in the legacy world, and sometimes overlooked by disrupters, can include:

- *Competitive positioning,* by developing a clear and compelling vision and strategy linked to core competencies and a viable profit-generating business model; seeking growth and scale/scope economies through mergers, acquisitions, restructuring, divestments, and capital investment projects; building on reputation and trust, supported by brand, marketing, and sales; and securing incremental innovation opportunities and intellectual property protections

- *Operational strategy,* including the levers of business, products, and services development; finance; asset optimization; systems and process efficiency, such as risk management, compliance, procurement, and logistics; and robust analysis, planning, and project management capabilities

- *Organizational culture,* as seen in governance arrangements that support vision and strategy; organizational values; people acquisition, development, and retention approaches together with relevant leadership capabilities; and performance alignment that connects the firm's critical priorities to its culture, systems, people, and clients

- *Macro levers,* including traditional regulation and policy management; identifying important corporate social responsibility initiatives; and understanding the implications of economic and market forces

DEPLOYING THE FIREPOWER

A leadership team with the Phoenix Attitude uses both conventional and contemporary firepower to create a Future-Facing Blueprint. The challenge is choosing carefully while building creatively because the elements can be combined in different ways for different purposes. For example, AI, one of the contemporary arsenals of emerging technologies, has many applications. It is used in one way in a Siri or Alexa device and in quite another way in high-frequency foreign-exchange currency trading.

Firepower arsenals are not a prescription for change—they are an opportunity to generate ideas. This can allow the organization to do things differently, and importantly, allow it to do different things altogether. Examples include Amazon's use of robotics to automate its warehouse operations to gain speed and efficiency, and Alibaba offering its retail technology stack as a service for mom-and-pop stores in China. Conventional mergers and acquisitions combined with platform capacity could change the scale and scope of an organization or market, as with IKEA (see Chapter 12). Another outcome from scanning contemporary firepower is the development of ideas for entirely new products and services, or ways of delivering them, that lead to additional innovation options. We include this in our list as disruptive and nondisruptive innovation.[3]

Such is the nature of firepower options and why considering as wide a set as possible is so valuable. In all, the weapons await the human imagination and aspiration that an Encounter Battlefield can unleash.[4]

One Encounter participant, Bram Jansen, the regional CEO for the Netherlands of one of the world's biggest fast-moving consumer goods companies, exemplified this outlook:

> We have actually included the Encounter war games role-play as a half-yearly strategic review exercise, as a structured part of our strategic planning process now. And as part of this, we have—let's call it a war game—where we actually challenge the team to attack our strategy vigorously as if they were a competitor or someone we had never even imagined. The objective is to make sure that our defensive strategies are in place. And then, apart from that, whenever we evaluate new projects, part of the review process is to say: Right . . . if someone else wanted to kill our project, how might they do that?

In Encounter exercises, we separate our scanning discussions of contemporary firepower from those about conventional elements because they are significant at different stages of the Battlefield debates. Contemporary arsenal opportunities are more deeply considered in the Extreme Attack stage, while conventional elements and combinations are more carefully considered for Horizon Defense options. Scans are also used when the strategic defense option review becomes related directly to the business itself as participants work out the Future-Facing Blueprint of priorities and transformation.

> ### The Firepower Metaphor
>
> Humans have used "fire" for more than 50,000 years—for heating, cooking, and light. In the Phoenix Encounter, we use the term "firepower" as a constructive metaphor. It encapsulates the fundamental fire that gives new life to the Phoenix-like leader and organization. In the Encounter Battlefield, "firepower" suggests a range of potential weapons and resources for both attack and defense.
>
> Firepower is available to the young and the old, the disrupter and the incumbent. We believe that scanning the arsenal for sources of firepower is essential for the Phoenix leader—and that the firelight can illuminate a valuable reflection or ignite a firestorm.

A WORD OF WARNING— BEYOND THE HYPE

Before we go further into firestorm disruptive technologies and business models, a word of warning. The idea of contemporary firepower (such as deploying a digital platform) reshaping the structure of an industry is an alluring one. However, leaders need to be extremely careful in understanding the true economic foundations of these business models to grasp the full extent of how emerging technologies and other trends could transform their business. This prevents another bias: "drinking the Kool-Aid."[5]

If a company wants to mirror the growth of technology companies such as Amazon, Google, or Facebook, it must keep in mind that it is not just technology and data, but technology combined with a business model and supported by culture, operations, and talent that makes the company what it is. These factors let the company enjoy low marginal costs, low capital investments, positive network externalities (more customers/platform users bring more value to each other), and decreasing customer acquisition costs, making its business highly scalable and hence profitable in cash terms. In the absence of such operational advantages, it is delusional to pretend to be a tech company when in reality you are not.[6]

This is vividly illustrated by the 2019 IPO woes of WeWork, a traditional real estate business trying to emulate technology firms without having its essential ingredients. For instance, there is no high-margin complimentary service that WeWork could offer its customers, the data that it collects from its facilities has limited business value, and switching costs for its customers seem low to nonexistent. It was a business with two dollars of costs for every dollar of revenue, and billions of dollars in long-term lease liabilities. In 2019, when WeWork tried pushing an IPO valuing the business at $47 billion, it met investor resistance even at a $15 billion valuation. Finally the company had to pull its IPO and enter a capital reconstruction with SoftBank, which was further subject to litigation during COVID-19. The market essentially compared WeWork to IWG (formerly known as Regus) as a traditional but transforming shared workspace real estate company—which was profitable, growing, and valued at $4 billion at the same time—not a technology company, as WeWork had attempted to position itself. As one market commentator remarked, the "version of alternative reality is coming to an end."[7]

We might ask the same question of firms such as Airbnb: Is its growth justified? Our short answer: It's more likely in the longer term. Airbnb doesn't own any assets and has the tech company operational approach. It fundamentally is a digital intermediary, operating a platform connecting accommodation owners and users that has propelled its business by creating an environment of trust and has steadily expanded its ecosystem to provide its customers unique and seamless experiences. (Knowing where you are going, with whom, and for how long lets Airbnb act as a platform for local services—tours, concerts, etc.—which only gets better as more renters and tourists get onboard with Airbnb.)[8] Its asset-light business model gave it a higher chance of survival than its analog competitors during the COVID-19 pandemic. As the travel industry recovers from the aftermath of this crisis, Airbnb's platform could seamlessly onboard certified third-party cleaning and disinfecting services, at lower transaction costs (thanks to its digital DNA), and further reinforce its core value proposition of trust for all stakeholders on its platform.

There are lots of startups where the jury is well and truly out. Peloton, a firm that sells high-end connected stationary bikes, is an example where the pre-COVID-19 market questioned its ability to grow due to consumer costs, even when the (small) segment of the market that could afford the bikes found value in the product. Late 2019 evidence showed significant growing market concerns.[9] However, global lockdowns during COVID-19 provided Peloton with a much-needed boost for more significant adoption of its product and services. Peloton could have a springboard to leverage scale in its business like never before. It could use its digital roots to create value-added services that ensure continuous customer engagement once lockdowns are lifted.

In summary, we think it's easy to get carried away by the hype of emerging technologies and trends. Leaders with a Phoenix Attitude need to consciously revert to fundamental economic principles. This includes the potential long-run impacts of catastrophic events such as a pandemic, when evaluating their options for action in the Future-Facing Blueprint.

INTO BATTLE—PROACTIVE SCANNING AND RADICAL IDEATION AT WORK

In the chapters ahead, we scan some firepower examples for Battlefield attack and defense ideas, including:

- Digital and social platforms and ecosystems

- Indispensable and emerging technologies

- Other contemporary trends, such as emerging markets and the workforce of the future

Although the central concept of this book is the Phoenix Encounter method, we believe the power of this method is difficult to comprehend fully unless you radically ideate about how some of these firepower examples could completely destroy your organization. Indeed, many leaders who have undertaken the Encounter exercise have found that these scans offer a rude awakening to their current blinkered state. For this important reason, the chapters in this part of the book are exemplars of what it means to undertake Proactive Scanning, something that is a must-have for any organization and leader of the twenty-first century to develop radical ideas for Extreme Attack and comprehensive options for Horizon Defense.

A major caveat: Chapters 7–12 in Part II are information scans of firepower and were current at the time of publication, but as noted in our introduction, the speed of change is accelerating and these will be out of date by the time you read them. Use these scanning chapters, but also consult the website resources (www.phoenixencountermethod .com) for updated versions.

The Phoenix Encounter method lasts. Its real-world examples will continue to evolve at speed.

The Battlefield Gets Real

For years, the director of service operations for a major customer transport firm in Asia Pacific, a man we'll call Gary Smithers, thought operational efficiency and labor management were his highest strategic priorities. There were two good reasons for this inward focus: Smithers's business unit was responsible for its back-office operations, such as luggage handling. It was a self-contained operation, and there was no competition in sight.

Then came Smithers's Encounter Battlefield exercise. After assessing his unit's strengths and weaknesses, Smithers entered the Extreme Attack stage. For the first time, he confronted the possibility that a company that he had considered a noncompetitor could, with sufficient scale advantage, perform all of the firm's back-office operations more efficiently. That possibility grew more discomfiting when he realized that (1) the imagined noncompetitor might already be providing value-added services to several transport businesses operating around Smithers's region; (2) the threatening service provider had sufficient capitalization and skills to deploy new AI technologies much faster than Smithers could; and (3) the competitor could build out its enhanced support platform with other service partners in mid-office operations (such as data tracking and data analytics) not currently available in Smithers's organization.

While Smithers was pondering the consequences of this imagined incursion, a cell phone call broke his concentration. Annoyed that a subordinate had interrupted his Encounter, Smithers was about to suggest that he call back later when he learned the reason for the call: an actual noncompetitor had, in fact, made a proposal that morning that was very much like the threat constructed during the Extreme Attack. For Smithers, the proposal was very bad news, but the coincidence was a revelation: the threat was very real. Fortunately, work in the Horizon Defense stage of the Encounter had helped Smithers carefully consider all of the proposal's implications. He knew exactly how to respond.

Following the Battlefield Exercise, Smithers determined to have deep conversations about the proposal with his firm's executive leadership. He was confident that his recommended course of action—which included new technology, new service partnerships, and capacity for data analytics—would be the best way to go.

the is D I G I T A L W O R L D is DRAWN ADS THE

SOCIAL & DIGITAL

1 — a POWER SHIFT from FIRMS to CONSUMERS

CONSUMER · FIRM

2 — NEW POSSIBILITIES

PARTNERS · BUSINESS MODEL · CONSUMERS · PRODUCTS & SERVICES

FIRM BOUNDARIES SHIFT UPSTREAM & DOWNSTREAM

3 — STAKEHOLDERS become CONTENT CREATORS & INFLUENCERS

FIRM

ZERO MOMENT OF TRUTH · FIRST MOMENT OF TRUTH · SECOND MOMENT OF TRUTH

INSTANTANEOUS POSSIBILITIES for
* ENGAGEMENT
* COOPERATION
* CO-PRODUCTION

CHAPTER 7

ALL DIGITAL FIREPOWER, ALL THE TIME

*We must respond to opportunities before
they become conventional wisdom.*

—SATYA NADELLA, CEO, Microsoft

The power of digital and social media to disrupt traditional businesses and industries is evident in every Encounter exercise we run. Consider the Extreme Attack contemplated by Doris Souwe, CMO at one of Japan's leading global cosmetic brands:

> Her Encounter started by leveraging the power of digital to create a personalized, high-quality body care product for women. The consumer could choose from a palette of five different fragrances, three different formulations, and three sizes. These would then be delivered (or available for pickup in store) in recyclable glass bottles with built-in sensors to measure consumption. If feasible, packaging could also be done using 3-D printing in the store. The service would be sold as a 12-month subscription.
>
> Fragrances, as well as refill formulations, could be changed with two weeks' notice. The creams, lotions, soaps, foams, etc., would have no palm oil. All soap remnants would be

used for second use production or distributed to the poor. All of the marketing for the new line would be through digital and social media. Consumers would be made coproducers of informational content. Spokesperson influencers for the new product would be active on digital and social forums focused on recycling and plastic bans.

DIGITAL IS BASELINE LEADERSHIP UNDERSTANDING NOW

Digitalization has set the world on fire. It is fuel for the phoenix. By early 2020, more than 4.5 billion people had access to the Internet. That represents more than a 1,000 percent increase since 2000. Even with that kind of growth, just over half of the global population is online. There is plenty of room for more growth, and more growth means more and faster change.[1]

One of the largest changes that Internet digitalization brings is unlocking the flow of information and knowledge across the world. That flow (Figure 7.1), according to a 2017 article in *McKinsey Quarterly*, is growing in a convex fashion even while the other major global flows of trade and finance remain relatively flat.[2]

The *DHL Global Connectedness Index 2018 Report* confirms this finding and suggests it is powered by the 55-fold increase in international Internet bandwidth available per Internet user since 2001.[3]

Unlocking information flows has significant consequences. One of the most profound is the quantum shift in the power balance from sellers to buyers, a phenomenon that is not limited to first-world commerce—it underpins the arsenal of customer power. We know this from both our research and our personal experience.

In 2008, Paddy spent Christmas break with his family in a small village on the west coast of India. Running each morning on the pristine beach, he noticed that as the local fishermen returned from their nightly fishing runs, they chatted on mobile phones. The fishermen, it turned out, were not just chatting with friends, they were talking to business partners at several local fish markets. They were learning the

FIGURE 7.1 Global Flows

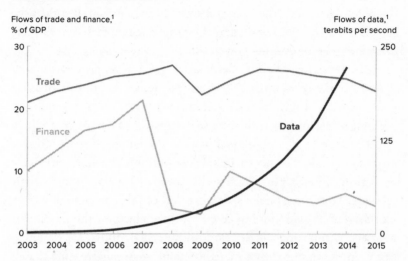

Flows of trade and finance,[1]
% of GDP

Flows of data,[1]
terabits per second

[1] Trade and finance are inflows; data flows are a proxy to inflows, based on total flows of data.

Source: McKinsey & Co

price that wholesalers were paying for each type of fish, and they then sent their catch to the market with the highest prices.

The practice, known to economists as "price discovery," freed the fishermen and their very perishable product from the shackles of mid-dlemen. (In the analog world, middlemen used their informational advantage to benefit from the oldest business model in the world: buy low, sell high.) The fishermen significantly improved their income.[4]

The cell phone advantage didn't stop there. Paddy also noticed that one fisherman had a very expensive phone—a Nokia E90 Communicator—identical to his own phone. "Why do you buy such an expensive phone?" Paddy asked. The Communicator offered a GPS application that provided a foolproof way of locating the nets the fisherman dropped each night in various places. Without it, the fisherman wasted valuable time searching for his nets, time that he could now use to drop and haul more nets.[5]

Paddy was amazed. As it turned out, his phone had the same GPS application, but he hadn't even noticed it. He found it interesting that a smart company like Nokia failed to exploit these potential sales and instead marketed the expensive Communicator just to higher-income urban areas. In Phoenix Attitude terms, Nokia's leaders had not seen the potential because they had not scanned the horizon. But the fishermen in a tiny village had, and their vigilance increased both their catch and their bargaining power.

In their report *Digital Planet 2017: How Competitiveness and Trust in Digital Economies Vary Across the World*, economists Bhaskar Chakravorti and Ravi Shankar Chaturvedi (2017) raise a number of strategic leadership issues relating to the growth of the Internet.[6] They say, for example, that developed markets are far ahead of developing economies when it comes to digital penetration.[7] The more surprising revelation in their report describes the speed of innovation in the digital space across these markets, or what they call the digital momentum score. Here, the developing economies are ahead of the developed markets. A consumer in Kenya, Philippines, or India, for example, can do more things with a smartphone or quasi-smartphone than a consumer in Germany or Denmark.[8]

The digital revolution—which is still accelerating—has helped developing economies overcome their infrastructure deficits and leapfrog into the twenty-first-century economy in ways that are still opaque to many observers in the developed markets. Consumers in these markets are empowered in ways that they could not imagine just a few years ago and, Phoenix-like, they are leveraging this to the hilt.

DIGITAL MOVES LIKE AN AVALANCHE

It's important to recognize that something beyond affordability and access is driving the growth of the new breed of digital upstarts; it's called "network externality effects."[9] We see it clearly in the evolution of WhatsApp. In 2009, Jan Koum and Brian Acton released WhatsApp, a smartphone application that let users send text messages via the phone's data network (also referred to as the over-the-top [OTT] network), as distinguished from an SMS message that goes over the telecom operator's cellular network.[10]

The economic significance of such externality can be seen in the $19 billion that Facebook paid to acquire WhatsApp in 2014 at a time when WhatsApp had all of 55 employees on its payroll. The company's small size masked its impact on the telecom world.[11] The growth of WhatsApp also shows us the disruption a single technology can wreak on legacy companies that are unprepared for the digital, globally networked world. The London-based research and analytics firm Ovum estimated that WhatsApp and similar over-the-top voice and messaging companies (e.g., Skype, Link) would cost global telecom operators about $386 billion in revenue between 2012 and 2018.[12] All this should remind readers how important it is that an organization's senior leadership have a clear sense of their tasks:

- Scan technology trends in the marketplace across industries and geographies.

- Leverage the power of the digital revolution to make their firm future-ready.

- Build the capabilities essential for digital innovation.

- Cultivate the digital transformation needed in every area of the firm.

Externality effects can also have important social significances, which equally small-scale operations can set in motion. Consider a single engineering professor and two graduate students at Johns Hopkins University in the early days of the COVID-19 pandemic. During a coffee-shop meeting in January 2020, the students shared their concern about the spread of a novel coronavirus in China, where they had family. They wanted to track the spread of the virus. Like the rest of the world, they knew little about it; their own research was in Measles, Dengue fever, and Zika. Their advisor, Dr. Lauren Gardner, knew even less, but she was Phoenix-minded by nature and in recent years had used her training in civil engineering to investigate how transport systems can spread infection.

Gardner instinctively looked into the future. Understanding exponential growth very well, she encouraged the students to find a digital solution to the tracking challenge. It took them just a day to develop a COVID-19 dashboard prototype. During the next several weeks they spent hundreds of hours inputting data from many disparate data sources, including news reports, government reporting websites, Twitter feeds, data aggregators, and an online community of Chinese healthcare providers (DXY.cn).

The dashboard went live on January 22, 2020, and soon was tracking approximately 7,000 data points and mapping the progress of the pandemic in real time. Neither Gardner nor her students were medical professionals or data scientists, yet together they found a way to curate a torrent of digital information of tremendous medical and social importance. The mapping website they created provided a more comprehensive and compelling perspective on the progress of the pandemic than anything that the United States, China, WHO, or any other stakeholders had yet built. It soon became the go-to site for anyone wanting to track the virus. In the early months of the pandemic, it was a major source of data for epidemiological modelling in the United States. In March 2020, the Johns Hopkins tracker recorded more visits than CNN, LinkedIn, or eBay.[13]

The diffusion of digital technologies is as global a phenomenon as any we have witnessed. There are no barriers of age, gender, religion, economic development, or geography. Not only are most of the world's people connected to one another and to a large chunk of the world's accumulated knowledge, but they are also contributing to the creation of further knowledge. This can be seen with Wikipedia (at a broad scale), in more specialized enterprises such as GitHub (a web-based hosting service that has become the world's largest portal of open-source code for software developers), or the many millions of do-it-yourself videos on YouTube. The consequence of this is clear: the consumers of today (whether business-to-consumer [B2C] or business-to-business [B2B]) are increasingly knowledgeable, demanding, sophisticated, and empowered.

DIGITAL MOMENTS OF TRUTH

Phoenix leaders build an understanding of how digital transforms the customer relationship and influences the "moments of truth" in these interactions.

For instance, readers with marketing experience might be familiar with one of the fundamental frameworks used to generate customer insight: the funnel model of the consumer decision-making process (Figure 7.2).[14]

FIGURE 7.2 The Funnel Model of Consumer Behavior

The idea is that as consumers decide what to buy, they follow a discernable process. Jan Carlzon, CEO of Scandinavian Airline System in the early 1980s, is widely credited with developing the notion of the "first moment of truth," or FMOT, which is perhaps an overly dramatic way of describing consumers' first point of contact with a product or service and the need for the firm to capture the consumers at this point (Figure 7.3).

FIGURE 7.3 The First Moment of Truth

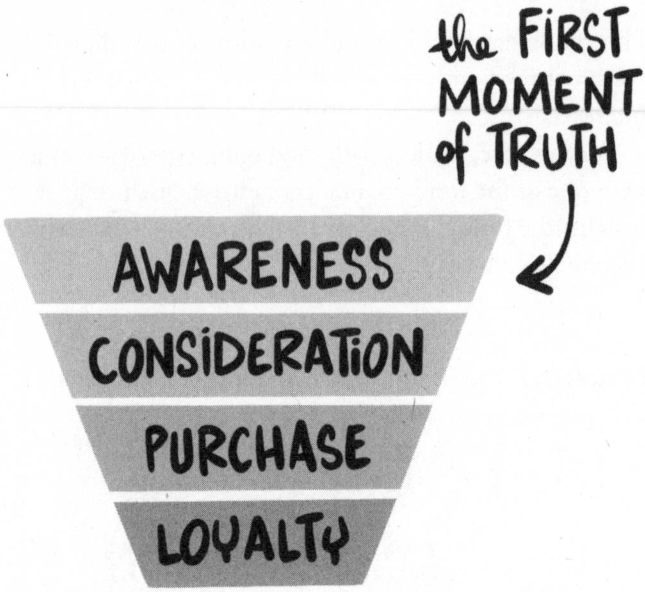

Though Carlzon popularized the concept of FMOT (and subsequently wrote a punchy book with the same title), there were leaders at many other companies, including Coca-Cola, Procter & Gamble, and Unilever, who were recognized for their mastery of this stage of the consumer's decision-making process. The FMOT approach depended on extensive marketing expenditures on advertising and promotions targeted at the end consumers (also referred to as "above the line," or ATL, expenditures).

The rise of modern retail and the growing clout of firms such as Walmart, Tesco, Carrefour, Dairy Farm, and 7/11 in the last decades of the twentieth century led observers to a second epiphany, known predictably as the "second moment of truth," or SMOT (Figure 7.4). Credit for the term is usually given to A. G. Lafley, the president and CEO of Procter & Gamble, who emphasized the importance of capturing consumers at the point where they first physically touched and felt its products—namely, at the point of sale (POS).

FIGURE 7.4 The Second Moment of Truth

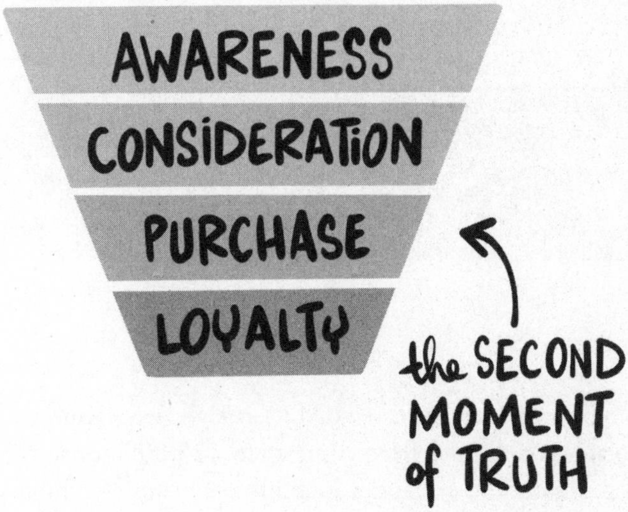

The importance of SMOT to firms is best seen in the growing share of below-the-line (BTL) expenditures (trade promotion expenditures such as listing fees or quantity discounts to retailers) in a firm's marketing budget relative to above-the-line marketing expenditures.[15] Increasingly, marketers were persuaded that while it was important to win at FMOT, it was just as important to win at SMOT.

What exactly do FMOT and SMOT have to do with today's digital world? They are the forerunners of "zero moment of truth," or ZMOT, the digital world's contribution to decisive consumer moments. ZMOT refers to the time *before* contact with a product, when consumers are looking for information to help them solve a problem (Figure 7.5). At that moment, they do something that all of us do every day—they search the Internet.

FIGURE 7.5 The Digital Moments of Truth

How important is ZMOT? Crucial. A McKinsey analysis based on data collected from more than 125,000 consumers across 350 brands and 30 categories found that consumers' choices in about 90 percent of the categories are driven by the brands they consider at the start of their decision-making journey.[16] The Nielsen 2018 CMO report found that 79 percent of the respondents ranked search as "very" or "extremely" important, followed closely by social media, at 73 percent. The numbers for traditional media make for interesting reading: TV was 51 percent, print was 25 percent, and radio was 23 percent.

DIGITAL CHANGES FIRMS— INDUSTRIES TOO

An example of digital's power to launch startups into a Phoenix orbit can be seen in the Instant Pot, founded in 2009.[17] The Canadian company with about 50 employees built a $300 million business, with no venture capital funding and almost no advertising. In practical terms, Instant Pot is a pressure cooker, one that distinguished itself from predecessors by emphasizing its safety. In brand terms, it's a monster, with a cult-like following created almost entirely in the digital world. "Without Amazon," says founder Robert Wang, "we wouldn't be here." Wang isn't exaggerating. The Instant Pot page on Amazon shows more than 28,000 reviews and user-generated answers to more than

1,000 questions.[18] The Instant Pot Facebook Group has more than 1.55 million members. Corelle Brands, which owns Pyrex, Corning-Ware, Corelle, and other brands, acquired Instant Pot in early 2019.[19]

The Instant Pot story also makes another important point about the opportunities the digital world can unlock. The digital world lets firms extend their business processes and systems far beyond the boundaries of their organization, all the way to their business partners and beyond. Amazon, for example, decides stocking quantities, shipping, and fulfillment for Instant Pot and handles its customer support. Amazon is also the source of many of the new product ideas and product reviews, and it develops answers to the most frequently asked questions about the product. The significance of this is enormous. The ability to seamlessly connect across the agents (i.e., consumers, intermediaries, and manufacturer) reduces information distortions across the value chain and leads to tremendous efficiencies and productivity improvements.[20]

The power of digital + social to transform industries is probably best seen in the impact that the COVID-19 pandemic has had on one of the most anachronistic and straitjacketed disciplines in the world: academic publishing in healthcare. Scientific journals have historically taken anywhere from six months to a year to conduct the peer review process that has been required to vet articles before publication. Under this regime, the value of academic publishing was understood to be expertise, discernment, authentication, and gatekeeping. COVID-19 turned all that upside down. At a time when the whole worried world was looking for the latest science on the virus, the old model of academic publishing seemed almost perverse. This new market demanded new value and a new model, one with a focus on raw data, speed, open sharing, and public knowledge.[21]

Suddenly, science publishing moved like greased lightning. Between March and May 2020, roughly 7,000 papers appeared on COVID-19, about 4,000 under sped-up peer review protocols through academic journals and another 3,000 on recently built online repositories called "preprint servers." The two biggest of these servers for COVID-19 publishing, bioRxiv and medRxiv (pronounced "bio-archive" and "med-archive"), took articles from all comers and made them available within hours of submission, after only basic screening, with no peer review required. Access to the articles was free and open to all, and anyone could comment. In essence, the Rxiv forums replaced peer review with crowdsourced wisdom.

Preliminary evidence suggests that the new publishing model worked. Readers quickly shared and built on promising results. They challenged suspect research. Lead time to publication dropped tremendously. Although changes in scientific publishing were already underway before COVID-19 (bioRxiv was founded in 2013, for example, 22 years after a similar archive was created for physics research), the virus dramatically increased the velocity of change in that sector and likely makes many of those changes permanent. In this example, not only did the world of digital + social move faster than an avalanche, it also created new moments of truth, highlighting the need for a coordinated public + private sector response to save lives, promote information sharing, and speed social and economic recovery.

DIGITAL IS FIREPOWER AT VELOCITY, NOT JUST SCALE AND SCOPE

The disruption wrought by digital and the opportunities presented by it are not limited to the B2C world; they affect B2B as well. Consider the Tesla battery solution example.

Twitter and Power Plays

In early 2017, South Australia was subject to something almost unheard of in a developed economy: power shortages, brownouts, and blackouts. Billionaire software executive Mike Cannon-Brookes (one of the cofounders of Atlassian, an Australian enterprise software company) took to Twitter in response:

Mike Cannon-Brookes (@mcannonbrookes), 5:04 PM, 9 Mar 2017: We don't need more gas peaker plants or ridiculous "clean coal." Let's solve it with software and innovation.

A few hours later, Twitter carried an article from the COO of Tesla's battery division:

Tesla battery boss: We can solve SA's power woes in 100 days.
The head of Tesla's battery division says the company could solve SA's power woes within 100 days, and do the same for Victoria.

Cannon-Brookes then tweeted:

Mike Cannon-Brookes (@mcannonbrookes), 4:01 AM, 9 Mar 2017: Lyndon & @elonmusk - how serious are you about this bet? If I can make the $ happen (& politics), can you guarantee the 100MW in 100 days?

Then came this from Tesla founder Elon Musk:

Elon Musk (@elonmusk), 10:50 AM, 10 Mar 2017: @mcannonbrookes Tesla will get the system installed and working 100 days from contract signature date or it is free. That serious enough for you?

It didn't take long for the then-prime minister of Australia to join in the conversation. Let's fast forward 100 days to a post from Tesla:

Tesla (@TeslaMotors), 8:20 PM, 6 Jul 2017: We are installing the world's largest lithium-ion battery storage project in South Australia

In fact, Tesla finished installing the storage power pack ahead of schedule.[22]

We are not suggesting that Tesla's battery solution was the optimal economic solution to the problem—there are both supporters and critics in the energy world on this. Rather, our point is that digital has the potential to change and accelerate every aspect of business. As John Donahoe, a former head of eBay, notes on the impact of software as a service companies such as ServiceNow, Atlassian, Salesforce, and Workday in the B2B space: "These are core, fundamental platforms. They're having the same fundamental impact at work that the FAANGs (Facebook, Amazon, Apple, Netflix, and Google) had at home."[23]

Digital presents challenges and solutions. Making digital commitments can be problematic because they can be expensive and take a long time to implement. Leaders with the Phoenix Attitude will gain advantage here because they and their teams will generate a much wider initial range of possible solutions and be more inclined to set up short pilot experiments that inform bigger digital transformation decisions. Further, when a leadership team is at the decision point on major digital initiatives, Phoenix leaders will stress-test each of these projects with an attack and defense Completely Opposite Viewpoints Debate before committing. Most importantly, leaders and their talent must recognize the range of digital possibilities as a baseline for future business models, not just as an add-on to their existing business model.

HARNESSING SOCIAL FIREPOWER

As digital technology has unlocked information flows around the world, it has enabled the creation of global communities that were otherwise unlikely to emerge. These social communities are transnational and transregional. From venues as diverse as small fishing villages on the west coast of India to the business office of the *New York Times*, social media has upset the balance of power. When we scan the horizon for opportunities that carry the greatest promise, social networks rank as one of the most important.

Facebook is just one example of how social media has upended marketing communications. Others include YouTube, WeChat, Instagram, QQ, Kakao, and TripAdvisor. In the not too distant past, companies used two primary vehicles for communicating with consumers and other stakeholders—paid media and owned media. Paid media referred to the marketing exposures a firm generated by paying for space in commercial media vehicles (e.g., print, radio, TV, etc.). Owned media referred to marketing exposures that a firm generated through its own media vehicles (e.g., brochure, website, in-house TV channels, newsfeeds, etc.). In the new world of social media, much of that is no longer needed. Digital technology has enabled anyone to create their own content and broadcast it to the world at large. That content is referred to as "user-generated content," or UGC, and it is the fastest growing source of media content today.[24] Consider that every minute, users upload more than 300 hours of video on You-Tube. Eighty percent of YouTube views happen outside the United States. The average number of YouTube views on mobile phones alone exceeds one trillion every day.[25] UGC lets consumers and other stakeholders become part of the production engine for content and information.

Content created on UGC is often more compelling (and more trusted) than what was available before the advent of digital and social. Wikipedia is a prime example of the power of UGC, instantly replacing predecessors Encyclopedia Britannica and Encarta.[26] In a similar vein, TripAdvisor and Expedia have laid waste to the travel publishing business as increasing numbers of users prefer sites populated by UGC rather than advice from professional travel experts. Wikipedia, TripAdvisor, and Expedia are proof of James Surowiecki's observation in *The Wisdom of Crowds* that, under the right circumstances, groups can be even smarter than the smartest experts.[27]

It's not surprising that most consumers rate UGC as a more reliable source of information and knowledge than "professionally generated content" (PGC) (e.g., company websites, advertising, and the like). In fact, our research on consumers' browsing behaviors reveals some interesting nuances on the relationships between these content types. Using data from a major European portal that offers both UGC and PGC lifestyle content for women and has about 130 million users per month,[28] our analysis showed that UGC consumption increases the rate at which users visit a website. Moreover, UGC and PGC can be substitutes or complements, depending on the type of search (e.g., exploring or revisiting). Different UGC formats (e.g., forums, blogs, or albums) also exhibit browsing consumption patterns that are very different from those of PGC. For example, high forum consumption promotes frequent revisits and increased PGC consumption, whereas blog consumption can detract from subsequent PGC consumption.

The power of UGC can be seen in its influence on corporate communication strategies and the challenges it presents for corporate leaders.[29] The "United Breaks Guitars" song is an example of the dangers of not having an active social listening capability.[30] The story begins when baggage handlers at Chicago's O'Hare Airport broke musician Dave Carroll's $3,500 guitar. United Airlines refused to pay compensation because Carroll failed to make the claim within the stipulated 24 hours. Carroll tried for nine months to make his case, and when his efforts came to naught, he did something that he was uniquely qualified to do: he wrote a song called "United Breaks Guitars" and posted it on YouTube. The video generated more than 150,000 views in a single day and close to five million views within a month. It was so persuasive that Bob Taylor, owner of Taylor Guitars, offered Carroll two guitars and other musical equipment, which Carroll used to come up with two sequels to the original song. The song became the number one hit on the iTunes Music store the next week. United ultimately offered Carroll compensation, which he told them to donate to charity, but not before their market capitalization dropped by $180 million thanks to "guitar-gate."[31]

The moral of the story is that corporate leaders must have an active "social listening" capability, as well as a clear plan to respond to what is being said about them, their products, their competitors, and the micro and macro environment within which they operate.

In the cleverly titled article "Mine Your Own Business," Oded Netzer, Ronen Feldman, Jacob Goldenberg, and Moshe Fresko describe the diagnostic value of UGC.[32] Using a combination of text mining and semantic network analysis tools, they show that UGC data can generate market maps and competitive insights without resorting to traditional marketing research techniques that rely on survey and/or sales data. In other words, scanning, listening, and sensing mindsets applied to the new world of digital can generate critical business insights.

The next challenge is learning to leverage digital and social to do things in ways they haven't yet done—such as using digital and social as a springboard for innovation and market leadership.

THE DIGITAL SPRINGBOARD

Companies in the analog world have long used tools such as focus groups to get input on potential moves, but the new world of digital and social allows companies to do this on a global scale and with unmatched speed. Two examples, one from a digital native company and another from an established incumbent, illustrate the opportunity to use digital + social as a springboard.

Brian Chesky, CEO of Airbnb, took to Twitter in December 2016 to ask his consumers what Airbnb should be doing better. Chesky's move was essentially a request to make his customers coproducers of the next series of innovations. And it worked. Within days, Airbnb was flooded with UGC on things that it needed to do next.[33] Many of the innovations launched in 2017, such as nightly meetups in major tourist destinations across the world, were based on these inputs.

The second example is documented by our INSEAD colleague David Dubois in an interesting case study describing how L'Oréal leveraged social media and social networks to generate ideas for innovation.[34] One of David's key observations is this: companies don't have to learn new skills all on their own. The new world allows for collaboration in ways that have not been possible before. In this case, both L'Oréal and Google gained from a partnership: Google taught L'Oréal how to leverage the possibilities created by digital + social, as they flagged L'Oréal that searches for hair-coloring were trending and tons of YouTube videos were being created by young girls on how to color hair in interesting shades. Fittingly, L'Oréal taught Google how these insights could be translated to successful business results by launching a new global brand, "Wild Ombre," that became a bestseller and allowed L'Oréal to move into a market segment where they were not present before. Another colleague, Dominique Lecossois (Global Asia Fellow at the Emerging Markets Institute, INSEAD, Singapore), found a similar pattern of symbiotic relationships between legacy retailers and startups specializing in e-commerce/m-commerce (mobile commerce) enablement across the world.

CAUTION IS NEEDED IN THE DIGITAL + SOCIAL WORLD

Though this new world can help build business very fast (e.g., Dollar Shave Club), it can make businesses stumble equally fast. The fashion industry offers us a great example. Star designer Alessandro Michele deftly leveraged digital + social to take Gucci to the top of the fashion world, but the negative response to his company's blackface "Balaclava" sweater launch, which was perceived as racially insensitive, resulted in steep drops in its social media strength and declines in sales. Prada and Versace have had similar incidents.[35]

Leaders must also make sure that the hype and hoopla about this new world does not get ahead of reality. Muted market response to Uber and Lyft IPOs and the pullback in WeWork's IPO are critical reminders that crowdsourced wisdom is often more meaningful than the hubris of charismatic founders and overenthusiastic early investors.[36] Though the new world of digital and social has unlocked flows of information, it has created a disturbing asymmetry in terms of data access. Consumers, businesses, governments, and regulators have yet to work through privacy issues in ways that satisfy all parties.[37]

In summary, the new world of digital + social has transformed traditional models of behaviors and traditional rules of business. It creates challenges that leaders in the analog world never had to consider (such as increased customer power), yet it presents growth opportunities that few leaders in the analog world ever imagined.

In defining your Encounter Extreme Attack and Horizon Defense options, are you maximizing the power of all digital + social, all the time?[38]

CHAPTER **7** CHECKLIST

Summary Thoughts

1. The digital world is awash in data. Data flows are growing faster than trade and financial flows. This unlocking of information combined with mobile connectivity shifts the balance of power from firms to their consumers, and consumers are leveraging this power shift to the hilt.

2. The digital + social world opens new possibilities for business models directly connecting customers, partners, products, and services that shift the boundaries of the firm or industries—upstream and downstream.

3. The world of digital + social creates instantaneous possibilities for engagement, cooperation, and coproduction between organizations and stakeholders from a digitally charged zero moment of truth (ZMOT) at time of search, together with the first and second moments of truth (FMOT and SMOT) where awareness and visibility of products and services occur. In this digital universe, stakeholders become content creators and influencers (e.g., user generated content).

Reflection

1. How is the unlocking of information flows in the new world of digital + social shifting the balance of power between your stakeholders (e.g., customers, employees, investors, regulators, etc.) and your organization?

2. What are the implications of digital + social engagement for your business? What does this mean for redrawing the boundaries of your firm or industry? Does this open up possibilities for doing existing activities differently or doing completely new things to create value?

3. What actions will you need to take to build the digital + social capabilities in every area of your organization?

NEW WAYS of DOING OLD THINGS

NEW VALUE PROPOSITIONS

NEW ENTRANTS

NEW PARTNERS

NEW BUSINESS MODELS

NEW ECOSYSTEMS

NETWORK of USERS

PLATFORM

DIFFERENT REVENUE MODELS

$

GROWING the USER BASE is the **KEY IMPERATIVE**

iT'S NOT JUST B2C!
× NEW INDUSTRIES
× NEW SECTORS
× NEW GEOGRAPHIES

WAYS of DOING THINGS that haven't been done BEFORE

CHAPTER 8

PLATFORMS: THE ECOSYSTEM FIREPOWER

*In today's hypercompetitive environment enabled
by technology, ownership of infrastructure no longer
provides a defensible advantage. Instead, flexibility
provides the crucial competitive edge, competition is
perpetual motion, and advantage is evanescent.*

—GEOFFREY G. PARKE, in *Platform Revolution: How Networked Markets
Are Transforming the Economy and How to Make Them Work for You*

Fifty years ago, the word "platform" described something you might stand on—perhaps a train platform. J. K. Rowling's mystical platform Number 9¾ at London's King's Cross Station in her Harry Potter books appeared by magic. That's no more wondrous than the new world of online platforms, which are rewriting the rules of business, starting with retail.

These platforms are not the kind one stands on; they are marketplaces that connect buyers and sellers of all types of products, services, and solutions. We believe that these platforms, and the changes they bring, will grow in scale and scope in the years to come.[1] Considering how platforms and ecosystems might work to attack or defend you is one of the Completely Opposite Viewpoints Debates every leader must have in the Encounter Battlefield.

Amazon, Taobao, JD.Com, Flipkart, Jumia, Mercado Libre, Naspers, Airbnb, Grab, Gojek, and WeChat have been eagerly adopted by consumers across the world and routinely hog business headlines across geographies. The strange thing, from a business perspective, is that while many of these companies produce nothing, some of them have market capitalizations that exceed those of many of the companies on the Fortune 500 list.[2]

We mentioned earlier that one of the key characteristics of social networks is their ability to grow in a viral fashion. Platforms can grow virally, too, but for a different reason. Because platforms need not be built from scratch, they make it possible to exploit an advantage that Hal Varian, chief economist at Google, refers to as "combinatorial innovation"[3]—basically the combination of any number of technologies, products, and services on top of one another to achieve competitive advantage.

Looking way back, David Hounshell provides a fascinating account of the combinatorial innovations spurred by the advent of interchangeable parts in the 1850s: the rise of modern mass production factories for everything from sewing machines to automobiles.[4] The key distinction between then and now is that the components of the Internet platform are digital, not physical. They are ideas, standards, protocols, programming languages, and software. Unlike physical components of long ago, these digital components never run out of stock once they have been created, and they can be shipped or changed instantly across the world. Web pages, chat rooms, email, file transfers, auctions, and exchanges can be seamlessly onboarded.

Amazon and Alibaba may be among the world's best examples of the power of platforms. For example, Amazon was once a retailer—a bookseller—but today it is much, much more. A quick look at Amazon's acquisitions and investments reveals CEO Jeff Bezos's vision for the ever-expanding Amazon platform.[5]

Acquisitions have helped Amazon build a portfolio of complementary assets into its ecosystems.[6] The acquisition of Audible in 2008 let Amazon catapult itself into the leadership business in the audiobook world. The acquisition of Twitch in 2014 gave it entry to the live streaming business. The acquisition of Souq in March 2017 broadened its e-commerce footprint into the Middle East. The acquisition of Whole Foods in 2017 let it offer a much more comprehensive assortment to its customers, in terms of both product categories and physical locations.[7] The acquisition of Ring in February 2018 let it marry smart-doorbell technology with omni-channel retail, while the acquisition of PillPack in June 2018 helped Amazon leverage its pharmacy licenses in the 50 US states and jump-start its push into pharmaceuticals and the drugstore retail space.

In China, acquisitions and investments tell a similar story about Alibaba co-founder Jack Ma's vision for the platform.[8] Jack Ma says, "In the beginning I just wanted to survive. For the first three years, we made zero revenue. I remember many times when I was trying to pay up, the restaurant owner would say, 'Your bill was paid.' And there would be a note saying, 'Mr. Ma, I'm your customer on the Alibaba platform. I made a lot of money, and I know you don't, so I paid the bill.'"

NOT JUST PLATFORMS BUT ECOSYSTEMS

Platforms and Ecosystems

A platform is a way of creating a connected community of stakeholders that can interact with one another to reduce frictions and create value. Platforms today are digitally based business model facilitators and can include social connectivity, e-retailing and e-wholesaling, business transacting, and marketplaces. An ecosystem builds out from the platform to extend reach and seamlessly integrate connectivity beyond boundaries of traditional industries, geographies, partners, and users.

WeChat (developed by Chinese startup Tencent) provides a glimpse of the potential of the platform business model to evolve in Phoenix terms as a firestorm ecosystem. WeChat is a mobile social network, very much like WhatsApp, but WeChat, described by the *New York Times* as the Swiss Army knife of apps, is a lot more than a social network. What many people don't know about WeChat is that it is one of the biggest players in the mobile banking business in China (along with Alibaba).

Mobile banking is a growing phenomenon in North America and Europe, where governments and businesses are encouraging their customers to move to a cashless society. In 2016, estimates put the mobile banking business in North America at about $100 billion and the same business in Europe at about 100 billion euros ($114 billion). In contrast, the mobile banking business in China was estimated to be about $12.8 trillion.[9] The size of that market gives WeChat and Alibaba access to revenue and profit pool opportunities that many of their competitors, such as WhatsApp and Amazon, just do not have.

COVID-19 has provided the stage to amplify the power of platforms and ecosystems. For example, you have probably never heard of Tobias Lütke, and yet his Canadian company, Shopify, saw its share price rise by a whopping 4,000 percent in the five years since the company was listed on the New York Stock Exchange in May 2015. That rise was nearly five times the increase of Amazon shares over the same time period. Interestingly, its share price has almost doubled since January 2020—a reflection of the market's valuation of its value-added in the pandemic world.

Shopify is an e-commerce platform that offers businesses the tools they need to build, market, and run their online stores. It works with more than a million small merchants and retail point-of-sale systems worldwide but also includes such giants as Heineken, Nestlé, and Staples in its client list. Its consumer app, called Shop, launched in April 2020 in the midst of the pandemic, groups its clients' online stores together so consumers can discover local businesses, get personalized recommendations, pay for the products they purchase, and then track the deliveries. The Shopify revenue model is based on a mix of fees including recurring subscription fees and payment-processing fees that grow with transaction volumes.

As the pandemic locked down brick-and-mortar stores and upended traditional shopping behaviors, Shopify saw traffic across its ecommerce platforms exceed Black Friday volumes every day. In early May 2020, that surge helped Shopify briefly vault over Royal Bank of Canada to become the country's most valuable company; that same week, the company raised $1.3 billion in a stock offering. Shopify's pandemic growth exemplifies the power of platforms to grow both swiftly and far, creating wealth and connection across industry and geographic boundaries.[10]

MAKING SENSE OF NONSENSE

The network externality effects (explained in Chapter 7) that we see in platforms such as Amazon and Alibaba allow them to scale their businesses using very different revenue and profitability models than those that have been available to many of their physical competitors. Many legacy firms consider new business initiatives, and when they don't make financial sense to their fixed mindset, they hold off. Most, for example, would never consider selling products below marginal costs. But in the platform and ecosystem world, as pointed out by Nobel Prize–winning economist Jean Tirole and his coauthor Jean-Charles Rochet, many traditional rules of economics do not apply.[11]

Paddy's own research showed us how platforms can run pricing and promotion tactics that seem to defy conventional business logic.[12] The data came from one of the biggest e-commerce platforms in Europe. Like Amazon, the company had sellers dealing with all types of consumer goods (music, books, apparel, etc.) and they also had lots of buyers. The data collected included weekly revenues and weekly counts of the number of new sellers, returning sellers, new buyers, and returning buyers, all of which was used to calculate one of the most closely watched numbers in the retail business: "customer lifetime value," or CLV, the profitability associated with each customer in the retailer's installed base.

Many leading retailers look closely at how this number evolves year over year, aware that a growing CLV means a growing share of customer wallets and increasing customer loyalty. In this instance, the CEO's concern was that the CLV of a new seller or new buyer was too uncomfortably close to the company's cost of acquisition. Was this a sustainable business model?

As the researchers dug deeper into the data, they found that the company was onto something very powerful. While the costs of acquisition versus profitability on an individual seller looked troublesome, that was only part of the equation. What had not been considered was that the value of every participant in the platform was a combination of *two* revenue and profit pools: the direct customer lifetime value (DCLV), generated via revenues from that customer's transactions on the platform, plus the indirect customer lifetime value (ICLV), the revenue that a customer generates by virtue of his or her influence on onboarding additional new sellers and new buyers to the platform. The latter was a measure of the indirect externality effects that they generate for the platform. In mathematical terms:

> *Total Customer Lifetime Value (TCLV) = Direct Customer Lifetime Value (DCLV) + Indirect Customer Lifetime Value (ICLV)*

The missing piece in the company's homework was an estimate of the indirect customer lifetime value. It was about quantifying the impact that seeing a new seller on the platform has on other sellers who think, *If that seller thinks it is worthwhile to list on the platform, then maybe I should too,* as well as on other buyers who think, *If that seller is on the platform, then maybe I should take a closer look at the site, as it may have interesting things on it.*

Their analysis showed that every time the platform gained one seller, it picked up three additional sellers. More importantly, each new seller led to 11 new buyers. In other words, focusing on each participant's direct profitability was shortsighted. When they combined the total impact of each seller from both the direct and indirect externality effects, they could show that the total CLV of a new seller was about 4.5 times its cost of acquisition.

IT'S ALL ABOUT VELOCITY OF GROWTH

The key to understanding the business model of a platform and its extension into an ecosystem is appreciating the imperative of growing the installed base on all sides of the platform (buyers/users and sellers/providers). Growth should be one of the drivers of change Phoenix leaders consider as they build their Future-Facing Blueprint. Every additional platform participant can create pull. This growth attracts more participants across all platform sides—two sides in the case of the company discussed previously, multisided in the case of the Amazons and Alibabas of the world.

Amazon naysayers have long questioned the sustainability of a business that did not generate profit even 20 years after its inception. Those people miss an essential point: Amazon does not need to make a profit on a particular seller or buyer. The additional buyer and seller are the means to an end—a bigger ecosystem—and multiple revenue and profit cash pools. It is not surprising that the holy words at Amazon's Seattle headquarters are "customers" and "growth." Nor is it surprising that profitability was considered a dirty word there. When Amazon started in the United States in 1994, the company was competing for less than 1 percent of the total personal consumption expenditure on books. As of 2016, it was competing in categories that accounted for almost 70 percent of the total consumption expenditures in the United States.[13]

The growth was possible because buyers and suppliers provide most of the necessary capital, happy to get on board and write a nice check for that privilege. Our calculations show that Amazon generated $17.3 billion in free cash flows in 2018 alone. Its business model lets Amazon run its business on other people's money and fund new business projects from Alexa to outer space. The analysis also reveals why it is critical that Amazon generate growth from other business spaces (e.g., cloud and geographies like India). The day Amazon stops growing is the day the free cash flow will start to dry up—and that will be the day that it will need to start thinking about modifying its business model.[14]

At the beginning, platforms focused on digital goods and services. Today, the world of platforms includes companies like Uber, Gojek, BlaBlaCar, and Didi for transportation; Airbnb for lodgings; Rent the Runway for designer fashion; and Primephonic for specialist classical music streaming and download. These new entrants have moved on from digital to a new combination of digital + physical that leverages the platform model for a wider swath of goods and services. Similarly, platforms are no longer a quintessential business-to-consumer (B2C) phenomenon—companies like Transfix in the trucking business, Upwork in the outsourced project management business, and Cvent in the business events marketplace show that platforms work just as well in the business-to-business (B2B) space. The bottom line remains the same: create growth in the ecosystem that will generate the money needed to fund further platform business growth.

COVID-19 has shown that it can accelerate platforms that are positioned to capitalize on a sudden demand surge. For instance, look at India's upstart company Think & Learn, founded in 2011 by Byju Raveendran. He was a onetime math tutor, with the goal of making compelling math and sciences teaching available online to K–12 students across India—everywhere from small villages to Tier 1 cities. Raveendran hoped to help democratize education in a country with a huge variance in the quality of primary school education.

In 2015 the teaching platform spawned an app, called "Byju's," which made some content available free to consumers for a limited time, with more content available by subscription. The lessons were rigorous but also upbeat and creative, full of live action, eye-catching graphics, game environments, and special effects (Byju partnered with Disney for the youngest grades' curricula) to appeal to parents and students alike. Even though Byju created its own content (unlike typical platforms), it strategically created a platform-like business model. Byju's modularized content lets students get a "personalized" learning experience. This creates a high degree of student engagement and satisfaction. Moreover its digital platform gives Byju's the capability to seamlessly integrate third-party services (e.g., pedagogical collateral, customized coaching, and college admission counseling), letting it leverage its platform-like business model to monetize the economic benefits of creating an ecosystem.

Already boasting 42 million registered students and 3 million paid subscribers in the early months of 2020, Think & Learn was valued at $8 billion and was considered a very hot ticket indeed. With the emergence of COVID-19 and India's stringent nationwide lockdown, the platform took off. Byju began offering free access to its online content in March 2020 and immediately attracted 6 million new students; at the same time it developed a new line of real-time classes to help students stay on track with their work.

As Raveendran observed, "Technology has always been there, but people are taking it up in the pandemic. What has not happened in years will now happen in months." It would seem Byju's fortunes are assured, whatever course COVID-19 takes. While many liken Byju's to Netflix, because of its creative content, there is a critical difference: Netflix must invest billions every year to create new content, while Byju's can depend on the enduring fundamentals of math and science. Once its content is created, Byju's can use it practically forever, only freshening it up a bit now and again. This is one reason that Byju's is one of the few platforms in the world that reports annual profits.[15]

QUANTUM LEVERAGE FOR GROWTH

Many e-commerce observers have heard about a retail phenomenon called "Singles Day" in China.[16] Started by young Chinese people as a celebration of being single, the day, November 11, has morphed into the biggest online shopping day in the world. Alibaba's online sites (Taobao and Tmall) alone sold more than $38 billion worth of merchandise on Singles Day 2019. The scale of this growth is enormous, but equally impressive is the accelerating speed and scope of the phenomenon—from $9.3 billion in 2014 to $38.4 billion in 2019.[17]

Consider that most of the sellers on these sites are small and medium-sized businesses, not big brands. Traditionally, access to credit has been difficult for these firms for a variety of reasons (e.g., identity, credit history, etc.). But Alibaba is in a unique position because it has the complete history of all the buyers and sellers who trade on its platforms and can use such data to create its own credit scoring system.[18] This allows the company to build layers of financial services that leverage its data about buyers and sellers, and it does that in ways that create more value for these platform participants than legacy financial institutions can bring to the game.

For example, Alibaba-backed companies (e.g., Ant and Alipay) offered credit to buyers and sellers.[19] Then it went one step further and created new revenue and profit pools by securitizing these loans. With the approval of the Shanghai Stock Exchange, it placed these securities (different versions with tenures of 3, 6, and 12 months, and yields of

3.35 percent, 3.55 percent, and 4 percent, respectively) with qualified institutional investors and asset managers less than two weeks later. Because Alibaba could rate the risk of these loans, the Shanghai Brilliance Credit Rating and Investors Service rated these securities as AAA grade.

These securities were close to twice oversubscribed prior to closing, as they offered rates that were better than anything offered by Chinese banks. We see in this example how the new breed of super platforms has leveraged the 360-degree data view of participants in their ecosystem to create new opportunities for monetization of big data.[20]

Incumbent legacy players with legacy systems and data are up against some formidable competitors. Piyush Gupta, CEO of DBS Bank, got the message. "The Chairman of ICBC wasn't worried," he said. "Citi and Wells Fargo people weren't concerned. But I was paranoid. Alibaba and Jack Ma catalyzed my paranoia. I knew I needed to think like them and be like them. Now I try to get everyone at the bank to ask: 'What would (Amazon's) Bezos do?' Not 'What would (JPMorgan's) Jamie Dimon do?'[21] This is Phoenix leadership thinking.

ECOSYSTEMS CREATE CONNECTIVITY ACROSS INDUSTRY BOUNDARIES

The bigger strategic leadership question for attack and defense is that the ambitions of the new breed of platforms and ecosystems extend far beyond e-commerce or m-commerce. They change the boundaries of firms and industries. Financial services providers would never have thought that they would face competition from firms like Alibaba or Amazon. This is what makes the platform model and ecosystems so powerful. With access to a variety of revenue and profit pools beyond just the sales of goods and services, platforms can do things that legacy firms in traditional industries have never dreamed of doing. While traditional firms are still in catch-up mode, this new breed of players are going far beyond simple trading. They are building an ecosystem of proprietary service providers across sectors and industries that cut across whole swaths of other industries and sectors.

Because platforms can grow in a viral fashion, they can leverage the direct and indirect externality effects brought to the game by all the participants in their ecosystem. They can spot opportunities across broad swaths of related categories and sectors, and they have the capability to muscle into new products, services, and industries. Consider Ping An, a Chinese insurance company that has created an ecosystem that provides a one-stop shop for its consumers, featuring insurance (Zhong An), finance (Ping An Bank), healthcare (Ping An Good Doctor), entertainment (Huayi Brothers), housing (Pinganfang), auto (Autohome), and peer-to-peer assets exchange (Lufax).[22] Leaders cannot afford to think that they are safe from disruption by platforms. They need to know how to respond and adapt to these players, or they risk becoming collateral damage in much the same way that makers of navigation systems were to search engine platforms that provided mapping functionalities on their apps.[23]

CAUTION IS ALSO NEEDED ON PLATFORMS AND ECOSYSTEMS

It's important for leaders and their organizations to keep in mind a few other aspects of this new world of platforms and ecosystems. Part of the power of the platform business model is its ability to avoid the constraints that characterize brick-and-mortar businesses. Platforms such as Amazon, Shopify, Alibaba, and Flipkart can feature unlimited product range and assortment. This allows them to cater to a very diverse set of consumers, but it also creates problems, such as difficulty in monitoring and controlling quality.[24] This can lead to one of the key challenges for platforms and ecosystems: building trust with stakeholders, which many legacy firms can use as a defense idea.

Another potential drawback for many platforms is that while they offer products and/or services that have been available elsewhere, they do it in a very different way, one that allows for creating unconventional performance metrics—which could be misleading.[25] The vast amounts of data that platforms collect on all the actors in their ecosystems and their activities also raise very serious concerns about privacy and data protection. European regulators are in the forefront of agencies trying to mitigate these risks.[26]

Seen from a broader legal and societal perspective, the network effects that underpin the platform business model can create a "winner takes all" outcome. That can lead to fears that platforms and ecosystems could build digital monopolies, with detrimental impact on consumers, businesses, and societies—more product choices through a smaller number of gateways. Platformization is still in its early days, and all participants (e.g., consumers, firms, regulators, governments, etc.) have yet to come to grips with many of the realities of this new world.[27]

There is probably no business model better suited for a pandemic than the platform business model. It is therefore not that surprising that some have referred to Amazon as "the new Red Cross" for its delivery of essentials to locked-down consumers across the world. But it is important to keep in mind that with Amazon's success should come business model scrutiny, whether it be the millions of jobs that offer insecure employment, its tax arrangements, or its use of data on independent sellers on its platform. The pandemic has shown us issues that Phoenix leaders need to keep in mind: security, responsibility, trust, and, lastly, engagement.

PLATFORM AND ECOSYSTEM BUSINESS MODELS ARE CENTRAL TO EXTREME ATTACK OPTIONS

In summary, the new world of platforms and ecosystems has shown that there are new ways of doing old things and there are ways of doing things that have not been done before. Platforms make it necessary for leaders to reexamine their basic assumptions about how to do business.

The benefits of scanning across the world of new possibilities—digital + social + platform, as well as the technology scans in the following chapters—in the Encounter process are evident in many attacks we have witnessed.

Platform Attack

Consider the attack developed by David Johnstone, head of business development, and his Encounter team members, on his business, one of the most respected pan-European motor insurance firms. It started with one of the world's largest e-commerce firms acquiring an insurance competitor. Leveraging its own data along with the acquired insurer's actuarial expertise, the new company developed original insurance products. And while it had no insurance sales force and no automobile dealership touchpoints, it did have close to 100 million customers, most of whom had automobiles purchased from some of these dealers. More important, while David's insurance company had incomplete data on their customers, the new company had comprehensive data. By leveraging the data across the new company's overall portfolio of online and offline services (e.g., e-commerce, travel, telecommunications, financial services, and investments), it created a more compelling customer loyalty program. That program minimized acquisition costs while maximizing the customer lifetime value by leveraging the network externality created by the multi-sided platform. David was clearly developing the Phoenix Attitude, complete with outside-in thinking, Proactive Scanning, and the willingness to question assumptions.

How are you going to use or become part of a platform or ecosystem in your Extreme Attack? Even more important, what might this mean for your Horizon Defense and future innovation or partner opportunities?

CHAPTER **8** CHECKLIST

Summary Thoughts

1. The new world of digital + social + platform is creating opportunities for:

   a. New value propositions

   b. New entrants

   c. New partners

   d. New business models

   e. New ecosystems

2. The economics of the platform world are quite different from those in the analog world. The direct and indirect externality effects of the platform's network of users is a key reason why they can drive their business using revenue models that seem illogical to their analog nonnetworked counterparts. Growing the installed user base is the key imperative for platforms.

3. Platforms and ecosystems are becoming ubiquitous. They are not just a B2C phenomenon. The viral reach of platforms extends into industries (B2B), sectors, and geographies that can seem far removed from traditional core businesses. This demonstrates the velocity of growth and connectivity of these new business models compared to legacy firm value chains.

Reflection

1. Is your organization capturing the new opportunities created by combining digital + social + platform? Can you leverage these possibilities for doing existing activities differently, or doing completely new things, or creating new value propositions?

2. If you are defending yourself, what makes more sense, becoming a platform company or becoming part of another platform ecosystem?

3. What are your organizational and leadership capacities for taking advantage of platforms and ecosystems? What are the knowledge and talent gaps?

NEW TECHNOLOGIES CREATE UNPRECEDENTED POSSIBILITIES!

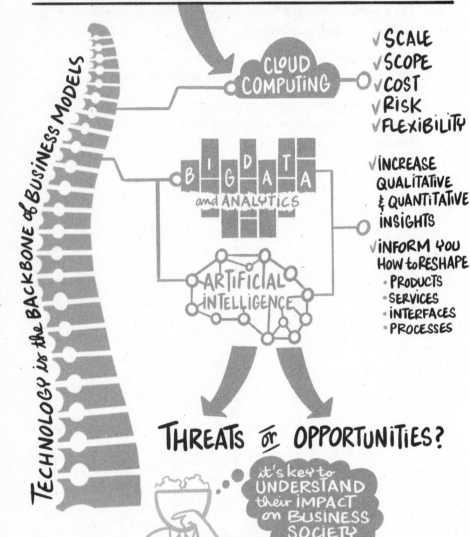

TECHNOLOGY is the BACKBONE of Business Models

CLOUD COMPUTING

✓ SCALE
✓ SCOPE
✓ COST
✓ RISK
✓ FLEXIBILITY

BIG DATA and ANALYTICS

✓ INCREASE QUALITATIVE & QUANTITATIVE INSIGHTS

ARTIFICIAL INTELLIGENCE

✓ INFORM YOU HOW to RESHAPE
  • PRODUCTS
  • SERVICES
  • INTERFACES
  • PROCESSES

THREATS or OPPORTUNITIES?

it's key to UNDERSTAND their IMPACT on BUSINESS SOCIETY PEOPLE

THE FIREPOWER OF INDISPENSABLE TECHNOLOGIES

AI is a tool. The choice about how it gets deployed is ours.
—OREN ETZIONI, CEO, Allen Institute for Artificial Intelligence

In December 2014, Apple stores began selling an intriguing product: a personal thermometer that connected to an iPhone. It was a nifty idea, and like many nifty ideas that thrive with the Internet of Things (IoT), it began to evolve the moment it was born.

Within two years, the ear thermometer, which a San Francisco startup called Kinsa manufactured, was synced to the iPhone app via Bluetooth. The app included the voice and image of Sesame Street's popular Elmo character, who spoke to children while their temperature was being taken. The app could be informed by a patient's medical history and could offer advice on what action should be taken, depending on the patient's temperature and history. Much of the data was, of course, collected by Kinsa, which could identify and track a particularly fevered population. It could also partner with companies like Clorox, which could target advertising for its disinfectant wipes to the most fevered zip codes. All of this happens in real time. It's sold on Amazon. It's all good, almost, because in the case of technologies like Kinsa, issues of patient privacy and user consent require very careful consideration. Leaders who develop such technologies must know exactly where the legal and ethical boundaries lie.[1]

Kinsa's smart ear thermometer combination technologies and extension strategies, not to mention Elmo and Clorox wipes, begs a question that is going to be asked more frequently in the next few years: What kind of product is this? Is it a medical instrument? Is it a marketing tool? Or as we saw with COVID-19, is it a public health warning system[2]? The answer could easily be "all of the above." Or it could be another question: Why does it have to fall into only one category? In the digital world, lines that have long delineated product categories have lost their focus. Data flows in many directions for many purposes. The only impediment to purpose is a lack of vision: the inability to see opportunity or threats.

For that reason, scanning the technology vista regularly is part of a leader's role in the twenty-first century. In the Phoenix Encounter Battlefield exercise, especially in the Extreme Attack stage, scanning these trends is essential to generate "out there" ideas of destruction.

In almost every Extreme Attack we have seen, technologies are central, often linked to platform/ecosystem business models. You can see this in the Encounter examples throughout this book. We have seen so many examples that there are simply too many to select one or two discrete vignettes. To give readers a sense of how diverse these options are, we have included some short examples for reference in this chapter and the next.

Indispensable Technology Encounter

Disrupting the Smartphone in an Extreme Attack

Smartphones transformed phones from a simple device for voice communication to a data-crunching handheld computing machine—their ubiquity (41.5 percent of all phones in the world) is a testimony to their global consumer appeal. But the new world of indispensable technologies could also portend the demise of the smartphone industry. Consider the attack conceived by Pham Ngoc, senior vice president at a global hardware manufacturer, who has a career in electronic engineering and marketing. Her extreme attack disruptor was a simple handheld device (like a phone version of the Google Chromebook) where nothing is stored locally and nothing is processed locally—everything is done in the cloud. The device is simply a pipe connecting the device's owner to the cloud; it becomes a commodity that anyone could make. The cloud is where the technology play happens, including sophisticated phone-dedicated artificial intelligence (AI) services. In this world, the competition is no longer between Apple, Samsung, Huawei, LG, Oppo, and Xiaomi. It includes the likes of Google, Amazon, Alibaba, Tencent, and Jio, among others, who can create a compelling ecosystem of cloud-enabled applications. In this world, phone manufacturer technology is no longer an advantage and their costs are a huge disadvantage.

TECHNOLOGY IS THE BACKBONE OF BUSINESS MODELS TODAY

The technological breakthroughs that are redefining the global business ecosystem have enabled the reinvention of business models and the birth of some previously unimaginable combinations. The investment banking industry, for example, has replaced "old-school" traders[3] with "new-school" algorithms. Michelin is experimenting in some markets with a pay-per-mile business model, rather than selling its tires. This would let it serve its customers by providing them access to tires as opposed to tire ownership. Financially, such a business model converts its customers' capital expense (CapEx) into an operating expense (OpEx). This also gives Michelin an opportunity to serve its customers with new value-added solutions derived from the data generated from real-time tire use.[4] Everywhere we look, we find that old rules no longer apply, and the new rules are being designed to make things faster, less expensive, and easier to acquire.

All of this matters to different people for different reasons. It matters to organizational leadership because leaders must understand what technology can do for their organizations. It matters to organizational management because managers need to know how to exploit technological advancement. It matters a great deal to corporate investors and boards, who want to change things up when they suspect an organization is underperforming.

Technology has always moved forward, of course, but it never moved as quickly as it has since the birth of the digital age. Today, as we write this, COVID-19 has accelerated technology's pace of change, in terms of speed, scale, complexity, and scope, to unprecedented levels. Google and Apple collaboratively working on an app would have been unimaginable in the pre-COVID-19 era!

To understand technology's transformational power, let's use the auto industry as an illustration. In the twentieth century, industry efforts largely drove technological advances, such as improvements to engines, braking systems, and fuel injection systems. Today the automobile industry is being transformed by technology developed outside the industry, all over the world, and for purposes that often have nothing to do with cars. Figure 9.1 contrasts the pre-autonomous technology automobile value chain with the post-autonomous technology automobile value chain.[5]

TECHNOLOGY SCANNING IS NO LONGER THE IT DEPARTMENT'S JOB

As goes the auto industry, so go many others, with technological advances coming from outside as often as from within an organization's value chain. That makes it hard, sometimes impossible, for inward-looking leaders to identify the tools and tactics that will push their organizations forward.

Today's leaders have no choice but to look outward. They must keep their heads up and their eyes on the horizon. The good news these days is that the development of new technologies is no longer solely the responsibility of in-house research and development (R&D). The bad news is that scanning for useful tools and strategies is now everybody's responsibility, and applying tools and strategies borrowed from the burgeoning universe of technological advancement is more important than ever. In our interactions with senior executives, we see that many are indeed seeking to understand the impact of technologies

FIGURE 9.1 Automotive Industry Value Chain Transformation

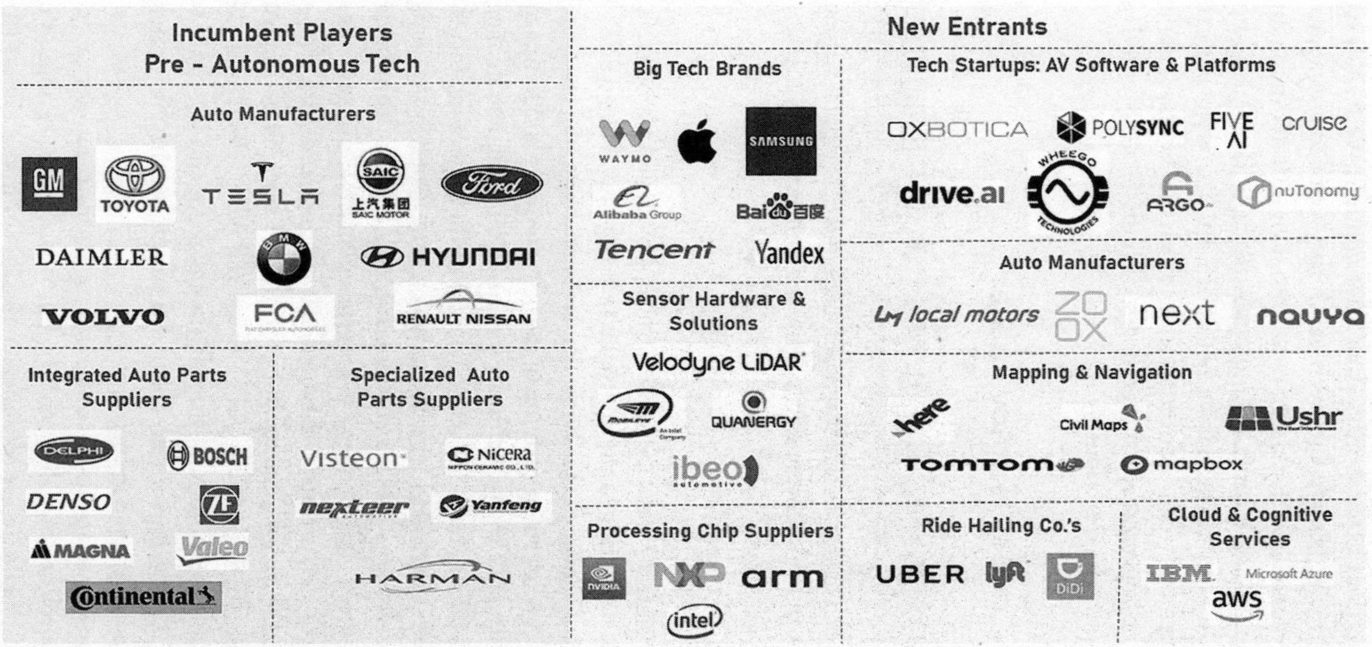

Source: www.mytechfrontier.com

within their vertical areas. That's not enough. We think executives should look beyond their verticals if they want to anticipate trends and technologies that might come into their industry in the future.

Next we scan some technologies that will likely play important roles in every future-facing enterprise. In fact, we believe they are indispensable firepower for attack and defense. Because proper scanning of the landscape should begin with the 50,000-foot view, we'll start with cloud computing.

The Cloud's Clear Advantages

What Is the Cloud?

The "cloud" refers to IT services supported by computer system resources that are housed remotely and accessed via the Internet.

Everyone knows about the astonishing growth of Amazon's retail sales, which has rocketed the company to being one of the world's largest retailers.[6] Fewer people know that retail now brings in less than half of Amazon's operating income. In the first quarter of 2020, Amazon Web Services (AWS), the company's cloud computing service, generated $3.08 billion, or 77 percent of all of Amazon's operating income.

AWS offers 70 IT-related services, and its advertisements boast of more than a million customers, including GE, Airbnb, Expedia, Dow Jones, and Kellogg's. Those heavy hitters didn't outsource their IT—servers, software, database, networking, and analytics—to the cloud just to save money.[7] A great deal of research persuaded them that cloud-based IT would be easier and more reliable than keeping the function in-house.[8] After all, the cloud does for IT what Michelin would like to do with tires—it takes something that has been a product and sells it as a service.

The concept of cloud computing, or leasing computer capacity, has been around for half a century, but it wasn't until Amazon created AWS, originally called Amazon Elastic Compute Cloud (Amazon

EC2), in 2006 that it became a viable commercial option. Since that launch, the advantages of the cloud have led to a major shift in the enterprise IT infrastructure paradigm.[9] That's not surprising. The cloud lets businesses access computing infrastructure on demand to meet all kinds of computing needs on a pay-per-use model, sparing organizations significant capital expenditure in IT infrastructure. In his book *The Big Switch,* Nicholas Carr compares the evolution of cloud computing to that of power plants. "In the early days," writes Carr, "companies usually generated their own power with steam engines and dynamos. But with the rise of highly sophisticated, professionally run electric utilities, companies stopped generating their own power and plugged into the newly built electric grid."[10]

With most of the world under lockdown during the COVID-19 pandemic, the power of cloud-based systems has been revealed to even the most reluctant adopters. The pandemic has shown organizations the world over how cloud systems can provide the agility needed to adapt their processes to support remote work, handle highly variable workloads without the exorbitant costs of creating buffer computing capacity, and process large-scale data sets in real time to reoptimize business processes. It's no surprise that cloud service providers like Twilio saw a more than 50 percent jump in their share price at the beginning of May 2020, and big tech cloud computing revenues saw year-on-year growth of 25 to 50 percent.[11]

Cloud Considerations

The advantages of cloud computing have been discussed for a long time now.[12] For example, cloud computing allows for seamless deployment of strategies that let firms integrate their own and third-party applications in ways that cultivate an ecosystem of co-innovation that's far more seamless than legacy in-house IT infrastructure.

Curiously, despite the advantages of cloud computing, adoption maturity still varies across businesses. According to the *RightScale 2019 State of the Cloud Report from Flexera,* while 94 percent of businesses say they have adopted cloud services, only 68 percent of large enterprises and 57 percent of small and medium-sized enterprises are in advanced or intermediate stages of cloud adoption.[13] Other evidence suggests that companies no longer view security, reliability, and performance as the biggest barriers to cloud adoption. Rather, uncertainty about costs of migration, finding the right talent, complexity of managing the change, and difficulty in accurately estimating the long-term benefits of cloud adoption now seem to be the hurdles.[14]

Perhaps more important, cloud computing is a baseline infrastructure required for building artificial intelligence (AI) and Internet of Things (IoT) applications, such as Kinsa's ear thermometer. The possibilities are practically endless. We can imagine, for example, a cloud-based virtual phone that applies Google's Chromebook concept to handheld devices. Such a phone would be faster, lighter, and more powerful than anything in use today. Harnessing the capacity of the cloud gives companies a faster track to enter the new machine age. We think of cloud adoption as a key arena that should be carefully evaluated by all executives who want to make their enterprises future ready.[15]

Big Data and Analytics

What Is Big Data and Analytics?

Big data typically refers to extremely large data sets, often created by integrating data from a variety of sources, and usually requiring sophisticated software and computational power to mine valuable insights.

Data analytics refers to examining raw data to discover meaningful patterns. It also includes using rigorous empirical methods to test conjectures, and using algorithms that facilitate data-driven decision-making.

Data, especially big data, has been on the strategic priority list of businesses for at least the past decade, with many enterprises investing heavily to grow their data assets and build them into their future strategy. Big data and analytics play a critical role in powering technologies such as artificial intelligence (AI) and robotics. Virtually all of the top consumer Internet and technology companies (e.g., Amazon, Google, Facebook, and Alibaba) have sophisticated data assets and supporting architecture—all requirements for any enterprise that hopes to maintain market position and expand into new verticals. Amazon's know-how and expertise, acquired by running its cloud computing business, operating data centers equipped with graphics processing units (GPUs), and handling large amounts of customer data, played a central role in the development of its AI-powered voice assistant, Alexa.[16] Similarly, Alibaba leveraged its user data assets and data expertise to expand into a completely new vertical—financial services.[17]

Data and analytics are also strategic priorities for a majority of top non-tech enterprises. According to New Vantage Partners' "Big Data and AI Executive Survey 2019", 92 percent of the firms surveyed reported increasing the pace of their big data and AI investments, and 55 percent of these firms plan to invest more than $50 million in these initiatives. Executives say fear of disruption from data-driven digital competitors and the need for agility are the top motivators behind their investments.[18] For example, access to real-time data and analytics is one of the key value-adds that fintech companies are offering customers, and the majority of the top banks have invested in data analytics solutions to build similar offerings. One can imagine what would happen to those banks if Google and Amazon were to apply their vast data resources and analytics to understand customer risk profiles and lifestyle preferences and then use that understanding to develop finely tailored, scalable products and solutions.

JPMorgan Chase has more than 300 data professionals (JPMorgan Intelligent Solutions) mining its proprietary data assets to drive value for its businesses.[19] Similarly, manufacturing companies are dredging their data assets (e.g., IoT data) for gains in operational efficiency, reductions in unexpected asset breakdowns, and transformation of their business models. Research firm IDC projected that manufacturing companies would be the biggest spenders on big data and analytics solutions after banking until 2020.[20] As Gartner research director Alan Duncan notes, successful firms of the future will be those that can effectively use analytics to convert their data into actions and, ultimately, improve the customer experience. "Algorithmic business is pivotal to competitive advantage," says Duncan.[21]

With cloud computing and advanced analytics tools, companies may not only tap into traditional data troves, they can also leverage new sources of data, such as video, image, audio, and text, to power their business algorithms. Airports are using video analytics to glean insights into traffic movement and improve the operational efficiencies.[22] The voice analytics firm Cogito is partnering with healthcare providers to analyze customer service calls to glean insights into customer stress levels.[23] More dramatically, digital startups and several established brands have begun to integrate geospatial imagery analytics to power their decision-making processes.[24] Figure 9.2 exemplifies the variety of ways in which data is being used.[25]

In an ongoing research project using customer product review data, Sameer found that incorporating customer reviews from online blogs helps explain a car's sales performance, and that different forms of review (text and star ratings) provide complementary information. In other words, combining different forms of data may lead to better decision-making, and high volumes of unstructured data, such as textual reviews, can be mined and analyzed at scale to yield actionable insights.[26]

While it's clear that big data generates value, and the majority of businesses continue to invest in new data sources, companies hoping to become more data-driven face many challenges. According to New Vantage Partners' "Big Data and AI Executive Survey, 2019," the majority (77.1 percent) of senior executives say that business adoption of big data and AI initiatives remains a significant challenge.[27] Executives cite a lack of organizational alignment and cultural resistance as the top challenges. Kaggle's 2017 survey, while a bit dated, provides a bottom-up perspective, citing challenges like lack of clean data, talent, managerial support, and clarity of problem statement that data scientists face in implementing data-powered applications and models for businesses.[28]

To remain competitive, organizations will have to make their data more accessible to their employees. Self-serve analytics platforms or

FIGURE 9.2 Industry Applications of Geospatial Data

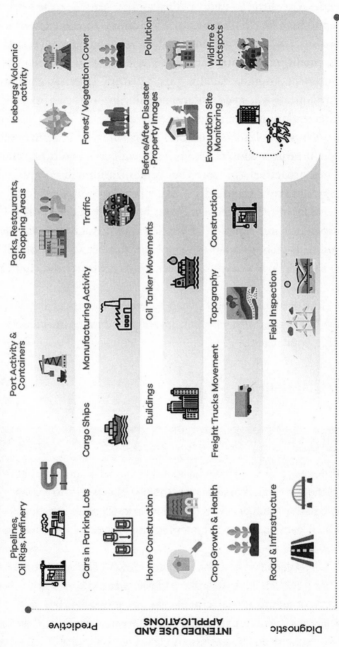

solutions, providing business users on-demand access to data, reports, and queries, have grown rapidly in the past few years, and the market is expected to hit $22.8 billion by 2020.[29] Business intelligence solution providers such as Sisense and Microsoft have rolled out conversational business intelligence solutions that let business users exploit conversational interfaces to mine data insights.[30] Natural language generation company Narrative Science's solution, Quill, automatically transforms data visualizations into intelligent narratives.[31]

Today's business leaders must also make sure that governance and oversight measures address user privacy concerns and other ethical issues and proactively prepare their organizations to comply with evolving regulatory standards.[32] The top tech companies in recent times have faced severe media and user backlash because of their lack of transparency and violation of implicit user privacy norms.[33] Many tech and non-tech companies have been subject to data breaches, leading to severe penalties and rebukes from regulators and consumer bodies.[34]

Data and analytics capability can be central drivers of an Extreme Attack. As a leader, how are you leveraging data as an incumbent defending your space?

Artificial Intelligence (AI)

What Is Artificial Intelligence?

In general terms, artificial intelligence refers to computer technologies that are capable of solving and training themselves to answer problems that traditionally required human intelligence and capabilities (e.g., learning, perceiving, inferring, communicating, and making decisions).

A formal definition from the Stanford study, *Artificial Intelligence and Life in 2030*[35] holds that "Artificial Intelligence (AI) is a science and a set of computational technologies that are inspired by—but typically operate quite differently from—the ways people use their nervous systems and bodies to sense, learn, reason, and take action."

The acronym AI is an umbrella term used to describe subdisciplines such as natural language processing (NLP), natural language generation (NLG), computer vision, automated speech recognition, and machine learning. As our colleague Theos Evgeniou wrote, "AI and its impact on business, governments and society may be today where physics was at the turn of the previous century. After breakthroughs in physics at that time, and later in biology and other fields, the world became very different from what it was for thousands of years before."[36]

We agree. AI promises to be the most transformational technology of the next generation of technological change. As Andrew McAfee and Erik Brynjolfsson from MIT say, unlike the first machine age, which primarily automated routine work, the current wave of technological advancements reveals that tasks previously considered unprogrammable (or not amenable to if-then rules) are next in line for automation, thanks to developments in AI and machine learning.[37] All the top major technology players, including Facebook, Google, Amazon, Microsoft, Alibaba, Tencent, Twitter, and Apple, have infused their products with AI capabilities. Facebook's newsfeed, Amazon's recommendation engine, and Apple's Siri online personal assistant all use AI. AI-powered solutions have enabled these companies to not only drive user engagement but also drive cost savings and, most important, set the stage for expansion into new business segments.

Intelligent conversational platforms that include applications such as voice-enabled personal assistants, smart home assistants, and chatbots have been the first wave of AI technologies, and they have been adopted across both business-to-consumer (B2C) and business-to-business (B2B) segments. Apple was the pioneer, integrating Siri in its smartphones, but Amazon was close behind with its smart home assistant solution, Alexa. Alexa gained rapid adoption and scale by building and leveraging the developer ecosystem to build custom skills for all types of home durables. That strategy worked so well that by 2018, most of the top home appliance makers had enabled control of their appliances via home assistants.[38] Along with consumer products, enterprise technology companies are integrating voice-enabled personal assistants across a range of functions. Amazon has announced Alexa for Business, a platform that will let companies build their own skills and integrations.[39] General Electric plans to integrate Microsoft's voice assistance technology into its 600K Digital Twins to shorten the time it takes to service critical machines.[40]

AI-powered solutions now support customer service, marketing, sales, employee collaboration and communication, finance, and human resources. We think it's just a matter of time before AI-based auditors and tax consultants start to threaten the Big Four accounting firms. Many companies (e.g., Skyscanner, Starbucks, Staples, UPS, and OCBC Bank) are using AI-based technology developed by third parties to interact with their customers. Human resource applications that leverage AI-powered solutions across talent sourcing, candidate interviews, candidate screening and selection, performance reviews, and employee engagement are beginning to emerge. Unilever is experimenting with AI-based tools for recruiting, and the company claims that the technology has led to the hiring of the "most diverse class to date." Unilever also reports that AI tools have led to a significant reduction in hiring lead times (from four months to four weeks) and to an increase in acceptance rates (from 64 percent to 92 percent).[41]

Business adoption of AI-powered solutions is not driven only by efficiency and productivity gains. AI is a source for creating competitive advantage. A 2017 BCG and MIT survey of 3,000 business executives found that 83 percent of respondents perceived AI as a source of strategic opportunity for their businesses.[42] Foxconn, the largest private employer in China, has said its ambition was to become "a global innovative AI platform, rather than just a manufacturing company."[43]

COVID-19 has been labeled both a pandemic and an "infodemic," meaning that it has spawned an epidemic of misinformation, most of it online and much of it dangerous. A fascinating example of AI's use to reveal these falsehoods comes from India. One of Sameer's collaborators, Dr. Tavpritesh Sethi, and other academics at the Indraprastha Institute of Information Technology Delhi (IITD) created an app called "WashKaro" that provides information about the coronavirus as well as best practices for hygiene. The app uses an AI-based system to power a chatbot, called Satya, that "busts fake news and myths" and delivers accurate and possibly life-saving information in various local Indian languages with the aim, according to Dr. Sethi, of giving "the common man the right information at the right time."[44]

We believe that knowing what AI can do for you today—and more important, tomorrow—should be at the front and center of your future-looking business model thinking, and it must be considered, at least in Extreme Attack options in the Encounter. Business leaders should prepare to face a steep learning curve and undergo a significant lag before AI technology truly transforms their businesses. These matters should be part of leadership teams' ongoing Completely Opposite Viewpoints Debates.

In the Encounter exercise, we hear frequently about the challenges faced by nondigital firms attempting to adopt AI technology, including their outdated IT infrastructure, their talent shortages, and their lack of agile organizational processes. Fear of these challenges often blocks the consideration of AI options.

AI models also need a critical amount of historically relevant and reliable data before they can be considered fail-safe, and leaders should be mindful that historical and user data carries with it new legal and ethical challenges. Historical and incomplete data, for example, could lead to algorithmic bias and discrimination. Enlightened early adopters of AI technology are instituting governance frameworks and redesigning organizational structures to reduce the impact of new risks posed by adoption of AI technologies.[45]

ANOTHER NOTE OF CAUTION ON "INDISPENSABLE" TECHNOLOGY

Organizational leaders will also have to consider the broader societal impact of technologies such as AI-powered solutions, including their influence on political campaigns, criminal activities, and information warfare.

Already, some widely used algorithmic-based ratings systems, such as COMPAS, which predicts criminal recidivism, have been accused of bias and criticized for their lack of transparency. There is the possibility—some say the inevitability—that humans will not fully understand and control how AI algorithms make decisions. In the early days of business AI adoption, author Stephen Hawking warned,

"The short-term impact of AI depends on who controls it; the long-term impact depends on whether it can be controlled at all."[46]

Notwithstanding our cautionary note, as you debate radical options for Extreme Attack and Horizon Defense, what ways might you use cloud computing, big data, analytics, and AI?

As we begin to recover from the pandemic and governments contemplate easing lockdowns, it appears increasingly unlikely that the world will revert to business as usual. Firms such as Twitter now offer employees the option of permanently working from home. Alternate work arrangements for knowledge work, like remote and gig work, may well be our new reality. At the same time, customers' expectations of greater digital engagement and their demand for a seamless, "phygital" experience will require firms to dramatically re-engineer their business processes. Cloud computing, big data, analytics, and AI are technologies that will let organizations deliver value for the customer under these new work arrangements. A Phoenix Attitude lets leaders proactively leverage these technologies and rethink organizational processes to create a formidable position going forward.

CHAPTER 9 CHECKLIST

Summary Thoughts

1. Core new technologies such as cloud computing, big data, analytics, and AI create unprecedented possibilities that can be both a threat and an opportunity for any organization. They can all be considered for attack and defense options.

2. Cloud computing services housed remotely hold the potential for scale, scope, cost, risk management, and flexibility advantages. Big data, analytics, and AI can increase quantitative and qualitative insights and inform the way you could reshape the nature of products, services, customer interfaces, and organizational processes.

3. Understanding the role of these technologies in reshaping the future of industries is fundamental for leadership teams today, including business implications and broader societal and people impact.

Reflection

1. How are the expectations of your customers or employees being influenced or likely to be influenced by AI-powered technologies? What advantage are you taking from the latest cloud computing solutions and big data and analytic capabilities? If none, why not? What new investments might your organization need in its data infrastructure, assets, and systems?

2. Would these technologies allow your organization to do different things or do things differently? What gaps does your organization need to address to tap into these technologies? Does your organization have leaders and talent with skills to engage and execute strategies that leverage these technologies?

3. Has your organization evaluated the negative consequences and implications of AI-powered technologies that might be adopted? Is your leadership team equipped to evaluate the ethical challenges or dilemmas resulting from new technology adoption? Does your organization have guidelines, processes, and policies to address concerns and issues reported by customers or employees, such as privacy concerns?

CHAPTER 10

TARGETED TECHNOLOGY FIREPOWER

*What new technology does is create new opportunities
to do a job that customers want done.*
—TIM O'REILLY, founder of O'Reilly Media and popularizer
of the terms "open source" and "Web 2.0"

For today's business leaders, technologies such as the cloud, big data, and artificial intelligence (AI) are no longer just interesting or things that might someday come in handy. They are central to the future for any organization that hopes to survive. That "not an option" status sets them apart from the technologies we scan in this chapter. These, while potentially transformational, may or may not be the right vehicle to support an organization's forward motion. In a Phoenix Encounter Battlefield exercise, these technologies could provide targeted options for an Extreme Attack and/or alternatives in the Horizon Defense (see *Targeted Technology Encounter*).

Targeted Technology Encounter

From Airport Parking to Mobile Fulfilment
    The new world of technologies and business models can combine in interesting ways to create formidable attacks and compelling

defenses. Consider how the Phoenix Encounter played out with Nicola Bianchi, CEO of EGNA Corporation, which manages airports across the world. Two of the biggest nonaeronautical revenue generators for airports are on-airport and off-airport parking lots. An attack combining autonomous vehicles with a sharing economy effectively laid waste to all of Nicola's real estate infrastructure. Her defense was a total repurposing of this real estate to e-commerce/m-commerce fulfillment centers. The shared autonomous vehicles that dropped passengers and cargo at the airport would pick up packages from the warehouses created in the parking lots and fulfil the last-mile delivery. The vehicles' arrivals and departures would be coordinated by real-time GPS/IoT synchronization with warehouse robots for picking and packing of consignments.

The scale/scope economies of the airport operators in pooling these functionalities across e-commerce/m-commerce platforms would drastically reduce the distribution costs for these players. In fact, one of Nicola's short-term embedding initiatives after the Encounter was to create a team focused on understanding the regulatory implications of such a move and creating a short list of viable technology engineering companies as partners.

We start the chapter with the Internet of Things (IoT), which has been on the emerging technology list for more than a decade.

INTERNET OF THINGS (IoT)

What Is IoT?

The Internet of Things refers to the digitization of the physical world (e.g., machines, vehicles, parts, and appliances) with technology solutions (e.g., sensors, microphones, cameras, etc.) to capture data (e.g., wear and tear, audio, pressure, temperature, etc.) and to control and operate IoT devices remotely (e.g., via the Internet). The data captured by IoT devices can then be used for business and customer value generation.

The IoT ecosystem now includes an extensive network of IoT platforms, cloud service providers, storage and software support providers, connectivity service providers, and communications solution providers. Customized platforms offering analytics, device control and management, and application development solutions have bridged a critical software gap.[1]

Advancements in IoT, along with other technologies such as machine learning, are changing everything from electric toasters to oil rigs. Oil and gas producers now use "digital twins" for real-time analysis of machinery to optimize production flow and preventative maintenance.[2] Hirotec America, supplier of automotive door hinges, partnered with PTC (an IoT platforms provider) to consolidate the sensor data (temperature) from multiple sources and let management see real-time data across global manufacturing facilities, improving operational efficiency.[3]

Companies across a wide range of industries, including consumer appliances, technology, manufacturing, automotive, healthcare, and farming, use IoT-powered solutions to reduce friction and automate processes, gain insights on product usage, drive efficiency, and develop new business models. Consumer appliance manufacturers have AI-powered smart home assistants that control smart home appliances with voice commands. Amazon's Dash Replenishment Service lets brands track product usage and allows users to auto-replenish household products (e.g., detergent and water filters). Similarly, consumer appliance companies, such as Nespresso, send product and service alerts to users and monitor product usage with connected appliances.[4]

Manufacturing companies that long relied on time-based or condition-based maintenance that required physical inspection now use IoT data and machine-learning algorithms for predictive maintenance. Downtime is expensive. According to a 2016 study by Aberdeen, the average cost of downtime for US manufacturing businesses was $260,000 per hour. IoT-enabled predictive maintenance solutions use real-time data from sensors and the environment to build predictive models that can determine an asset's likelihood of failing.[5]

IoT has fueled the emergence of several new service models. HP has rolled out its Instant Ink subscription service for customers with HP printers outfitted with sensors. For a fixed monthly subscription fee, the company tracks the ink usage and auto-replenishes ink cartridges. The function enables HP to establish direct communication with customers and monitor product usage and model future services.[6] And as mentioned earlier, Michelin is experimenting with using sensors in its tires to collect data on fuel consumption, tire pressure, temperature, speed, and location of client vehicles—data that it uses to make recommendations to fleet managers and train drivers on how to use less fuel when driving. The company claims truck fleet managers could save 1.5 liters of fuel for every 100 kilometers driven. The IoT has driven a fundamental change in Michelin's business model: moving from a product seller to a provider of services and solutions.[7]

The rollout of 5G technology will improve connectivity, download speeds, and computing infrastructure and usher in the next generation of IoT solutions. It will speed the adoption of connected cars, smart city technologies, and industrial IoT solutions. In the near future, we expect to see IoT-enabled traffic systems, as well as streetlights and garbage bins. This presents opportunities to innovative private players, who could create entire operating systems for cities, eliminating the need for some government sector departments. IoT is a strong potential tool on the list of Extreme Attack options.

However, despite such advantages, IoT's impact on businesses has been elusive to date, largely because of challenges to companies' data use. A 2015 McKinsey study revealed that an oil company used only 1 percent of the data 30,000 sensors generated when deployed at a particular oil rig.[8] IoT data has been one of the top contributors to the "dark data" phenomenon, wherein data captured by IoT sensors is not analyzed and used for decision-making. Other challenges for IoT include new security and privacy concerns as well as organizational resistance that often accompany IoT implementations.[9]

Leaders should be mindful that greater IoT adoption has the potential to exacerbate several business challenges, such as making organizations vulnerable to cybersecurity threats. In contemplating any IoT-based Horizon Defense options, companies have to make sure that processes would be in place to tap into data and insights and manage security. They would need to foster a culture to navigate the new business models and opportunities IoT generates.[10]

AUTONOMOUS VEHICLES AND MOBILITY

What Are Autonomous Vehicles?

The term "autonomous vehicles" refers to vehicles that rely on technology to partially or fully replace a human driver in navigating from the origin to the destination, avoiding obstacles and hazards, and responding to traffic conditions.

Technological advancements, particularly those in AI, computing, and sensor technologies that drive the IoT, have dramatically altered the automotive industry value chain, and new players now bring us innovations that weren't anywhere near the drawing board in the twentieth century. Intel and NVIDIA provide processing capabilities for cars, Mobileye makes sensor technology, Civil Maps offers mapping services, and Ericsson and Qualcomm sell connectivity services.

Silicon Valley executives tell us that these companies have reshaped views about the role of automobile manufacturers in the automotive value chain. For many of them, a car is mainly a device into which they plug their software so they can sell consumers new services and algorithms. This new kind of car can be seen in Waymo's autonomous ride-sharing service launched in December 2018.[11] In fact, most of the legacy carmakers say they will have some form of advanced autonomous vehicles by 2023. Of course, technology validation is just a first step. Regulatory issues (e.g., autonomous car liability[12] and ethical concerns) are challenges that will need resolution.[13] Recognizing the upside of autonomous technology, a few market regulators (such as those in Germany, Singapore, and New Zealand) have begun to create guidelines.[14]

Despite the challenges, the scale of investment and progress by automotive and technology companies makes autonomous technology adoption inevitable.[15] Silicon Valley–based venture firm Loup Ventures projects that by 2040, 90 percent of new vehicles sold will be highly or fully autonomous.[16] Another study published by Intel and Strategy Analytics predicts that driverless vehicles will enable a "Passenger Economy" worth $7 trillion by 2050, spread across consumer mobility and business mobility services.[17]

When we consider likely early adopters, mass transit services are high on the list. Automotive and emerging companies are already exploring "microtransit services" powered by autonomous technology.[18] No fewer than 20 cities, including Amsterdam, Tokyo, Singapore, Paris, Perth, and Boston, have tested autonomous buses and shuttles. NAVYA, a French manufacturer of autonomous shuttles, has been operating fixed-route self-driving buses in various European cities, including Paris, since July 2017.[19] Having completed a period of pilot testing, autonomous shuttles are now available for public use in Singapore, Las Vegas, and Helsinki.[20]

Several startups are focusing on parcel delivery, and some are testing different kinds of autonomous vehicles, including drones and robots. Starship, Udelv, Toyota, and Ford have announced partnerships with food delivery and ecommerce companies to build autonomous mobility platforms.[21] In China, Alibaba and JD.com are using drones to ship packages to remote areas.[22]

Autonomous driving technology also shows great promise in industrial applications. It's being tested for supply chain processes such as raw material handling, warehousing, first-mile logistics, long haul, and last-mile logistics. Autonomous long-haul freight vehicles, which are expected to save 75 percent of labor and fuel costs, could transform supply chain logistics and prompt a wholesale reconsideration of supply chain strategies.[23]

Amazon is rumored to be planning hyper-localized, dome-shaped fulfillment centers whose inventory is replenished by trucks and drones to complete the last-mile logistics within an hour of receipt of the customer order (Figure 10.1).[24]

FIGURE 10.1 Amazon's Autonomous Fulfillment Center of the Future?

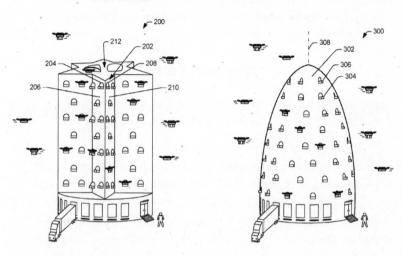

Source: Amazon Patent Application (US 20170175413 A1)

The Chinese platform JD.com has asked the Canadian government for permission to use drones to transport processed seafood from plants on Canada's east coast to airports for shipment by air to cities in China.[25] Several startups and a few established companies, including Airbus, Boeing, and Uber, are testing autonomous flying vehicles.[26] On the radical edge of new transportation is Hyperloop, a system of sealed tubes through which pods carrying people or freight will move at high speeds.[27] The concept, proposed by Tesla and SpaceX, is being explored by several cities.[28] Cargo Sous Terrain, a Swiss company, is said to have completed a successful feasibility study for an underground cargo tube for autonomous delivery carts, and the company is expected to have a logistics infrastructure in place in Switzerland by 2030.[29]

Despite significant investment in driverless vehicles, they are not likely to be available to consumers for several years, if not decades. Interim developments (e.g., semiautonomous vehicles) and technology associated with autonomous vehicles, such as robotics and computer vision, are likely to have a far-reaching effect across many verticals.[30] Future-focused leaders should (1) be aware of the implications of these developments for their transportation needs and supply chain logistics and (2) prepare their organizations to leverage these technological developments for competitive advantage.

3D PRINTING

What Is 3D Printing?

3D printing, or "additive manufacturing," in manufacturing parlance, refers to a manufacturing process or technology used to build products or parts layer by layer with digital (computer-aided) design as the input. In contrast, traditional manufacturing processes (termed "subtractive manufacturing") typically cut and join smaller pieces of raw materials.

While manufacturing companies have used 3D technology since the 1980s—primarily for product prototyping—recent advances in software, hardware, and materials have greatly expanded its applications. 3D printing is aiding (and in some cases driving) manufacturing in companies across the industrial spectrum, and in some verticals (e.g., automotive and aerospace), firms have integrated the technology across multiple applications.

In the healthcare sector, 3D printing is now widely used for devices such as hearing aids, dental braces, and prosthetics. These applications benefit from personalization and customization that ensures improved fit and patient comfort. Established workflows now enable doctors to integrate measurements and scans and build 3D-printed products with faster turnaround times.

Bioprinting, or 3D printing technology that makes artificial or engineered tissues that imitate natural tissues in structure and composition, is enabling the development of new applications. For example, Merck is partnering with Organovo to bioprint tissues used in testing drug effectiveness and impact. Similarly, L'Oréal is investing in research to leverage artificially constructed tissue for cosmetic testing.

In the food production space, startups Novameat and Redefine Meat are developing plant-based, 3D-printed meat substitutes that are similar to animal meat in texture, taste, appearance, and nutrition.[31]

Local Motors is using 3D printing to help manufacture passenger shuttle buses, upending a decades-old automotive manufacturing and supply chain. The company, which is building a network of microfactories, invites customers to get involved in automotive design. Its microfactories, with distributed manufacturing made possible by 3D printing, portend a potential disruption of the traditional manufacturing setup.[32]

The clearest advantage of 3D printing technology is the ability to make things on demand. A consortium of companies, including Maersk, is planning a pilot project that will deploy 3D printing technology on ships instead of carrying spare parts on board.[33] In an arrangement that would reduce inventory and distribution costs, Caterpillar and John Deere are partnering with Silicon Valley–based startup Carbon to evaluate the feasibility of setting up warehouses with designs stored in the cloud and printed on demand.[34]

Companies like MakeXYZ and Xometry allow entrepreneurs, tinkerers, and designers (demand side) to connect with a global third-party network of specialized 3D printing designers and printing facilities (supply side).[35]

3D printing clearly has the potential to rewrite many of the rules, not just of manufacturing, but also of supply chain management.[36] While companies like Zara (Inditex) have built an empire by ensuring speed to market—in Zara's case, with manufacturing facilities co-located within their primary market in Europe—3D printing takes co-location to the next level, offering the capability to create a distributed network of hyper-localized "manufacturing" units. Those units need not be owned; they could be borrowed from a shared ecosystem of 3D printing shops. All of which begs the question about the future of manufacturing firms: Will design be their only real value-added function?

Recent breakthroughs in 3D printing technology, such as metal printing systems, make it possible to mass-produce parts with complex design and specifications. Industry insiders believe the 3D printing technology has potential to rival the productivity and quality metrics of traditional manufacturing processes. Of course, this strategy is not for every product, but the more customized the product, the more viable such a strategy could become. Considering the increasing desire for customized products, it's hard to ignore the implications of 3D printing in developing customer-focused options for Extreme Attack and Horizon Defense.

ROBOTICS

What Is Robotics?

Robotics refers to the field of design, construction, and use of robots, as well as computer systems for their control and information processing.[37] Robots are programmable machines capable of responding to their environment to automatically carry out complex or repetitive tasks with little direction.[38]

Robots are simply machines that perform physical tasks as instructed by computer programs. They are the digital, algorithmic, AI, and physical firestorm version of automation. Automation was a major driver of industrial efficiency throughout the twentieth century, and robots were quick to get in on the act. The first rudimentary industrial robot was put to work in the 1930s, and robotic manufacturers, such as KUKA and ABB, have been building robotics solutions for industry since the 1970s.[39]

Today's robots are very different creatures. They perform surgeries, repair machinery, and execute hundreds of functions that were long considered nonautomatable. Aided by the developments in complementary technologies, such as AI, sensors, autonomous navigation technology, and cloud computing, robots now handle intricate and complex tasks in warehouses as well as customer interactions in retail businesses.[40]

Startup Kindred Robotics is partnering with retail and e-commerce companies to test a robotics solution that can quickly and accurately sort products in warehouses. Kindred uses machine learning to teach robots to grasp products of various dimensions and sizes.[41] Companies are also deploying a new generation of robots powered by natural language processing and deep learning algorithms to handle customer interaction tasks. Lowe's sales robot, OSHbot, lets customers type on its touch-screen menu to find a particular item they want. It then guides them, with the same navigational technology found in driverless cars, to the right aisle and shelf. Softbank's Pepper line of robots uses facial recognition software that can recognize joy, anger, and surprise, and is even learning to distinguish nuanced expressions, such as telling smiles from smirks.[42]

Japan's Mizuho Bank has robotic tellers with AI-based functionality that are capable of advising customers on loan application processes or helping them with simple investment products. The bank uses a robotics platform that leverages IBM Watson's natural language and other cognitive capabilities to personalize the Softbank robot called Pepper and its interactions with customers.

Concierge and service robots gained media attention with their promise to replace human workers in customer interactions, but with the few exceptions we've described, these solutions have not seen rapid adoption, mainly because robots can't yet handle complex customer queries. So far, businesses largely make do with robots that manage simple, standardized, repetitive tasks rather than those that automate complex and changeable tasks.[43]

Logistics, e-commerce, and retail companies across various markets are tapping smart robotics solutions to improve their warehouse employees' efficiency and productivity. DHL's warehouse facility in the Netherlands, for example, estimates that it saved employees about 32 kilometers of walking per day by moving packages with autonomous robots made by Fetch Robotics.[44] Fetch uses navigation sensors such as LiDAR and 3D cameras to identify and navigate obstacles and collect inventory data. US grocery chain Kroger is partnering with the UK-based robotic automation firm Ocado to build automated warehouses with layout and structure that help robots operate efficiently.[45]

Unsurprisingly, leading robot suppliers are deploying cloud robotics, which connect robotic systems with cloud computing infrastructure, to build an "intelligent brain." Those systems, which use the same technology as autonomous vehicles, offer value-added services such as predictive maintenance to avoid downtime.[46] Startups such as Hirebotics and inVia Robotics are offering a "robot as a service" option where companies pay on usage basis and avoid upfront capital costs.[47]

We believe the collective effort of all of these players will vastly expand the scope of applications that can drive value for businesses. Figure 10.2 provides a quick visual scan of the state of the adoption of different robotics solutions available today.[48]

FIGURE 10.2 A Snapshot of Robotic Adoption— Current and Future State

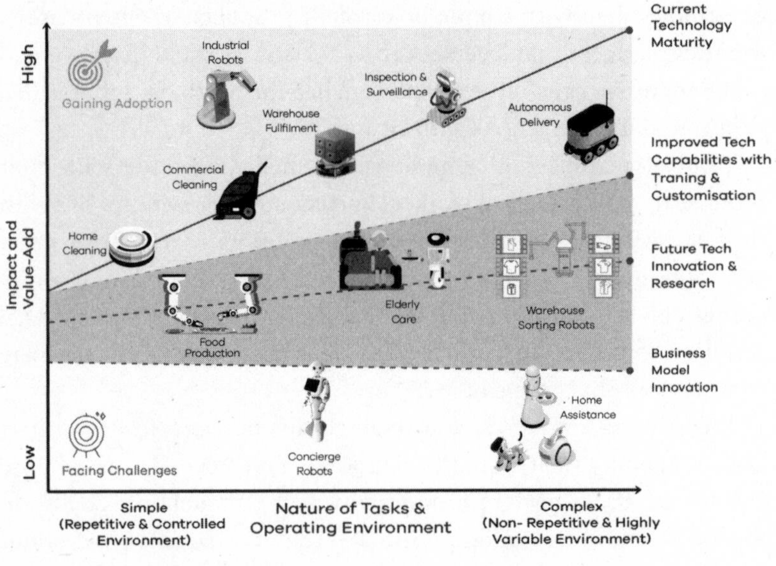

Source: www.mytechfrontier.com

BLOCKCHAIN

What Is Blockchain?

A blockchain is a peer-to-peer distributed electronic ledger for transactional data, which is encrypted and stored in blocks of

specified size. The ledger does not have one owner who is responsible for verification and updating of transaction records. Instead, a
well-defined incentive-compatible mechanism ensures that recorded
transactions are valid and that consensus is reached between different parties (all or part) sharing the ledger. A blockchain facilitates
automated transactions using "smart contracts." In some business
applications, access to the ledger is limited to a prespecified set of
parties known as permissioned blockchains.

We find that many senior executives fail to distinguish blockchain
from cryptocurrencies such as Bitcoin. Although blockchain is the
backbone technology for cryptocurrencies, it has great potential for
noncryptocurrency applications.

For the sake of simplicity (because blockchain's technical details can
be overwhelming), blockchain can be thought of as a digital, distributed ledger. At its core, a blockchain is a set of algorithms that allows
for securely and immutably storing transaction information that can
be accessed and verified from anywhere. From a business perspective,
a blockchain can play a critical role where intermediaries are needed to
facilitate transactions (e.g., lawyers to ensure a secure transfer of legal
deeds and money in a land sale-purchase transaction), but such intermediaries are too expensive, too slow, or not trustworthy.

Let's look at a few examples of how that can work. In 2015, technology entrepreneur Leanne Kemp used IBM's blockchain system to
create a global registry for diamonds, using several features of each
diamond for identification and creating a digital alternative to the
existing paper-based processes. Kemp believes that her company,
Everledger, can further reduce the exchange of conflict diamonds.

In 2016, BitFury, a Bitcoin mining company, and the Republic of
Georgia's National Agency of Public Registry announced a partnership to pilot a blockchain land titling project that could help people in
underdeveloped countries where legal titles to land are either unreli-
able or nonexistent. BitFury CEO Valery Vavilov believes blockchain
will help do three things. First, it will add security to the data so the
data cannot be corrupted. Second, by powering the registry with the

blockchain, the public auditor will also make a real-time audit, so the auditor will audit the registry not once per year but every 10 minutes if so programmed. Third, it will reduce the friction in registration and the cost of property rights registration because people could do this on their smartphones. According to *Forbes*, buyers or sellers of land in Georgia can pay up to $200 just to have the transaction notarized.[49] BitFury hopes to reduce that cost to 5 to 10 cents. Phase two of the project, which is aimed at further integrating blockchain technology in the process of land sales and transfers, was approved by the Georgian government in early 2017.[50]

We believe blockchain has the possibility to be tremendously disruptive, but it is at a very early stage. In fact, we believe blockchain could disrupt the disruptors, including the platform giants like Uber.

Blockchain Fells Uber?

In preparation for a full Encounter exercise in an American energy company, we had the Encounter team do an imagined Extreme Attack on a different company and industry, Uber, where they practiced Radical Ideation and produced the following scenario.

You buy an autonomous vehicle. Using IoT-enabled systems in your car, you register it on a blockchain system. You also add parameters of a "smart contract" on the blockchain system, which essentially is an algorithm that will determine what it costs for someone else to use your car. In that contract, you specify that when you are not using your car (i.e., when it is sitting in a parking lot), someone else can use it, provided that the trip does not take your car more than a certain distance away and that the car returns to you immediately after completing a trip if you request it.

If you want additional control, you can also specify that only people with a phone registered in your city or country can use your car. Pricing can differ by time of day, time taken to complete the trip, distance, and so on. Now a person living in your city can use the system to look for available cars when he or she wants to travel from A to B.

This person finds your car, sees your offered contract, and decides to book it.

The car autonomously drives to the client's location for pickup, which you can easily verify by checking the coordinates of phone and car. The car drives the passenger to the destination, which you can also easily verify, and the passenger makes an automatic digital wallet payment over the blockchain—also easily verified. We might not need an intermediary like Uber anymore. The car could even be insured on the blockchain system via a peer-to-peer mechanism for underwriting the risk of a particular trip.

The imagined scenario in the box *Blockchain Fells Uber* would disrupt several industries at once and requires hurdling several regulatory barriers, but it would take only one or two countries to experiment with such a system before others start considering it seriously. Like any other sharing economy example, this scenario would need a layer of trust for car owners and their customers to transact. Fortunately, there is a whole new economy called the trust economy that is being developed today. Startups like Trooly (acquired by Airbnb in 2017) use AI and data from a variety of sources online (e.g., social media) to codify trust.

Blockchain has also been used to improve product provenance and authenticity in supply chains, manage loyalty programs with crossover points from partner organizations, track trades in finance industries, verify identities, and catalog educational records. These cases illustrate the industry drive to use this technology widely, though we have to be careful in overgeneralizing its current business impact.

Before considering blockchain as a solution for an existing pain point, we must ask the question of whether other, significantly simpler or cheaper technologies could equally address those pain points. In many cases, the answer to that question is yes, as shown by SWIFT's global payment innovation initiative in the financial payments world.[51] Consider cases where adoption of blockchain technology in supply chains has been pushed to increase provenance.[52] We believe that blockchain technology really doesn't solve the issue of provenance of physical goods unless each unit is uniquely identifiable, in which case a unique digital twin of that good can be created. If each unit is not uniquely identifiable, then it's hard to perfectly verify whether the good being sold indeed is the same one represented by its digital footprint. Even where each good is uniquely identifiable, such as diamonds, blockchain-based solutions may not be the most effective way to reduce conflict diamonds.

Take one example from Sameer's ongoing research, where blockchain technology is heralded as a way to create tamper-proof certificates of origin for diamonds.[53] In theory, this should eliminate practices that have plagued the industry: slavery, child labor, armed conflict, and environmental harm. Yet the same innovation also lets retailers segment the market into customers who care about responsible sourcing and the many who do not. As Sameer's research demonstrates, the supply for cheap, nonresponsibly sourced diamonds could actually rise as an unintended outcome of this technology.

Nonetheless, this is a technology that has some firestorm disruptive properties. If good economic cases can be identified—a setting where an intermediary is too costly or slow, or not seen as fully trustworthy, and the transaction involves an exchange of either digital products or physical ones that may be uniquely identifiable—blockchain technology may have a role to play. In undertaking your Encounter debate, at least ask yourself how an attacker might use blockchain to release stakeholder pain points or digitally build trust.

POST-COVID-19

Many of these targeted technologies played instrumental roles during our struggle to overcome the COVID-19 pandemic. Robots worked in healthcare facilities with COVID-19 patients, did last-mile deliveries of household essentials in cities under lockdowns, monitored public spaces, and served as ambassadors for social distancing. 3D printing sped the manufacturing of urgently needed medical and quarantine facility equipment. IoT technology enabled healthcare workers to remotely monitor and operate tele-ventilators, keeping workers safe. IoT facilitated temperature screening and contact tracing, two important practices that helped to curb the contagion.

While COVID-19 revealed the advantages that these technologies provide in terms of agility to respond to demand and supply shocks during a pandemic, the unit economics of these technologies in post-COVID-19 normalcy has yet to be demonstrated. Will the immediate advantages last? Sameer addresses this question in his 2020 article "Are Robots Overrated?" in the *Harvard Business Review*. It's is crucially important that Phoenix leaders understand how COVID-19 may change the rules of the game for technology deployment and experimentation when we emerge from the crisis.

For example, let's revisit our discussion of how blockchain technology could disrupt disrupters like Uber. COVID-19 has shown us how access to platforms for many businesses can provide the flexibility to respond to demand and supply shocks. But many of these platforms have been too expensive for the neighborhood mom-and-pop stores. Could this be the favorable wind that an open-source, decentralized, blockchain-based platform was looking for? Imagine the potential of a technology platform that enables trusted transactions and connects buyers and suppliers, designers and 3D printers, experts and consumer needs in a seamless, low-cost, and scalable manner. Will this be a game changer for some? How are you considering these firestorm technologies in your organization's Phoenix future?[54]

EXPANDING THE ARSENAL OF FUTURE TECHNOLOGY IN ATTACK AND DEFENSE IDEAS

Our aim in this and the previous chapter was to provide a broad scan in what is happening in the world of technology (at the time of publication) to be used as stimuli for both the Extreme Attack and Horizon Defense options in your Encounter debates. What might you use for radical ideas in attack and savvy defense moves, including pilot projects and experimentation?

There are also many other emerging and potentially highly impactful technologies (e.g., gene therapy, augmented and virtual reality, metamaterials, and nanotechnology) that we have not touched on here. Some of these technologies could fundamentally change many of the assumptions that you take for granted when thinking about the rules for engaging customers, competition, new product development, and the like. For example, in Google's 2019 demonstration of "quantum supremacy,"[55] it showcased a quantum computer that could solve a complex problem within a timeframe that is inconceivably fast for even the best-in-class supercomputers that use the classical computation system. This is touted by some as a moment that will fundamentally lead to a paradigm shift in what can be achieved by machines going forward. As this technology matures further, it will invariably have a profound impact on organizations, their business models, and the velocity of connectivity.

Phoenix leaders should generate wider option sets that include technologies beyond the immediate for attack ideas and taking far-sighted insights into their Completely Opposite Viewpoints Debates. The vitality of continuous, Proactive Scanning cannot be stressed enough for Phoenix Attitude leaders and organizations.

CHAPTER **10** CHECKLIST

Summary Thoughts

1. Scanning technologies beyond those directly related to your own industry is a must for leaders. Emerging technologies by themselves may at first seem to provide marginal benefits, but when combined with innovative business models could yield disruptive outcomes that can threaten the future existence of entire industries.

2. The breadth, depth, and pace of technology innovation is unprecedented. You should understand how technologies in mobility, IoT, 3D printing, robotics, and blockchain could fundamentally alter the nature of your firm and industry. Also consider how these technologies could create new options for your future attack and defense.

3. A Phoenix leader scans not only for existing technologies and their business model implications, but also for technologies in their embryonic stage that could reshape the future.

Reflection

1. What areas within your current business could take advantage of autonomous vehicle development, mobility services, IoT, 3D printing, robotics, and blockchain technologies? Would these have a positive, negative, or neutral impact on existing processes and policies and the workforce? For example, what potential changes would you need to reposition your business in a way that creates additional value using these technologies?

2. Might any of your competitors (actual and potential) or downstream and upstream partners leverage these technologies or be likely to do so? How would this impact your business, your people, your market position, your supply chain, your fleet management, and the like?

3. Would these technologies (or future embryonic technologies) allow your organization to do different things or do things differently? What gaps should you address in your organization to tap into these technologies? Does your organization have leaders and talent with skills to engage and execute strategies that leverage these technologies?

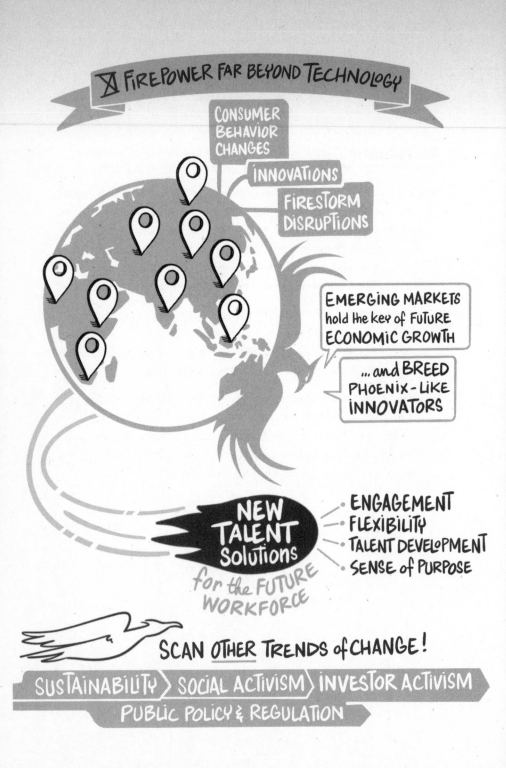

CHAPTER 11

FIREPOWER FAR BEYOND TECHNOLOGY

The first resistance to social change is to say it's not necessary.
—GLORIA STEINEM, American feminist, social activist, and journalist

While the technologies discussed in earlier chapters bring the kind of advantages that are now necessary to survive, there are other forces that could spell the difference between boom or bust. These are not technologies, and they are not even new, but used strategically, they can be as powerful as the latest artificial intelligence (AI) developments. These can all be used in Extreme Attack and Horizon Defense Radical Ideation.

What we scan for here are broad and fluid forces such as emerging markets, demographic diversity talent trends, activism, sustainability, and regulation. These are the social and economic forces that are fundamentally changing the business environment, and the more leaders know about them through scanning, the more likely they are to create future-ready organizations. We scan some of these here and suggest scanning for others beyond this book.

EMERGING MARKETS, EMERGING OPPORTUNITIES

Most Western business leaders have a general understanding that there is great promise in emerging markets, but relatively few know what it takes to realize that promise. There are many reasons for that. For one thing, developing markets can be confusing, shaped by local politics or customs and subject to the kind of economic shocks that keep leaders of traditional Western enterprises up at night. For another, after decades of globalization, they enjoy newfound prominence in the global economic order.[1] Figure 11.1, adapted from the IMF, captures this neatly.

FIGURE 11.1 Emerging Markets

Source: IMF Data Mapper, January 2018

Many emerging economies are now home to dynamic changes in consumer behavior, innovation, and firestorm disruption. In fact, as developed economies grapple with flat growth or no growth and with greying populations, emerging markets hold the key to the world's future economic growth. Their populations are young, their middle class is expanding, their consumers increasingly demand more and better goods and services, and they have the income to pay for them.

More important, it is no longer the case that local firms in developing economies compete only by leveraging social capital and local regulations. Many of these firms have global ambitions and the wherewithal to realize them. Enterprises in the developed world that ignore these dynamic local emerging market firms do so at their peril.[2]

To seek attack and defense ideas, we urge leaders to scan the horizons of emerging markets to (1) identify opportunities for engagement and (2) identify the implications of these forces and trends for potential transformation of business models and growth, cost, and risk agendas.

A GLOBAL MINDSET SEES OPPORTUNITIES DIFFERENTLY

Because three of our authors live and work primarily in Singapore, we'll start this discussion with some findings about that part of the world, acknowledging that many of the lessons apply to emerging economies on other continents as well.

An ASEAN report on economic prospects documents some interesting changes.[3] Until recently, firms looking to leverage growth in ASEAN focused mainly on the big cities (e.g., Singapore, Bangkok, Kuala Lumpur, Jakarta, and Manila). The report, which compares the growth rates of these cities from 2015 to 2025 with those of lesser-known cities in the region, finds that the cities expected to grow the fastest over this period are smaller metropolitan areas like Samut Prakan (Thailand); Batam, Denpasar, and Tasikmalaya (Indonesia); Vientiane (Laos); and Can Tho and Bien Hoa (Vietnam)—places that even people familiar with ASEAN would have a hard time finding on a map. Many of the companies that we consult with tell us they prefer the faster growth rates in the lower-tier cities over the big metros.[4]

That's important for leaders to keep in mind, and so is another important dynamic of these emerging markets: the fastest growing cities of today are not going to be the fastest growing cities of tomorrow—someone else will wear that crown. Economist Danny Quah's work illustrates this nicely. Quah has studied populations and production in different parts of the world and used that data to pinpoint the world's economic center of gravity (WECG).[5]

FIGURE 11.2 World's Economic Center of Gravity over Time

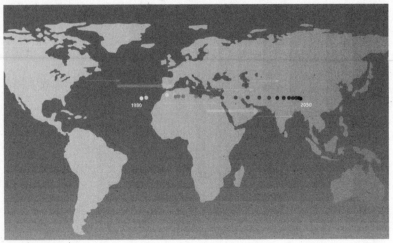

Source: Danny Quah

Quah's map of the world in Figure 11.2 shows the shift in the distribution of economic activity over the past decades. In 1980, for example, the WECG was in the middle of the Atlantic Ocean. By 2010, it had moved to a point just west of Minsk, capital of Belarus. Extrapolating growth projections of population and output, Danny predicts that by 2050, it will lie between India and China. In another measure of the influence of the emerging markets, a 2017 UBS/PwC report found that Asian billionaires outnumbered their US counterparts for the first time in modern history.[6] All of this means that leaders must know more than where their business centers will be. They must know what capabilities will be needed in that location to ensure relevance and competitiveness.

THE GAME CHANGER FOR THESE MARKETS

Perhaps the greatest change in emerging markets since the early 2000s is the diffusion of telecommunication and digital technologies—in particular, the rapid spread of feature phones and quasi-smartphones.

While the iPhone and Samsung remain largely unaffordable in these markets, consumers do have access to phones that provide most of the important functionalities at a fraction of the price of an iPhone. A consumer in Bangladesh, for example, can buy a smartphone for $123—about one-fifth of what a consumer in Germany would pay— and a smart-feature phone for around $40.[7]

These technologies have enabled consumers to leapfrog infrastructure deficits and enjoy better livelihoods, lifting large sections of society out of poverty. Hannah Ritchie and Max Roser track the diffusion of technologies such as fixed landline and mobile telephone subscriptions across different countries—for example, comparing the developed economy of the United Kingdom and the developing economy of Gambia.[8] They show that fixed landline subscriptions in the UK peaked at 60 subscriptions per 100 people in 2000, before mobile subscriptions raced past it. In fact, it took mobile about 20 years in the UK to surpass 100 subscriptions per100 people. The contrast with Gambia is striking. Fixed landline subscriptions there hadn't crossed single digits in 2015, but mobile subscriptions raced past about 140 subscriptions per 100 people, giving Gambia a higher tele-density than many developed economies.

Firms across the board have seized the opportunities provided by the diffusion of telecommunication in these markets. Gojek, an Indonesian unicorn (the name is a pun on *ojek*, the local name for a motorcycle taxi), is a classic illustration of this. The company, which has more than two million drivers on its platform, allows Indonesians to access everything from rides to food to massages and hairdressers without negotiating the traffic snarls that choke the world's largest island country.[9] It's worth noting that the infrastructure deficits that helped create these new breeds of entrepreneurs are invisible to most observers in developed markets because they never had to deal with such constraints.[10]

What3words is another example of these technologies' impressive ability to overcome infrastructural bottlenecks. By dividing the world into 57 trillion squares, What3words uses a three-word address to identify any location in the world. In a country like Mongolia with a vibrant nomadic community and largely nonexistent street addresses, What3words has become the official addressing system used by banks, post offices, taxis, Airbnb owners, and food delivery outfits.[11]

This new breed of emerging economy firestorm disruptors think and act very differently from those in developed countries. Their success has not come from aping innovative ideas from the developed markets and hoping the first mover advantage will take care of everything else. It has come from a determination to take on whatever obstacles might stand in their way and create a radically different business model: Phoenix fueled by technology.

The fire is accelerating. In the first quarter of 2020, India was hit not only by the COVID-19 pandemic but also the failure of three big banks. Yet despite the anxiety that usually accompanies such ordeals, the demand for cash has been subdued, largely because of the popularity of Unified Payment Interface (UPI), an app-enabled real-time electronic payments network. Until recently, cash was king in India, but the efficiencies of UPI, and the fact that it charges no fees for person-to-person transactions, have encouraged more than a billion transactions in every month of first-quarter 2020. Outside India, similar payments are handled by private firms (e.g., Visa, Mastercard, American Express, and now Alipay and Tencents), which own the network and charge heavily for its use. In India, however, UPI is forbidden by law to charge merchant fees.

Unsurprisingly, in November 2019, Google wrote to the Federal Reserve urging it to endorse a similar system for the United States. The Bank for International Settlements (a financial institution owned by central banks) concluded in December 2019 that India's digital financial infrastructure was so well designed that it had the potential to transform emerging markets as well as advanced economies. We have seen this phenomenon before. As we've pointed out, some of the most innovative developments in digitalization and technologies are happening in emerging markets. Leaders who pay attention to such innovation will be the first to unlock opportunities that would otherwise go unrecognized.[12]

EMERGING MARKETS BREED FIRESTORM COMPETITORS

The implication is obvious: do not underestimate local firms' potential in emerging markets. Gone are the days when companies entering these markets could safely assume that their competition would come only from other multinationals. The fiercest competitors in these markets are the local firms, and they have several advantages. For starters, most operate at much lower costs. They have been raised to run a lean ship, and that practice works to their great advantage.

More important, many have invested heavily in research and development (R&D) and in local distribution capabilities, making them more agile and entrepreneurial than most newcomers from developed markets. For them, the rest of the world is the next stage. We see this in traditional industries, in companies like the Chinese phone maker Transsion and the South African insurer Discovery. We also see it in the startup space. The world's largest Internet restaurant company is India's Rebel Foods, which pioneered the cloud kitchen concept in 2015 and is now being imitated by the likes of Deliveroo and CloudKitchens.[13]

One telling fact about these local firms is that their industries are more competitive and contested in their economies than are the same industries in the advanced economies.[14] A few statistics from the McKinsey Global Institute's analysis of corporate performance across sectors and regions help quantify this observation: the best performing emerging market companies derived 56 percent of their revenues from new products and services. In advanced economies, that number is 48 percent. Emerging market companies also invest twice as much (measured as ratio of CapEx to depreciation), make investment decisions faster, and are bolder in prioritizing geographic expansion outside their home markets.

> The following quote comes from a CEO, James Klarger, at one of the leading specialist mining companies in West Africa: "While we are very successful in developing markets across Africa, the Phoenix Encounter made us realize that we have an opportunity given our business model and elements of it that work very well in our environment to be a disruptor in markets such as Canada or New Zealand, where our type of approach has not been used in the past."

One final observation on emerging markets is relevant to scanning these for Extreme Attack and Horizon Defense ideas. Over the past decades, many Western multinationals have established captive outfits in these countries to outsource basic activities and benefit from cost arbitrage. That mindset needs to change. Leaders of these organizations need to realize that going forward, these hubs can be a powerful source of innovation that can elevate their organizations in ways that were previously inconceivable. When you are devising Encounter attack and defense options, what can you foresee from the emerging market world that would either "eat your lunch" or give you a "leap-frog advantage"?

New Firepower Born in Emerging Markets

DCF Investments, one of the world's largest asset managers, created a Global In-house Centre (GIC) in India in the early 2000s to support its global business. Like many other Western multinationals operating offshore support operations in emerging markets, DCF (USA) determined what work would be done by DCF (India). Chandra, one of our program participants, had worked at DCF India for more than a decade and happened to attend a major IT convention where one of the speakers (a senior VP at the GIC of another multinational) showcased its "Bi-modal IT" initiative. In essence, this meant that 95 percent of the GIC staff worked on the operational issues of the day while 5 percent thought up new ideas for the future. Energized, Chandra went back to work and pitched the DFC (US) CIO, Shelley Torello, the idea of a 0.5 percent team working on ideas for DCF global five years out. The pilot was to run for a year, and a decision would be taken at that point on what to do going forward. The CIO was intrigued and approved the pilot.

Chandra spent a month crafting a diverse team of five members, including two IT engineers, a business analyst, an MBA with a finance specialization, and a person who had spent most of the past five years helping run media campaigns for politicians. The Phoenix-like team started their journey with extensive business research with the goal of radical business ideation leading to prototypes, not full-fledged products. The team came up with three breakthrough ideas in their first year, impressing the CIO enough for her to pledge support for another three years.

As the team matured, their dreams became bigger. One of their scans revealed that DCF had a big generational gap in its retail client portfolio. The vast majority of its clients were more than 40 years old. When it came to the millennials, DCF's market share was miniscule, in contrast to disrupter startup players like "Friendly-Robbers" that had grown to several million in three years. The reasons for this became obvious as the team pressed ahead with its ideation and research. Friendly-Robbers (and its peers like "Be-Mazed") ran very simple apps that were mobile-based, could be used on the go, and offered only basic financial products (stocks and mutual funds) with the simplest trading functionalities (e.g., only buy and sell). The result was customers could apply and get activated on Friendly-Robbers in a matter of minutes. The existing DCF app in comparison was complex and the website even more so. The average consumer had to spend up to two hours to fill in eight to nine forms at DCF for account opening. It could take an additional seven days for the account to be activated and two to three more days to move money.

The idea of coming up with a new app for DCF was a no-brainer, but the breakthrough moment for the team was the realization that all that was needed to fulfil the know-your-customer norms in the United States was sitting in US government–issued identity cards. Building an app that scanned this card and using an API connected to the credit scoring companies' databases meant the team now had the ability to open and activate accounts in a matter of minutes.

Chandra, along with a couple of team members, flew to the United States. The CIO arranged a meeting with a group of senior DCF management and asked them to bring their adult millennial children as well. The senior leaders and their family members were given the apps and asked to play with them. The younger generation loved the new app; it was everything the DCF app was not. The result was a $25 million budget and a rollout expected to go live across North America in the next year. It will be the first retail product for DCF (USA) conceptualized by DCF (India). The realization among senior leaders in DCF (USA) is that DCF (India) is no longer just a place to park the grunt work. It could be a key contributor to DCF's Phoenix Breakthrough, taking ideation and agility from emerging markets into the core.

This was not an easy journey. Along the road there were moments where senior US leaders would challenge the team members: Who gave you the license to think? Why are you thinking beyond your mandate?

The moral of the story is clear. Unlocking the Phoenix Breakthrough requires leaders with the Phoenix Attitude, like Shelley and Chandra. It calls for teams of Dreamers and Doers: people with the habit of Proactive Scanning and radical startegic debate, people who are willing to attack and defend, as well as break any counterproductive orthodoxy—of gender, race, culture, and generation.

GLOBAL TALENT AND ORGANIZATIONAL RENEWAL

Having the right talent in place has always been an imperative for a successful enterprise. In the past 20 years, the "global war for talent" has only intensified. With people more mobile and connected more than ever in the global marketplace, the contemporary firepower of developing highly effective "talents solutions" should be part of every attack and defense option set.[15]

In 2009, INSEAD professors Schon Beechler and Ian together published "The Global 'War for Talent.'"[16] This research article described the need for modern organizations to take account of the sharply shifting demographics (intergenerational, cultural, and gender diversity, together with global mobility and connectivity) of the future workforce. In the decade since, the debate about the kinds of talents and capabilities required in the digital world has become increasingly urgent. It's clear today that many of the talents and capabilities that were emphasized in the past are no longer as valuable. Leaders must think about talent as what will be needed, not what legacy models have required.

For example, most leaders who venture into emerging markets do so with the understanding that they will need talent, but many don't realize how much that talent will cost. In Asia, especially, talent doesn't come cheap. Figure 11.3 is from a 2016 IMF report.[17]

FIGURE 11.3 Wage Premiums: Asia vs. Rest of the World

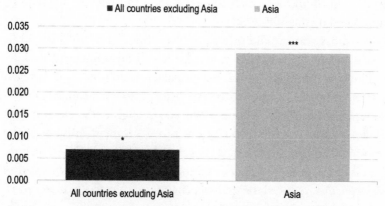

Note: Bars represent coefficients of regression explaining the Gini Index. The bar for Asia reflects total effect of the policy variable(s) on Asian countries, which is the sum of the average coefficient and the coefficient for the interaction term.
*** p<0.01, ** p<0.05, * p<0.1.;

Source: IMF

The figure shows the difference in wages that an employee with a credential (e.g., high school certificate, undergraduate, etc.) commands, relative to an employee without that credential, and compares that difference across Asia and other countries excluding Asia. The implication is clear: getting good talent in emerging markets is going to be difficult and costly. But big changes to the talent landscape are everywhere.

FAST-EVOLVING WORKFORCES

The nature of the workforce is changing fast, and it is connected to the world's most potent change agent: technology such as AI and robotics. While the discussion in popular media around this topic focuses mostly on job displacement, we believe that in the short to medium terms, only a minority of jobs will be completely automated. Most of the jobs, however, will be transformed, with technology-enabled automation taking over structured and predictable tasks. Human workers will take on higher-value tasks that the machines cannot perform. New technologies will also create jobs that require new skills and involve new tasks. A study by consulting firm PwC estimates that 30 percent of jobs across all countries and industries are likely to be automated by the mid-2030s.[18]

For those reasons and others, the workforce of tomorrow will be very different from that of yesterday. It will be connected, mobile, and intensely diverse—intergenerational, cross-cultural, and of mixed gender. Historically, when there have been profound advances in technology, such as the invention of the steam engine, the electric light bulb, or conveyor belt production, those advances influenced the workforce for roughly the next 30 years. After World War II, technological development took off, and that acceleration, plus widespread social change, reduced the span of generational clusters to closer to 15 years.

In 2019, we see for the first time that four relatively different generational groups (baby boomers, Generation X, and Gen Y or millennials, as well as older traditionalists) are operating across workplaces together.[19] Another generation, Gen Z, which has had Internet connectivity since birth, will join the workplace during the coming decade.[20]

Though these groups have much in common, their differences can be significant. Diversity perspectives are essential in the Completely Opposite Viewpoints Debates of the Encounter. We see some trouble ahead with leadership teams that are not actively scanning for or addressing talent and diversity options in their strategic agendas. One problem will emerge as baby boomers, compelled to remain in the workforce by inadequate retirement funds, good health, and greater life expectancy, try to hang on to senior roles that younger workers covet. After all, it's not that unusual these days for 23-year-old CEOs to run startups. Nor is it unusual for those young digital natives to do their jobs very well. Many also do their jobs differently than workers did a generation ago. Instead of following a designated career track that might lead to a corner office, they collaborate and iterate. Accustomed to 24/7 connectedness and aided by applications like Slack and

Zoom, they work in teams aimed more at advancing a product or idea than individual careers.[21]

Academic research identifies six areas where intergenerational differences are likely to influence the future workplace: communication and technology; work motivators or preferred job characteristics; work values; work attitudes; workplace/career behaviors; and leadership preferences or behaviors. Other research notes intergenerational differences in personal values, psychological/personality traits, turnover intentions, and organizational commitment.[22]

Going forward, greater flexibility will be the key to the successful workplace, and we see changes that will require such flexibility coming faster than ever. Those changes will affect how talent is attracted and acquired; how it is developed, motivated, and rewarded; and how it is retained.

Even changes to the modality of working are increasing. Those include the growing use of telecommuting (the proportion of people in the United States regularly telecommuting grew 115 percent in the decade to 2017, and that excludes the self-employed). During the COVID-19 lockdown periods, the proportion of remote work increased dramatically, with the Gallup organization reporting around 70 percent of US employees working remotely in May 2020. Another modality change is the increasing movement of people between profit and social enterprises (global recruiter Michael Page found that its Gen Y candidates were more likely to take a job with lower pay if they believed it was meaningful); and the popularity of new kinds of coworking office spaces, such as IWG.[23]

TALENT SOLUTION AGENDAS

Four areas of discussion should be a part of your strategic leadership debate today and must be considered in developing your Phoenix Encounter attack and defense options:

- *Career pathways and organizational structure adaptation.*
  Historically, businesses have focused teams on projects. Looking ahead, we see lateral, matrix-based teaming as part of the

general organizational design. This facilitates learning, as mentoring is now a two-way street with reverse mentoring of senior employees by juniors is becoming commonplace. Millennial mentorship or reverse mentoring could be considered a formalized, mildly absurdist version of the advice juniors give older colleagues on new technologies, emerging markets, and developing new products. It works; companies clearly benefit from millennial mentoring.

We have also noted that executives' interest in being mentored by Generation Y or Z has led to an assumption that Gen Z will seek to replace millennials at an accelerating pace once they are substantively in the workforce in the next two decades.[24]

Talent and skill challenges await both legacy and disruptive firms. At the end of the day, companies still need the technical skills to do things like chemical engineering, mechanical engineering, and actuarial studies, even if they are aided by new technologies such as AI. Fewer millennials are coming along with such skills. There also seem to be a few gaps in sophisticated soft skills together with technical skills, usually those built from extended work experience. Surprisingly, a study from the Educational Training Service in 2016 found that US millennials "consistently score below many of their international peers in literacy, numeracy, and problem solving in technology-rich environments. Equally troubling is that these findings also represent a decrease in literacy and numeracy skills when compared to results from previous years of US adult surveys."[25]

Looking at this from 50,000 feet, a traditional company planning to digitize would need to become the employer of choice in any area based in traditional skills, adjusted for generationally different styles of working, because the pool of younger people with these skills is likely to be smaller, and the number of firms competing for these people will be greater. If you are a Gen Y or Gen Z with a traditional set of skills, you will have a broad set of choices, not just the entrepreneurial choices. Organizations whose human resources leaders anticipate a talent war, as opposed to developing talent solutions that engage across the generations, will face serious talent acquisition and retention issues, as well as higher costs.[26]

• ***The skills and competencies for the jobs of the future will be very different, and the modes of employee engagement are changing.*** This paradigm shift will challenge not only recruitment and retention policies and procedures but also ongoing learning, development, and training. A 2017 McKinsey survey of young people and employers in nine countries found that educational systems have not kept pace with the changing nature of work, and many employers say they cannot find enough workers with the skills they need. Forty percent of employers said lack of skills was the main reason for entry-level job vacancies, and 60 percent said new graduates were not adequately prepared for the world of work.[27]

Another important trend is the increasing growth of online platform-based employment and freelancing, as noted by the World Economic Forum. Its work suggests that by 2025, more than half a billion people will benefit from digitally connected employment. Close to 60 million Americans were freelancing in 2018.[28]

• ***Watch out for generational squeeze and stress.*** Gen X, which is much smaller in number than millennials and baby boomers, has both ambition and digital skills and is knocking on the doors of baby boomers who hold senior jobs.[29] We see very limited planning of how best to integrate Gen Z workers, who started to arrive in tertiary education and workplaces from 2015 and will arrive in force by 2025. One 2018 survey showed that 77 percent of Generation Z say having a millennial manager is their preference over Generation X or baby boomers.[30]

TALENT INVOLVES LEARNING AND EVOLVING

One thing is clear: the time of the absolute learning organization has more than come. Aided by the growth mindset (Carole Dweck) discussed in Chapter 4, tomorrow's Phoenix leaders will need to challenge themselves and their organizations for accelerated learning with intense curiosity.

The concept is hardly new. It was put forth three decades ago by Peter Senge in his book *The Fifth Discipline*. In 1993, Harvard professor David Garvin posited that a "learning organization is an organization skilled at creating, acquiring, and transferring knowledge, and at modifying its behaviors to reflect new knowledge and insights."[31] In his work with other researchers, he identified three building blocks required to build the learning organization: a supportive learning environment, concrete learning processes and practices, and leadership that reinforces learning.[32] We believe that these same building blocks are essential and consistent with the Phoenix Encounter method and tools (like scanning and opposites debate) and that they should be reinforced by:

- Developing a culture of learning from failing, while encouraging intense sharing of different perspectives and knowledge

- Promoting a "learning HQ," where there is dynamic interplay between HQ and its markets and regions (not just centralization of thought)

- Engaging with a wide range of stakeholders—customers, partners, thought leaders, and employees—all from diverse generational, gender, and cultural groups

- Making continuous learning agility a core and personally derived competence routine across the entire Phoenix workforce

Any serious Encounter Extreme Attack or Horizon Defense has the talent and people dimensions at its heart. For example, one of our Encounter participants, Hans Schroder, a specialist in a manufacturing business, devised an attack that poached the incumbent's best young talent with the promise of accelerated promotion and mentored development. This attack offered a fully flexible, grow-and-learn talent process that rewarded these people with equity shares, including bonuses for acquiring further new talents for the new business, as well the chance to participate in a "shadow board of millennials" to challenge every real board decision.

During the COVID-19 pandemic, major trends in talent acquisition and workplace expectations began to move even faster. Virtual working and real-time teamwork created a prominent sense of purpose. Now it appears the benefits of crisis-driven practices have made a lasting impression on some leaders. In April 2020 Tata Consulting Services (TCS), India's largest IT firm, announced that post-COVID-19 the company would work toward a goal of having 75 percent of its 450,000 staff working from home by 2025. TCS's chief operating officer NG Subramaniam has made clear that the company does not "believe that we need more than 25 percent of our workforce at our facilities in order to be 100 percent productive."

In the same month as Tata's announcement, dozens of CEOs, including those at Mondelez, Nationwide, and Barclays, acknowledged the likelihood of permanent work-from-home flexibilities beyond the pandemic. A Gartner survey found that 74 percent of CFOs expect some of their employees who were forced to work from home because of the coronavirus will continue working remotely after the pandemic ends. In May 2020, Cisco launched a Future of Work initiative focused on sharing thought leadership on remote flexible working experiences well into the future.[33]

Phoenix leaders who can engage people have never been more important, especially considering early indications that remote work experiences driven by COVID-19 have improved productivity, colleague communication, collaboration, and flexibility. Phoenix leaders understand that these practices will lead to cost and operating model changes, and inevitably to regulatory reforms relating to employment policies. These leaders will want to have an opposite viewpoints debate: not "how to return to business as usual," but "how should we work in the future, and what do our people and our other stakeholders want?" Will some talent demand the opportunity to do at least some of their work flexibly? Will the world after a COVID-19 vaccine see alternative working arrangements, where offices and home working spaces coexist with satellite remote work sites, providing flexibility and shorter commutes, yet also opportunities with a distant company? Will your organization's defense include the leadership capabilities and technology systems to sustain virtual collaboration at magnitude?

SCAN FOR OTHER TRENDS SUCH AS ACTIVISM, SUSTAINABILITY POLICY, AND REGULATION

Some massive forces of change in today's world don't make the strategic dialogue list often enough for legacy leaders. These include activism and sustainability, policy and regulation, as well as the macro forces of dynamic geopolitical and economic power tilts. In our book's online resources, we provide additional scans to promote thinking about Extreme Attack and Horizon Defense options in these arenas. These topics lend themselves to books on their own and we do them an injustice in our text here. However, we raise a couple of examples to stimulate Encounter thought now.

Activism is not new. From the suffragette movement of the nineteenth century to the civil rights and environmental movements of the later twentieth century, activism and social consciousness has led to major changes—in those cases, changes for the better. Today, social media exponentially boosts the influence of activist campaigns. In addition to social activism, the activist investor, often exemplified by the 1980s corporate raider Carl Icahn, is another potential influence on modern corporations. We see investor activism as another form of firepower, one that has been elevated to that status by its increasing scale, scope, and velocity. In any attack and defense ideation and debate, ask yourselves:

- What might the forces of environmental sustainability mean for your firm and industry, and how might a disrupter harness this?

- What might an activist investor say or do about your business, and what obvious ideas, blinkered by your status quo bias, contribute to value creation?

The intersection of government, public policy, regulation, and organizations is a big and busy place, a must-see in the scanning process. We see many opportunities to use regulatory advocacy in Extreme Attack. It could be used to engage in the public policy and regulatory process to influence future regulations that would be beneficial to either deploying a new business model or new technology. The banking industry, for example, long heavily regulated, faces even greater regulation from national, regional, and international levels—from Basel III to Basel IV. Bankers hate it, but we suggest they heed the advice "Be careful what you wish for." Regulation and capital adequacy requirements are in many cases the only things standing between legacy banks and the waiting wave of disruptors. Ant Financial and several others have already entered the financial services space. In your Encounter option generation, ask: What regulations or policy settings could be beneficial in both attack (to remove incumbent advantage) and defense (to buy time to change)?

There is a wide world to scan. Do it at breadth first, then at depth, where most relevant insights emerge. Always ask What if? and What might be? Then ask how you can combine the contemporary world of change with the conventional levers of business performance. We turn to this in the next chapter as we combine contemporary and conventional firepower for attack and defense.

CHAPTER **11** CHECKLIST

Summary Thoughts

1. Emerging economies are now home to some of the most dynamic changes in consumer behavior, innovation, and firestorm disruption. Their entrepreneurs leapfrog incumbency and devise totally new ways of doing business. These are formidable future competitors who have Phoenix innovation built into their DNA because they have no other legacy choices.

2. The diverse intergenerational workforce of the future requires talent solutions that engage, provide flexibility, focus on talent development, and give a sense of purpose. People and technology are synchronous in a much more mobile talent market than the past.

3. Leaders should also scan other unstoppable trends of change to search for breakthrough options in either their attack or defense strategies. These include sustainability, social activism, and investor activism as well as government or public policy and regulation.

Reflection

1. What do you know or understand about the dramatic changes occurring in the business landscape of emerging economies? In thinking about these markets, are you seeing them simply as expansion possibilities, or are they incubators of new ways of doing things?

2. What will be your talent solutions approach to attract, develop, and retain the people your organization will need into the future? How will the talent capabilities and needs for the future of your organization differ from the past? Can you imagine using the Phoenix Encounter method as a strategic thinking and leadership development exercise for your high-potential talent?

3. Are you actively considering the implications and opportunities of crucial forces of future change, especially sustainability, activism, and public policy? Are you looking at these trends well beyond the scope of your traditional industry and geographic operations?

LEGACY FIRMS have ASSETS ...
- ✓ Access to Customers & Data
- ✓ Trust & Reputation
- ✓ Balance Sheet
- ✓ Business Systems

... to COMBINE with CONTEMPORARY FIREPOWER

CONVENTIONAL FIREPOWER e.g. M&As

+

CONTEMPORARY FIREPOWER e.g. DIGITAL Technology

NEW DEFENSE OPTIONS

NEW WAYS of CREATING VALUE

SCAN the POSSIBILITIES of COMBINING the DIFFERENT FORMS of FIREPOWER

FORTIFY your CORE BUSINESS

RELEASE RESOURCES for FUTURE INNOVATION SHIFTS

FIREPOWER FROM COMBINATORIAL INNOVATION

*We started combining the use of light and the use of
theatrics and the use of as many art forms as possible,
and it's still growing—that's the whole idea of it.*
—ALICE COOPER, American rock music legend

As you come to consider your Horizon Defense options in the Phoenix Encounter's Battlefield debate and think about your Future-Facing Blueprint, it's time to tap deeply into potential latent strengths of the traditional business world.

Amid all the hype about the disruptive influence of the forces of digital, social, platforms, and technology, it's easy to think that the future could be a place where legacy firms are no longer relevant. That would be a serious mistake. While digital innovation has seriously damaged many old dogs—*Rolling Stone* magazine and the *New York Times*, Borders, Blockbuster, Tower Records, the Limited, Aeropostale, and Wet Seal—the profits of these industries in their prime (circa 1997) accounted for less than 2 percent of the profits of the S&P 500 index of big legacy American firms.[1] This, united with the 2019 peaks in the valuations of legacy firms (and the IPO valuation pullbacks of many disrupters), suggests that markets believe the future for incumbents is far from the bleak picture that the digital zealots predict.

It's also important to remember that legacy incumbents have assets that can help them harness the forces of disruption in their favor, such as trust, reputation, and balance sheets.[2] As Ginni Rometty, Executive Chairman IBM, points out, incumbent firms own 80 percent of the commercial world's data—and most of this is beyond the reach of the FAANG-type platforms (Facebook, Amazon, Apple, Netflix, and Google). They also have more resources, such as cash flows, than the FAANG-type platforms, and they can invest those resources in big data, machine learning, and artificial intelligence (AI) to better leverage their data assets. In short, there is ample evidence to suggest that legacy firms will remain relevant in the years ahead—if, of course, they can learn to adapt and innovate. Many of them can.

In this chapter, we look at some firms that did just that. We also present legacy firm case studies on the website for this book (www .phoenixencountermethod.com). One tells the story of Naxos, one of the leading Western classical music labels in the world, and one describes the turnaround of Cisco's troubled telecom business in India. Both show readers how legacy firms can thrive by leveraging the conventional levers of business. By that, we mean the fundamental disciplines of business, such as strategy, marketing, operations, finance, and accounting, as well as organizational and human resource management.

HARNESSING COMBINATORIAL INNOVATION[3]

Successful companies make it a habit to think about innovation as a multidimensional construct, one that involves choreographing a bespoke set of forces across conventional and contemporary firepower. This is "combinatorial innovation" in its most potent form. These firms know that transformation is a consequence of bold reimagination of activities, actors, and resources—what we have referred to in earlier chapters as redrawing the boundaries of the firm.

IKEA is a great illustration of the combinatorial approach. As a disruptor in the furniture world starting in 1948, it changed the way consumers bought furniture. IKEA co-opted consumers to become co-producers—driving to the stores and picking and assembling in return for affordable design—and went on to become a global giant in the furniture retail business. However, the growth of e-commerce and changes in consumer shopping habits meant that the erstwhile disruptor was in danger of getting disrupted. IKEA's response to this threat has been to create a Phoenix-like defense built on a combinatorial portfolio of business model tilts leveraging contemporary and conventional firepower.

IKEA and the Combinatorial Innovation Playbook

In 2017, IKEA acquired the Silicon Valley startup TaskRabbit, a platform website that connects consumers with freelancers who perform many household tasks, such as assembling IKEA furniture. At one level, the move reflects the understanding that IKEA's traditional model, based on co-production, would need to evolve. It also reflects IKEA's ability to combine multiple insights: (1) a growing number of younger customers are not willing to build their own furniture and (2) the gig economy lets customers and retailers leverage a new labor force that performs assembly cheaper, faster, or more conveniently than the customer can manage.[4]

IKEA then co-opted Reform, a Danish startup, and bootstrapped it into IKEA's business model to help consumers create designer kitchens at a fraction of the price charged by kitchen designers. The company lets customers buy cabinet doors, panels, and counters designed by some of the world's foremost architects and put them on top of basic IKEA kitchen modules. As a *New York Times* article said, this was the birth of IKEA hacking or IKEA bling. As part of the ecosystem, Reform's success in selling kitchens across 20 countries has encouraged it to expand its offering to other rooms, including bathrooms. IKEA's combinatorial response has several other elements: smaller city center stores, furniture rental versus ownership, and a new platform. Press reports suggest IKEA is thinking about introducing "furniture as a service." All these things strengthen the overall IKEA ecosystem against the forces of firestorm disruption. The power of combinatorial defense can be seen in IKEA reporting its highest ever annual revenues of 41.3 billion euros in September 2019.[5]

From Encounter exercises, we have seen far more companies (incumbents and startups) generate competitive advantage through multiple innovations than with a single strike. This is the heart of Phoenix combinatorial innovation, an approach where the whole is much more powerful than the sum of its parts. In what follows, we scan examples of legacy firms, as well as startups, that have used such approaches for dealing with disruption and, more important, for innovation, growth, or advantages around cost or risk.

Firestorm disruption is rarely an overnight event. Most often it unfolds over time—sometimes it takes years or decades, and in some instances, it never happens at all. All leaders need to be ready for it in their business model defense and Future-Facing Blueprint.[6] In doing so, they need to think very hard about two fundamental issues: (1) how to take care of and fortify the core business during the transition to a disruption-proof model and (2) what things should be very different in tomorrow's organization to leverage innovation and enable growth. Ensuring the health of the core (even if it may be disrupted or destroyed in the future) is critical for the maximum exploitation of current resources—people, processes, and assets—all needed to propel the desired transformational changes. This implies a view of defense as a series of horizons for the blueprint—immediate action and the short term, medium term, and long term. As the following examples illustrate, incumbents can combine many of the conventional and contemporary sources of firepower in innovative ways, not just to ensure survival, but to achieve new growth.

Access vs. Ownership

Sometimes, changing the provision of a product or service from customer ownership to customer access can lend competitive advantage. Mahindra & Mahindra (M&M), one of the biggest manufacturers of farm equipment in the world, leveraged the access versus ownership model via its subsidiary, Trringo. M&M sells its machines in 40 countries, but its headquarters are in India. As in many emerging markets, farms there are small.[7] The vast majority of Indian farmers cannot afford to own a tractor, but thanks to Trringo, they can now get their hands on one. Trringo is the first-of-its-kind farm equipment rental service that helps small farmers mechanize operations instead of relying on manual and animal labor. Farmers can call a toll-free number or use an app on their phones to request the type of farm equipment that they would like to have at a specific time (and request an operator for it, if they need one). M&M uses its installed base of franchisees and other renters of farm equipment (who may carry products made by its competitors) to service this demand.

Uber is the best-known example of the potential of leveraging the ownership versus access trade-off. Uber (and equivalents like Lyft, Grab and Gojek) is easy to use: the consumer downloads the Uber app and requests a ride from one point to another. The app responds with a price for the ride and the details of the car and the driver who provides the ride. Consumers don't pay in cash; the fee is paid with a credit card that is kept on file. The massive appeal of Uber became apparent in 2015 when it completed its one billionth ride just four years after launch. The impact of Uber on the taxi industry was also easy to see: a taxi medallion that sold for $1.3 million in 2013 was on sale for $241,000 in early 2017.[8] Fundamentally, what both M&M and Uber did was not a new idea. They served as intermediaries between demand and supply, and in doing so, they got rid of the cost-quantity trade-off in markets with demand uncertainty and shifted the risks of asset ownership.

Co-production

Co-production invites agents external to the firm, like customers, to become part of the production of a product/service.

A classic example is McDonald's, as well as several of its peers in the quick service restaurant, or QSR, business. In a McDonald's, consumers do several things that were traditionally done by the staff at legacy restaurants: they walk up to the counter, order what they want, pick up the prepared food, seat themselves, and clean up when they are done. By empowering customers to become part of the production process, McDonald's unlocked value, reduced inefficiencies and costs, and improved the overall experience.

In the digital world, TripAdvisor, Expedia, and related startups in the online travel space have leveraged co-production and disrupted legacy businesses. Before their existence, consumers had to work their way through many agents to organize a trip. There were friends offering their recommendations, travel agents to book flights and hotels, and other intermediaries to take care of insurance, car rentals, and tours. The new world lets TripAdvisor and similar sites offer a one-stop shop that leverages co-production—in this case, user-generated reviews and other advice to create trust and reputation as well as such ecosystem functionalities as booking engines and payment gateways—all of the things that have disrupted hotels, airlines, and travel agencies.

New Suppliers

New suppliers have always brought new opportunities. Today, with technology thrown into the mix, those opportunities are plentiful. Technology lets companies create new businesses by tapping new service provider segments and offering those services to new user segments.

TransferWise, a London-based fintech startup, is disrupting the international money transfer business with its digital applications. Traditional money transfers move money from sender A in one country to recipient B in another country. TransferWise looks for a recipient C in the same country as sender A. Recipient C is expecting a transfer from sender D, who is in the same country as recipient B. By avoiding currency conversion and cross-border transfers, Transferwise eliminates several costs and commissions that have historically plagued the international money transfer industry.[9]

Utilities, among the oldest traditional industries, are big fat targets for firestorm disruption. Net metering is a simple bidirectional metering system that allows consumers who generate some or all of their own electricity (e.g., from roof-mounted solar) to offload their surpluses to the grid. Households can contribute energy to the economy and encourage utility companies to create new opportunities for business development and growth.[10]

Mergers, Acquisitions, and Divestments

Organizations facing the forces of disruption often recognize that the capabilities and assets they currently have are not going to fend off firestorm disruption. In some cases, a good mergers-and-acquisitions approach can help firms combat disruptors. In fact, leaders who actively practice proactive scanning are usually the first to see trouble ahead and develop their mergers and acquisitions (M&A) strategy.

Some Big Four accounting firms are doing that now; they are quietly preparing for a disruption of law firms. That's because, unlike the consulting or accounting space—two concentrated markets characterized by a handful of very large firms—there is no small set of dominant law firms. It's also because, as revenues from their traditional audit and tax business have flattened, the Big Four accounting firms have been looking to other areas for growth and scale. As their customers globalized, the value of a one-stop shop offering a combination of audit, tax, legal, and consulting services has gained strength. Deregulation across countries such as Britain and Australia that allows multidisciplinary practices (MDPs) has added impetus to such a move. Ernst & Young, for example, has expanded from 23 countries to 64 since 2013 through mergers and acquisitions, and others, including Deloitte, PwC, and KPMG, are eager to grow.[11]

Facebook's purchase of WhatsApp and the serial acquisitions of Amazon and Alibaba, detailed in Chapter 8, show how M&A can help a platform player maintain a leadership position. The strategy has been so effective that it has prompted many commentators, academics, regulators, business leaders, and politicians to voice concern about potential monopoly in these markets.[12]

Divestment and restructuring are another effective defense against firestorm disruption. It may sound drastic, but radical action is sometimes necessary. In 2017, Honeywell was under tremendous pressure from Third Point Fund activist investor Daniel Loeb to overhaul its business and maximize returns. Following an internal portfolio review by the management and the board, the company announced it would split its home and global distribution unit, which sold HVAC, fire, and security products, and its transportation systems unit, which focused on technology inputs into cars, trucks, and other vehicles, into two separate listed companies, while retaining ownership of its aerospace technology operations.

In Encounter debates, we find many leaders comfortable with contemplating acquisitions in their defense options. However, most leaders in these exercises resist thinking about divestment, even when it is blindingly obvious that someone else is a better owner of a business in a decaying industry. This is an example of the psychological issues that we discussed in Part I.

Vertical Integration

In instances where an industry value chain involves many layers of participants with all kinds of services, vertical integration could create competitive defense advantages.

Consider Carrefour's foray into emerging markets. The company's entry into Asia started in Taiwan in the late 1980s, when modern retail was the preserve of high-end Japanese department stores at one end and Japanese convenience stores at the other end. Our colleague Dominique Lecossois was one of the team leaders at Carrefour that pioneered the "farm-to-fork" model that is now widely imitated. As part of this vertical integration with a range of ingredient suppliers, Carrefour agreed to purchase all their production in return for commitments on quality. The deal worked wonderfully. It enabled Carrefour to cement its value perception as the freshest purveyors of these products in countries where freshness has long been synonymous with quality.

For another strategy that integrates defense and growth, consider the London Stock Exchange's (LSE) $27 billion takeover of Reuters Eikon data service. The deal adds foreign exchange and fixed-interest trading platforms to LSE's traditional strengths in equities and derivatives. The rise in its market capitalization of about $5 billion since the announcement reflects the payoffs from smart integration moves. For instance, the combined entity could allow a hedge fund to use LSE data and analytics to generate trades on the LSE platform and then settle them via the LSE clearinghouse and measure the investments performance against LSE indices—with LSE, in effect, becoming a one-stop shop.[13]

Partnerships

While many legacy companies can see that firestorm disruption is happening faster than ever, they don't know how to protect themselves. Partnerships may be a real saving grace. Airbus has created a new venture to manufacture drones and self-driving cars with Local Motors Industries, a 3D printing startup in San Francisco. Dirk Hoke, chief executive of Airbus Defence, said the joint venture brings together Airbus aerospace engineers with decades of experience with the radically different tools of Local Motors. The 50/50 joint venture would also be open to working with other partners, he added. "As a big company, you struggle to have a good story on how to drive innovation compared to little startups," Hoke said. "Here is a good combination: an open ecosystem for co-development, prototyping, and inviting other companies."[14]

In 2017, Airbnb entered a partnership with Veritas Investments, one of San Francisco's biggest landlords, to let its tenants rent out their units on Airbnb. The deal offers access to the home-sharing economy for a community of apartment residents. It also makes housing a bit more affordable in a very costly city by allowing residents to generate extra income. The partnership includes another independent startup, Pillow Residential, that helps tenants and landlords manage Airbnb listings by arranging for cleaning services, recording rental transactions, and giving guests a point of contact if something goes wrong.[15]

Platforms essentially create partnerships. In many Encounter defense plans, we see leaders considering these much more vigorously.

Branding, Trust, and Reputation

Having a brand that resonates with its core constituency of consumers can be an enormous source of competitive strength for a firm. It also offers a company the freedom to do things its own way, rather than follow conventional wisdom.

Consider Sriracha, a spicy dipping sauce with origins in Asia. When David Tran started Huy Fong Foods (named after the refugee ship that brought him out of Vietnam) in Los Angeles in 1980, he figured immigrants of Vietnamese ancestry would stock his sauce at pho shops and that the occasional American might squirt it on a hot dog or hamburger.[16] Twenty years later, Sriracha was one of the coolest food sauce brands on the market, with a cult following that cuts across cuisines and boundaries—and entire cookbooks devoted to it. There is even Sriracha memorabilia, from T-shirts to iPhone covers. The privately owned company does not spend any money on advertising and has no sales force; it relies on the same network of distributors it has used in the past.[17]

Singers Taylor Swift and Adele are contemporary exemplars of the power of branding, which, as they show us, can overcome prevailing trends in the music business. Spotify and Apple Music have more than 100 million subscribers paying for streaming, which accounts for 63 percent of US music consumption today, compared to 23 percent in 2014. Physical music sales and digital downloads have been declining for years. Yet Adele's album *25*, released in 2015, was withheld from streaming for seven months. Before her *1989* album, released in 2014, Taylor Swift removed her entire catalog from Spotify—it was only restored in June 2017. Her November 2017 release, *Reputation*, was similarly withheld from Spotify and still sold two million copies worldwide in the first week; it became available on Spotify three weeks later.[18]

In many Encounter defense debates we witness, there is much discussion on what trust and reputation value can be leveraged by legacy firms as digital providers, compared with upstarts with no track records.

Renaissance

Many iconic brands of yesteryear that had been considered marginal players in today's world are showing us that their brand strength and older products can span generations and centuries.

Levi's, which pioneered riveted jeans in the late 1890s, became a hugely popular brand among young adults between the 1950s and the

1980s. Since then, a combination of competition and legal and financial difficulties left Levi's a much-diminished company in the ensuing decades. Levi's has since embarked on a new strategy that leverages its history, and it seems to be paying off. The Levi's Authorized Vintage collection of 50,000 jeans from the 1960s through 1980s (priced at $300 a pair) competes successfully with other purveyors of archival denim. Women, who now make up 60 percent of Levi's customers, compared to 30 percent two decades ago, have helped propel Levi's to four straight years of growth. Millennials are another significant vintage fashion trend driver.

Another renaissance revival example is the spectacular growth of interest in vinyl LP records, the 12-inch ancestors of digital music played on analog turntables. In 2018, roughly 4 million chart-eligible LPs were sold in the UK alone, and the number was expected to be around 4.5 million in 2019. Most of these buyers are millennials who grew up in the era of first CDs and then digital streaming. Though still a small proportion of overall music sales, the retro-style interest in vinyl is a trend that has led labels such as Sony Music to resume in-house production. Among the most popular vinyl are Beatles albums such as *Sgt. Pepper's Lonely Hearts Club Band*, originally released in 1967 and the highest-selling LP 50 years later in 2017.[19]

New Products/Hybrids

In many cases, incumbents respond to the firestorm by creating hybrid products that combine old and new technologies. Typewriter makers, for example, added a CRT display, disk drive, and memory to create a hybrid word processor to respond to the disruption created by personal computers. Our INSEAD colleague Nathan Furr argues that the conventional view—that hybrids are an indicator of an organization's inertia—may be misplaced.[20] This work shows instead that hybrids can serve as sophisticated learning tools that shape organizational adaptation to technological discontinuities. For example, Prius is a hybrid between internal combustion engine and electric vehicles. It gave Toyota a way to learn about the future and helped the company adapt to technological changes.

Canon and Nikon have used this approach to preserve their market positions in the face of digital cameras. The two companies recognized that while the digital photography available in smartphones would disrupt the camera industry, it probably couldn't meet the high-performance needs of the professional segment. They combined the benefits of a raft of analog components such as sensors, light meters, and special lenses with essential digital capabilities such as transmission and storage to create a new breed of hybrid DSLR (digital SLR) cameras that now dominate that market segment.

In the second quarter of 2018, CNN President Jeff Zucker, the same person who once warned that the television business couldn't afford to trade "analog dollars for digital pennies," announced plans to launch a series of tiered subscription offerings for its digital news business.[21] Historically, TV networks treated their digital operations as a recycling engine for content created elsewhere. CNN's new approach is very much a hybrid, one that will give subscribers access to specially curated content on specific topics such as CNN Politics and CNN Money, which are built around CNN's TV network personalities.

Redefining Capabilities

Redefining capabilities can open doors to previously untapped markets. For instance, in Panama, the century-old canal is a legacy player that is leveraging new capability to access new shipping industry segments. Prior to a $5.4 billion expansion that was completed in 2016, the canal could only handle ships of 5,000 twenty-foot equivalent units (TEUs). Now the canal moves ships almost three times that size. The widened canal has brought in tens of millions of additional dollars in tolls to the canal authority because it gives shippers, shipping lines, and ports across the East Coast of the United States faster access to ports across Asia than transit through the Suez Canal, as can be seen in the 23 percent increase in transiting tonnage in 2017. However, the expansion's collateral damage includes write-downs of billions of euros in shipping assets by banks that had financed traditional Panamax vessels.[22]

Stockholm-founded BIMA is leveraging mobile technology in ways that disrupt the insurance industry and drive financial inclusion across the emerging markets. Before mobile phones were popular, accessing these consumers and administering insurance services were prohibitively expensive. Now, however, BIMA sells a range of insurance products through mobile phones. The products can cost as little as 60 cents per day, offer payouts of up to $1,000, and take just a few minutes to sign up. Microinsurance is now available in 16 countries across Africa, Asia, and Latin America.[23]

Unbundling

Unbundling recognizes that many parts of products and services create unnecessary costs. When parts that subtract value are bundled with those that add value, consumers are forced to compromise. Scoot, a low-cost, long-haul airline launched by Singapore Airlines in 2012, shows how a legacy airline can leverage unbundling to defend its business and create growth. Scoot passengers are guaranteed a basic seat. Everything else—better seats, baggage space, food, drinks—comes at an additional price, as is the case with low-cost carriers across the world. By carefully choosing the route structure, Singapore Airlines has effectively managed the disruption that companies such as Air Asia, Lion, Malindo, Cebu, and Indigo have created in the commercial aviation space.

Priceline is a digital startup that leveraged the power of unbundling. Before Priceline appeared, people who wanted to book an airline ticket started with a destination and a timeline and then searched across the universe of airlines using travel agents. Priceline turned the complicated process upside down by asking consumers where they wanted to go, when they wanted to go (with some flexibility), and what price they were willing to pay for that trip—all with the proviso that they would be given a seat from an acceptable set of airlines, but the choice of the airline was up to Priceline, not the consumer. They hawked this offer to airlines until they found one that would agree to that price point given their circumstances. Then they went back to the consumer with an offer specifying dates, times, and other rules of carriage. Through unbundling, Priceline opened up new segments of demand while giving airlines a way to sell excess capacity without cannibalizing their regular channels.[24]

Bundling

If unbundling is good, then bundling must be bad, right? Not necessarily. Bundling assumes that under certain conditions, a one-stop solution offering many products and services creates value for consumers by reducing their costs relative to acquiring each item separately. Ideally, it also improves efficiencies for producers by creating scale and scope economies through a one-stop window for disparate services.

Disney is a legacy player that has used bundling to consolidate its position. Across the world, media production houses have traditionally let cable and satellite operators supply their content to consumers. But largely in response to the growth of Netflix and related startups in the streaming business, Disney announced in August 2017 that it would launch its own series of streaming services that would deliver its entertainment products, including films and sports, direct to consumers—essentially bundling delivery into its content creation services. That move was powered by Disney's acquisition of majority ownership in BAMTech, a company that specializes in streaming video technology, for $1.58 billion.[25]

WeChat, launched in 2011, is a new-world social media company that used bundling to build an active user base of nearly a billion consumers in less than six years. In addition to standard messaging features, WeChat offers other features, all within the app. It has a social feed of friends' updates called Moments. WeChat Pay lets users pay bills, order goods and services, transfer money, and pay in-store. City Services allows booking transportation, making medical appointments, and even paying traffic tickets. WeChat's remarkable viral growth stemmed from its ability to add more and more features, bundled within its app. A WeChat user can spend the whole day on a mobile using this single app.[26]

Ecosystem Expansion

Many innovators and legacy firms can create value by augmenting their ecosystems with new players and capabilities.

Apple is a classic legacy example of the competitive advantage that can be created through an ecosystem. It has built a compelling portfolio of partners, as well as value-added services, that amplify the benefits of its products: phones, tablets, watches, computers, and so on. The ecosystem includes apps that work seamlessly across devices, content of all types, social networks, payment gateways, and productivity tools that leverage the vast trove of data within the ecosystem.

Uber Eats (and versions such as Deliveroo and Food Panda) was born when Uber added new services to the mobility platform ecosystem it had created. The app essentially adds a new set of participants—restaurants and food suppliers—who offer complementary services to people who are already using the platform. Consumers can open the Uber Eats app and browse restaurants in their vicinity for the kinds of food they are interested in at that instant. When they place items in the shopping cart, the app shows them the price and estimated delivery time. If they place orders, the app charges the cards that the consumers have placed on file. The app also lets consumers track the progress of an order, including food prep and delivery via an Uber partner.

Process and Asset Optimization

Processes that are optimized to deliver value can lend an organization a tremendous opportunity to capture value that's there for the taking. Narayana Hrudayalaya (*hrudayalaya* means "heart center" in Sanskrit) is one of the best examples of this. Dr. Devi Shetty, known as the Henry Ford of Heart Surgery, created a highly focused, high-volume, high-quality cardiac surgery hospital in India, exploiting the economies of specialization and related efficiencies.[27] Careful process optimization has led to a system where the average price for a coronary bypass can be 10 times lower than what US Medicare pays, with success rates that are better than the US average.[28] This is the remarkable power of careful process optimization—for attack or defense.

There are many other examples that tell the same story: Southwest Airlines became what is perhaps the most profitable airline in the United States by running its operations like a tightly timed marching band. Zara has created processes that gives it unparalleled speed in the fashion industry. Carefully optimizing processes can lead to a significant competitive advantage for organizations. Many times, these are overlooked options for fortifying the core in defending legacy businesses.

Regulation and Policy

Businesses have never been shy when it comes to exploiting the power of lobbying and regulation. They shouldn't be because those efforts can pay off quite well. Marc Levinson's history of container shipping, *The Box*, provides a fascinating account of the challenges faced by Malcom McLean, inventor of container shipping, which revolutionized the global transport industry. The *Ideal-X*, arguably the world's first container ship, carried 58 containers from Newark to Houston for the same cost as sending just one box by road. But it would take decades for it to revolutionize the industry because lobbying and regulators worked to protect the incumbents.[29]

Ichiro Kawanabe, chairman of the Japanese taxi operator Nihon Kotsu, is familiar with the power of lobbying and regulation to defensively ward off disruption. Taxis are strictly regulated all over the world, but in Japan, those regulations are administered by the national government, rather than local authorities. Ichiro focused on eliminating the ride-hailing apps by cherry-picking their innovations under the cover of regulatory protection. He launched a taxi-sharing service with reduced prices for riders who share the same vehicle.[30] Another innovation is an all-you-can-use service for urbanites willing to forgo their own cars.

The success of the London taxi industry in persuading London's employment tribunal that Uber drivers are not independent contractors is another example of the force of lobbying and regulation in defending against disruption—and buying time.[31]

COMBINATORIAL OPTIONS ARE ESSENTIAL FOR AN ENCOUNTER DEFENSE

The examples we've cited are not an exhaustive collection of possibilities for combinatorial innovation, defense, or Future-Facing Blueprint actions. This is a high-level scan of possibilities. Taken together, they highlight the incredible conventional firepower that can help both incumbents and startups deal with firestorm disruption.

As our IKEA illustration shows, combining multiple firepower elements lets companies create value, competitive advantage, and the ability to deal with disruption head-on. The Phoenix Attitude emerges. Disruption is not something to be feared; it is an opportunity for renewal and transformation. The IKEA story also highlights the fact that the process of renewal and transformation must be staged carefully over time.

The final phase of the Encounter method, the Encounter Breakthrough, focuses on taking the implications of insights from the Extreme Attack and Horizon Defense and using them to set the organization on a renewed course. It is about turning the Radical Ideation of attack and defense into a Future-Facing Blueprint for realistic actions, as we describe in the book's final part.

CHAPTER **12** CHECKLIST

Summary Thoughts

1. Amid all the hype about the disruptive influence of the forces of digital, social, and platforms, it's easy to think that the future could be a place where legacy firms are no longer relevant. This is not true. Leaders should consider using their traditional strengths (such as financial resources or process optimization) in new ways to create value and defense options.

2. Formidable defense opportunities (and sources of new value creation) exist in combinatorial innovation, where contemporary firepower (such as digital and technology) is conjoined with conventional firepower (such as mergers and acquisitions).

3. Scanning the possibilities for combining different forms of firepower is essential for providing options for transformative change and for fortifying the core business to release resources for future major innovation shifts (e.g., combining physical business and digital platforms, taking digital business models and adding physical infrastructure, and optimizing assets and processes).

Reflection

1. Are you scanning how traditional forms are using their conventional weaponry (such as asset optimization or divestments) to release resources for future innovation growth initiatives?

2. Is your leadership team brainstorming ways to combine traditional strengths (such as balance sheet, market position, trust, or reputation) with new technologies, partners, platforms, and ecosystems?

3. Are you planning defense moves (including offensive new strikes) against firestorm disruption, as a phoenix would—using as much available firepower as possible?

PART III

PHOENIX RISING:

Encounter Breakthrough

CHAPTER 13

BLUEPRINT FOR BREAKTHROUGH

I want to ask you a question, and that is:
What is your life's blueprint?
—MARTIN LUTHER KING JR., American
minister and civil rights activist[1]

In Part I, we established the need to switch attitude and conduct the Phoenix Encounter's Completely Opposite Viewpoints Debate, which contemplates a Phoenix-like combustion of the existing organization. Part II described the intense Encounter Battlefield exercise, in which Extreme Attack and Horizon Defense stages employ Radical Ideation, supported by Proactive Scanning for firepower that could present threats or opportunities.

In Part III, we urge leaders to focus on the options set generated from these debates. This includes preparing a Future-Facing Blueprint, with prospective actions based on the attack and defense stage insights, and the revised agenda for delivering a Phoenix Breakthrough. We also describe the all-important role the leader plays in enabling the organizational transformation required to embed the Phoenix Attitude in cultural DNA.

To understand how this works, we look at the Dvorak Finance Corporation (DFC), a company that we worked very closely with in 2018, and see how its Future-Facing Blueprint and embedding are playing out.

PUTTING THE PHOENIX INTO ACTION

Group CEO Halder Thomson offered a brief and candid view of his company:

> DFC began life as a captive internal provider, financing major dealers of DFC's parent company, Dvorak Engineering—a household appliance and farming equipment supplier in Eastern Europe. Leveraging its base in the rural market, a "blue ocean" at the time, DFC gradually diversified into rural housing finance and insurance for the "bottom of the pyramid."[2] The company expanded its services to include financing non-Dvorak-supplied household appliances, farming and construction equipment, and automotive (personal and commercial), for both small and medium-sized businesses. It also provided asset management and loan services for retail customers in the region's tier 2 and 3 rural cities and villages.
>
> By 2018, DFC had a $4 billion market capitalization. The company's key strengths were its relationships with appliance and equipment dealers, its local knowledge of specific rural markets, and its wide reach within countries. DFC aspired to be a leading financial services player in semi-urban and rural parts of the region by 2025, hoping to take its market capitalization to $15 billion. Its long-term goal was to become the gateway to customers in the rural and semi-urban market.
>
> DFC's growth targets were aggressive, and leadership understood that their journey was not going to be easy. Some in the leadership team weren't even sure that DFC could maintain its current performance, given the rapidly changing dynamics in the social and economic landscapes. Recent trade disputes led to an economic downturn, and that, combined with government policy uncertainties, had taken a toll on consumer confidence. Moreover, leadership was aware of the fate of several legacy players in other parts of the world and the dramatic change wrought in the financial services sector by technological innovation. Their concerns, however, were

not shared across the organization. This divide set up the call for the Phoenix Encounter.

A Chinese proverb reminds us of the important lasting impact of personal involvement: "Tell me and I'll forget; show me and I may remember; involve me and I'll understand." DFC brought together 30 leaders from different parts of the business to take part in the Encounter Battlefield exercises. The leaders split into six teams that worked simultaneously and then shared the results of each stage: Groundwork, Attack, and Defense.

Before entering the Battlefield debates, each of the senior executives prepared an initial business analysis and SWOT separately. Everyone then calibrated their views from these, generating a shared set of insights about their business vulnerabilities. This initial exercise stirred a sense of unease among the participants, whose discouragement was evident in the opening plenary before the Battlefield stages of Extreme Attack and Horizon Defense. Opinions expressed included "too inward-looking," "lots of confusing priorities," "past strengths are being overplayed," and "serious lack of innovation." A major discussion about leadership altitudes led to a realization that everyone needed to elevate their thinking from below 50 feet to 50,000 feet.

The teams then began Proactive Scanning sessions that searched for threats and opportunities wrought by technology, digital, platforms, regulation, talent, and emerging markets. To their credit, they went well outside the boundaries of their home business—financial services—and their local region. This was followed by the Extreme Attack phase of the Phoenix Encounter, where particular attention was given to the opposite viewpoints debate rituals of Radical Ideation and the Separation Imperative.

Imagining a Devastating Attack

As we have seen in many other Encounter exercises, the Radical Ideation of the Extreme Attack stage led the Dvorak teams to visualize the complete destruction of DFC by a "Newco" using a portfolio of contemporary firepower. Their imagined scenario unfolded like this:

1. A leading e-commerce platform available for the country (something like an Alibaba, Amazon, or Rakuten) obtains a nonbanking financial service license from the regulator and acquires an insurance company. That company can now provide a suite of financial services, in addition to its vast assortment of mobile-enabled products and services. The explosive diffusion of mobile technology across the country allows Newco to access all parts of the country without incurring the cost of building brick-and-mortar rural infrastructure. The new platform, as a digital native, has a significant strategic advantage over DFC's traditional product focus in its ability to aggregate and analyze data and integrate the latest technology (e.g., artificial intelligence [AI] and machine learning [ML]) with its platform to personalize financial solutions.

2. On another front, Newco encourages a set of activist investors to attack the senior management, board, and other investors of Dvorak Engineering, warning that it makes no sense to have a captive financial services arm and that the capital tied up in that arm could earn a much better return on investment in other parts of Dvorak Engineering.

3. One of the leading local private sector banks, one with a significantly lower cost of capital than Dvorak Finance, decides to enter the financing and insurance business in rural markets in partnership with the platform. It begins with a price war and then adds cobundled and mobile-enabled banking products.

4. Newco develops a new suite of products, including whole-of-life financing support, to take care of different needs, including microfinance loans tailored to different stages of careers for different members of the same family and dynamically available, revolving-reward facilities based on actual, data-based loan performances (such as early payments).

5. Newco aggressively poaches the most talented younger generation of data-savvy Dvorak employees—essential workers who had been held back by senior management—and offers them equity involvement in the new venture.

As the participants gathered in the plenary room at the end of the Extreme Attack stage of the Encounter and reviewed their experience, they realized that their sense of unease about the state of DFC's business at the start of the Encounter had led, in the Attack phase, to the alarming realization that while Newco was fictional, much of it could be a reality in a very short period of time.

The combination of macro forces shaping the economy (rapid expansion of literacy and education, improved agricultural productivity, increased rural income and consumption, and seamlessly mobile-enabled economies) and Newco's capabilities meant that many of the current pain points for DFC's stakeholders (consumers, employees, and partners) would actually be relieved by Newco's accelerated growth, increased value creation, lower costs, and better risk management.

> Piotr Belicz, the CEO of DFC's loan subsidiary, crystallized this fear as he spoke to a somber room. "Newco has so many things that we do not have," he said. "Do we realize that Newco can do many things that we cannot do? In fact, it can do many things that we have not even imagined before."

Ideating Their Horizon Defense

Piotr had effectively articulated the burning platform for the Dvorak team. The DFC teams were now raring to go to the next stage of the Phoenix Encounter: defense. They imagined all the elements of this Extreme Attack playing out, and they brainstormed ideas for their Horizon Defense, aided by further scanning the types of combinatorial defense maneuvers highlighted in Chapter 12. They made a list of immediate actions: prioritize their "Hot List" of prospective options, subject these to detailed data analysis, and stress-test the ideas with other strategy tools. Then they sketched out their defense ideas over time horizons—short term, medium term, and long term. Three hours later, their high-level plan looked like this:

1. Develop an all-encompassing vision captured in the call to arms, "Your Lifetime Money Partner—Family, Farm, and

Future." Transform DFC to a one-stop shop for all personal/business financial services requirements of a rural household—region-wide, alongside targeted and adjacent international expansion.

2. Integrate products with life-cycle financing enabled by mobility and connectivity. Create a new value proposition that offers personalized and solutions-based lifestyle and life-cycle financing that includes combination "digital-physical" offerings. These would leverage their current local physical distributor presence with extended and maximized digital mobility and would differentiate them from the competition.

3. Create an enterprise-wide, non-siloed, seamless customer experience, from needs to sales to services, entirely digitized support operations, and effective communication in all directions.

4. Reexamine aspects of the current go-to-market model and consider what major changes will be needed for the renewed customer value proposition. For example: Is there a need for appliance and equipment dealers? If yes, what should describe the dealer's new value propositions for the consumer?

5. Build a high-level digital infrastructure—cloud, big data, data processing, external data sources, and so on—and find a partner to accelerate this.

6. Evaluate offering platform accessibility combined with a comprehensive ecosystem of complementary business partners in other products and services (such as repair and maintenance).

7. Recruit a young, motivated workforce with targeted employee skills (app development, computer science, data science, etc.).

8. Strive for a forward-looking, dynamic, stakeholder-centric, and agile organizational culture with a permanent cell for futuristic technology and innovation incubation.

Selis Techier, team colleague in charge of marketing, summed up the promise of their defense vision:

> This could be a truly exciting and motivating prospectus for a high-growth business ahead and a great call to purpose for the talent we will need.

Getting to Their Future-Facing Blueprint

Enlightened and emboldened by their attack and defense ideas, the team revisited their blueprint, this time with a future-facing view that spans all the altitudes: 50,000 feet, 50 feet, and 5 feet. Their objective was the renewal of their future value propositions and strengths from the perspective of their stakeholders, including customers, employees, partners, investors, regulators, and local communities. Soul-searching by the senior leadership team led to a series of possible pilot projects that spanned the horizon of defense—immediate, short term, medium term, and long term.

Their Future-Facing Blueprint initiatives included a long-term view of developing a platform-based business as a single point of contact for customers' total financial needs across the life cycle. These also included offering customized solutions and digitally personalized service by harnessing new data analytics capabilities, while leveraging the existing partner network and personal touch points. This would be their "digital-physical" business model. In the immediate and short terms, they would run a pilot in one region of Slovakia. To make that pilot feasible and the future full-scale platform viable, they would need a series of staged projects with short- to medium-term horizons.

1. Go beyond customer centricity.

   • Map the current customer activity cycle across the funnel (see Chapter 7) and remap it in a fully digitized, more mobile way. Build a dynamic customer insights analytic engine that maps actions to outcomes and benchmarks and can make recommendations that include new offerings and service modes.

2. Exploit alternate ways to score credit.

   - Develop the capability to allow for personalized products and services in the unique Eastern European rural lifestyle. Create a new data bank of customer characteristics (leveraging private and public data records and marrying it with internal data). Build a new scoring system to enhance consumers' financial and social well-being. Reduce credit assessment costs and time.

3. Attack the legacy assumptions and recreate products, services, and systems to fulfill the new value proposition.

   - Question the dominant industry view that systematic investment plans (e.g., in actively managed equity and bond funds) should be the default option for consumers hoping to accumulate financial wealth. Does this make sense in a world of automation (e.g., robo-wealth managers) and alternative investments?
   - Fortify the core as urgently as possible by moving from manual to automated systems for digital data input, processing, and recommendations that are tailored to client needs. Progressively deploy artificial intelligence (AI) and analytics-driven approaches with credible third-party digital solution providers as partners.

4. Break up all silos and develop cross-selling and cross-data capabilities.

   - Internalize learnings from the customer centricity project across the organization.
   - Consider implications for new products in the medium term (e.g., microinsurance, animal stock loans, crop and harvesting loans).
   - Evaluate using digital data capabilities to map geospatial data, weather data, commodity markets data, and news/entertainment data to create new value-added services for the expanded client base.
   - Consider spinning off the data unit into a separate entity with an alternative capital structure in the long term.

DFC leaders had a long discussion to ensure that these would not be one-off projects. They determined that, in order to embed a continuous innovation culture in the organization, the company would need an internal innovation unit. This internal unit would foster the Phoenix Attitude within the organization and encourage business units to initiate pilot projects and create the capability to reinvent themselves in ways that would ward off future firestorms.

The Dvorak team members decided to designate other ideas generated in their Horizon Defense options list as priorities for further investigation, quantitative analysis, and business case development. These included new microfinance products, the potential to crowdfund a series of rural-based social initiatives linked to the towns and villages of the customer base, and the potential to either acquire or develop a digital bank with integrated services on the platform.

Placing these thoughts in the context of the strategic leadership thinking that permeated this organization reveals much about the company. To many outsiders, few of the first-round projects would be radically innovative. But as CFO Gayle Rickard said:

> Our focus has always been on the trenches: How do we lower our costs? How do we push our foot soldiers to deliver more? It has always been the same, year in and year out. The Encounter pushed us to think differently, consider new possibilities, new contingencies, and new agendas—to stop focusing on the obvious and think about fast-riding the curves in the road ahead. The Encounter has made what we should be doing blindingly obvious.

INNOVATION AND FORTIFICATION— HAND IN HAND

The DFC example clearly lays out the activities beyond the Battlefield phase of the Phoenix Encounter. First, participants distill the Horizon Defense conversation into a series of action items for investigation across short-, medium-, and long-term time horizons. We also ask them to sketch their expectations of high-level outcomes, if these action items are successfully implemented. You can see this in the list created by the DFC teams earlier in the chapter.

Participants update their Encounter Journal with a Future-Facing Blueprint that incorporates insights and their implications for strategic leadership and organizational priorities that work across all the altitudes—50,000 feet, 50 feet, and 5 feet. Next, they identify the actions they must take (e.g., pilots, further analysis, and resource mapping) to make the priorities realities. The checklists, templates, and questionnaires that we use with Encounter participants in the post-Battlefield phase are available in our online resources at www.phoenixencountermethod.com.

Ideally, an Encounter Blueprint will hold many possibilities for innovation, and participants should carefully consider every one. This becomes increasingly important as the shelf life of competitive advantages and competencies shrinks. Leaders must be prepared to manage a multidirectional portfolio of innovation initiatives, including those that are experimental, disruptive, nondisruptive, incremental, reverse, and resuscitative. Leaders must also understand that these different innovation approaches come with varying degrees of risk, time investment, cost of developing, prototyping, and reward. The first three are more associated with contemporary firepower and the other three with conventional firepower. All require creativity, commitment, resources, and focus. They also require a leader with the foresight to spot turbulence ahead and the equanimity to ride out the waves, learn along the way, and navigate to the new front.[3]

A Spectrum of Innovation Approaches in Business Practice

- **Experimental Innovation.** Firms that embrace design thinking, such as the Chinese electronics manufacturer Xiaomi, produce products in small batches and then make a series of rapid changes to the product based on consumer feedback. This type of innovation requires sufficient organizational agility to allow for an unimpeded flow of information, rapid learning, and quick response.[4]

- **Disruptive Innovation.** Some innovations are so disruptive that they make existing products, firms, industries, and business models obsolete. WhatsApp has done this, to the detriment of SMS and traditional telephony. Though this is a favorite approach of new entrants, disruptive innovation is often hard for incumbent firms to embrace because it can cannibalize existing products or business units. This conflict is the famous "Innovator's Dilemma."[5]
- **Nondisruptive Innovation.** This approach emphasizes non-disruptive creativity. It exploits the potential for creating new markets where none existed. This innovation does not lead to disruption or destruction. It generates new demand, as with the launch of microinsurance by firms such as BIMA, the life coaching industry, and even the development of Viagra.[6]
- **Incremental Innovation.** Japanese automakers such as Toyota push the cost-quality frontier using streamlined business processes such as lean manufacturing and Six Sigma. This type of innovation is often bottom up, as in-line managers are incentivized and empowered to launch productivity improvement initiatives on a continual basis.[7]
- **Reverse Innovation.** Firms like Tata, Nestle, and GE have innovated in emerging markets in ways that cater to needs in a resource-constrained environment. Then they extrapolated those innovations into developed markets.[8]
- **Resuscitation Innovation.** This is the kind of emergency innovation that Cisco adopted when its telecom offerings failed to gain traction in India. Instead of exiting this potential bonanza market, the local team switched from equipment sales to a service model. Ten years later, Cisco had nearly 100 percent market share in India. Though an extreme path, resuscitation innovation generally faces little stakeholder resistance because it is practiced when the firm is in a do-or-die situation, including an extreme crisis that necessitates innovation solutions. Still, it may face resource and capability constraints.[9]

REWARDS FROM EMBEDDING

Ultimately, Piotr, Selis, Gayle, and the other members of the Dvorak teams experienced a phenomenon that we have seen hundreds of times following the Encounter Battlefield debates. They felt a heightened sense of urgency that major change is not only required but overdue, and they understood that "Altitude Sickness" is the hidden disease holding everyone back. With a revised blueprint, clarity on strategic intent, and a list of strategic and business model priorities or actions in hand, they looked forward to the work required to get things underway, which has been accelerated during the COVID-19 pandemic. That work included:

- Engaging in serious Encounter-based discussions with the most senior leaders and decision-makers in the parent organization, including conscripting these people into altitude and attitude assessment, Proactive Scanning, and bringing them into Phoenix Encounter Battlefield debates.

- Creating a bench of project leaders and teams to identify pilots and experiments and start building the case for them. Embracing the idea of failing fast, which is essential for experimental innovation.

- Rebuilding the KPIs to fit the remote working reality: appraisals, productivity, engagement. Leverage the moment to instill a more data- and process-driven culture.

- Challenging the boundaries of thinking, the COVID-19 situation has heightened the need for discussion on dynamic innovation approaches (e.g., partnerships and customer co-production), as well as strategic debate that promotes cross-altitude thinking and opposite viewpoints.

- Encouraging deep reflection on the personal leadership development agenda and objectives needed to lead the transformative change that is a Phoenix Breakthrough—in perpetuity.

From our perspective, DFC's to-do list looked very promising and also very familiar. Many leaders' Encounter lists look a lot like theirs, and that similarity is unsurprising. After all, the forces threatening organizations are very similar, and the firepower options with which they have familiarized themselves are practically identical. Although the context-specific solutions devised by leaders are necessarily very different, the road to those solutions has been the same: the revelatory and often uncomfortable path of a Phoenix Encounter.

The other DFC team realization (which we have also seen many times before) is that delivering on the promise of the Phoenix Breakthrough involves working toward a culture that seeks and embeds change as a continuous process across the organization. Delivering the Phoenix Breakthrough in legacy organizations requires focus on two things: fortifying the core of the business and identifying the actors, actions, and activities that will enable its transformation into a future-ready organization. Embedding that into the organizational fabric as leaders is the focus of our next chapter.

CHAPTER **13** CHECKLIST

Summary Thoughts

1. Deriving a Future-Facing Encounter Blueprint requires the leadership and Encounter team to systematically move from initial battlefield options stocktaking, through Battlefield Attack and Defense stages, to consolidating their new ideas into a blueprint of actions and priorities.

2. The Future-Facing Blueprint will include a fully revised future value proposition for stakeholders, an updated SWOT (contrasting with the original SWOT) that emphasizes the strengths needed for the future (set against growth, cost, and risk criteria) and the gaps in the present, and a description of the transformed business model and the ways value will be created and captured.

3. The Future-Facing Blueprint documents the Phoenix Breakthrough plan and includes revised future strategic leadership and organizational priorities, immediate actions (such as board engagement, analysis, and pilots), and time horizon action items (short term, medium term, and long term) for exploration or execution.

Reflection

1. Does your strategic debate and dialogue consider questions related to the advantages of attackers like Newco, with unconstrained firepower?

2. Do you have a blueprint with a future-facing view of your strategic priorities, business model, value proposition, strengths, value creation, and capture, as well as approaches to innovation?

3. What changes will you and your team need to make in the way you will lead in the future as a Phoenix champion of developing and executing innovation?

XIV PHOENIX LEADERS: DREAMERS & DOERS

KILLS its OWN BUSINESS ...and Gives it REBIRTH

50,000ft

50 ft

5ft

RISE above the DAY to DAY THINK & DEBATE DIFFERENTLY about the FUTURE

DREAMER and DOER

PRIORITIZE EXECUTION

ORGANIZATION needs

LEARN from FAILURE in a SAFE ENVIRONMENT

DREAMERS (EXPLORERS)   +   DOERS (EXPLOITERS)

NO ALTITUDE SICKNESS

COLLABORATING to ACHIEVE TRANSFORMATION and FORTIFY the CORE

PHOENIX LEADERS: DREAMERS AND DOERS

Dreams are extremely important.
You can't do it unless you imagine it.
—GEORGE LUCAS, American film director and producer

Walt Disney, remembered as one of the most creative leaders of the twentieth century, was also admired for his ability to make things happen. "The way to get started," he famously said, "is to quit talking and begin doing."[1]

Creative imagination like Disney's is film producers' stock in trade. It is not quite so common in operational executives, who are generally very good at getting things done. The ideal leader, of course, possesses both imagination and the ability to execute. For that reason, these two attributes play critical roles in the Phoenix Encounter method, which elicits a Completely Opposite Viewpoints Debate that focuses on dreaming and doing. The powerful dynamic aims to unlock the Phoenix Attitude—the "aha" moment when the leader grasps the possibilities and strategic options afforded by the opportunities of Radical Ideation and wholesale renewal.

The Phoenix leader is unusual in that she or he is both a Dreamer and a Doer, someone who is not trapped in the separate worlds of imagineering or engineering, but capable of combining both. As if maintaining that perspective is not enough of a challenge, it is that leader's job to create a coterie of Dreamers and Doers. That requires some distinct approaches in leadership development.

IN PURSUIT OF THE PHOENIX LEADER EVERYWHERE

Embedding the Phoenix spirit of renewal within an organization is not a trivial undertaking, and it is particularly difficult for legacy organizations. That's because legacy organizations generally maintain two competing considerations: (1) they must ensure that legacy business continues to perform (which is why fortifying the core must be part of their Future-Facing Blueprint) and (2) they must realize the agenda for major renewal and innovation. These competing objectives map into two very different sets of capabilities:

- Enabling business transformation and innovation requires leader managers who are skilled at "exploration." These are the Dreamers—people who are comfortably at home with scanning, experimentation, risk-taking, discovery, and curiosity.

- Enabling business performance at scale and scope requires leader managers who are skilled at "exploitation." These are the Doers. Their home turf is a land of continuous improvements, operational efficiencies, and disciplined execution.

These two capability sets thrive in different environments. For example, the Doers will perform very well in what Robin Hogarth describes in his 2001 book, *Educating Intuition*, as "kind" learning environments. Patterns repeat over and over, feedback is accurate, and learning can be rapid. On the other hand, Dreamers would work very well in Hogarth's "wicked" learning environments, where rules of the game are unclear or incomplete; there may or may not be repetitive patterns, and they may not be obvious; and feedback is often delayed, inaccurate, or both.

Dreamer and Doer capabilities are not mutually exclusive, of course, and we have found that they coexist, to some extent, in every leader. Our classification is based on individual inclinations toward being more of one rather than more of the other. Phoenix leaders, unburdened by Altitude Sickness, more easily find the "sweet spot" that balances both capabilities. They apply both their leadership art and management skills. They do not engage in the kind of shallow dreaming that leads companies to change their names to "Blockchain Inc."; they do not bury their heads in the existing business. They are bigger than that. As Jim Hackett, CEO of Ford Motor Company, said, "Corporations tend to reward actions over thinking, but the truth is, you'll find the companies that didn't do the deep thinking and acted quickly have to redo things." This thinking is also echoed by David Epstein in his book *Range,* where he emphasizes the critical nature of diversity of experiences and thinking in creating the right balance of what we describe as Doers and Dreamers.[2]

The capabilities of a Dreamer and Doer happen to map very neatly into the leadership altitudes discussed in Chapter 3. The 50,000-foot thinkers are the Dreamers and explorers. The 50-foot thinkers are the Doers and exploiters. We have found that both Dreamers and Doers need the profound self-awareness of 5-foot thinking, and they need a personal leadership development agenda to match.

As James March's seminal article on organizational learning pointed out, leaders at legacy organizations must be extremely sensitive to the fact that the traditional business practices prioritize exploitation at the expense of exploration, with the result that they are set up for short-term success and at serious risk of long-term failure.[3] This has been well known for decades, but curiously, it is still a problem today. We believe that the Phoenix Encounter, which presents a systematic method for leaders to grapple with this challenge, can help solve the problem.

Leaders with a Phoenix Attitude build organizations that encourage Doers and Dreamers to focus on what they do best while continually exchanging ideas (the opposite debate). This is one reason why involving both Dreamers and Doers in the Encounter Battlefield exercise produces tangible results. Each type has an opportunity to practice the other's style of thinking throughout the Encounter process.

For me, especially, when you were challenging us to get our thinking a lot higher, my initial response was, "I can't do that, you know; that's complete nonsense." That's just too far out. I can't do anything with that because straight away, I'm thinking "task." And, I'm thinking 50 feet. But, until the Encounter took us there and forced us to think that way, and talk that way, and then I had that light bulb moment where one of our shareholders could do this to us very soon if they wanted to. It became real all of a sudden . . . it wasn't BS. And then I started taking it a lot more seriously and found myself engaging the what-if game as the primary way to think.

—Mark Sugden, CEO, High End Retail,
New Zealand

When left to themselves, Doers and Dreamers often have fundamentally opposite default positions, and each can fail to appreciate what the other brings to the table. The Doers are brilliant at leveraging the conventional firepower of management (e.g., strategic planning, marketing, finance, operations, and human resources) to constantly improve the core of the business over time. The Dreamers, on the other hand, are brilliant at exploring the answers to questions such as: Isn't there a way to do things better? What is new? What are the implications of "new" for customers, products, services, solutions, ecosystems, and so on? If Doers represent the sharp, hardworking managers who have carefully worked their way up, then Dreamers invoke the crucial strengths of the creator, entrepreneur, and adventurer—talents needed to ignite and forge innovation or transformation.

In his book *Loonshots*, Safi Bahcall illustrates the power that comes from getting the combination of "doing" and "dreaming" right, as seen in the role played by Vannevar Bush during World War II.[4] Bush, then the leader of the Office of Scientific Research and Development (OSRD), was charged with revitalizing the Allied military effort that ultimately contributed to victory. The military equivalent of the Doers, the generals and the officers, Bahcall writes, ". . . made it utterly clear that the scientists or engineers employed in these laboratories were a lower caste of society." Their path to victory called for producing more of the same: more planes, more ships, and more guns, all of which replicated the weaponry already in use. Bush, along with Winston Churchill and others who had watched with alarm the growing technology gap between the Allies and Germany, had a bigger idea.

Bush agreed with the generals that the Allies needed to be good in the trenches, but he also believed they needed to be good at giving the people in the trenches more effective tools. He created a structure that allowed the people in each group, the Doer generals and the Dreamer scientists, to feed off each other. To describe that accomplishment, Bahcall uses the metaphor of water at 32° Fahrenheit. Below that temperature, he tells us, water freezes into ice. Above that temperature, ice melts into water. At 32°F, ice and water coexist. The two sets of molecules circle back and forth in a dynamic equilibrium—molecules in ice patches melt into adjacent liquid water pools, just as molecules of water swimming by an ice patch lock onto them and freeze.

Bush built a structured environment that supported this kind of equilibrium, a key deliverable for any leader in any company in any era. As Bush recalls, "I made no technical contribution whatever to the war effort. Not a single technical idea of mine amounted to shucks. At times I have been called an atomic scientist. It would be fully as accurate to call me a child psychologist." It's interesting to note that Bush's description of his role reveals two other important elements in a leader's ability to lead his or her organization to a Phoenix Breakthrough: self-awareness and humility.

> My industry is very high margin, and we have a very high product share. So for me, it's very difficult to think about very different things. It's difficult to get away from success. Quite frankly I'm a go-getter to get things done. Dreaming is for our design department. My Encounter showed I am dead wrong, when just six new ideas killed me within a year.
>
> —Charleston Crane, CEO, Specialty Cosmetics

One particularly vivid illustration of the equal importance of Doers and Dreamers can be found in the evolution of Steve Jobs's mindset when he was at the helm of Apple. Before his first stint at Apple ended with his forced exit in 1985, Jobs exemplified the worst traits of the know-it-all leader. He lionized those who worked on the next generation of Apple products as the "artists" or "pirates" while dismissing those who worked on the legacy Apple II franchise as "Regular Navy," or worse, "bozos." As Walter Isaacson writes in his biography of Jobs, "Steve Jobs had a tendency to see things in a binary way. A person was either a hero or a bozo, a product was either amazing or shit."[5]

The Jobs who returned to Apple 12 years after his dismissal was a different leader. He had learned how critical it was for Apple to nurture both the Dreamers (Jony Ive and his artists) and the Doers (Tim Cook and his army). Isaacson's book includes a Jobs quote that captures our embedding idea perfectly: "I discovered that the best innovation is sometimes the company, the way you organize."

During the first peak of the coronavirus pandemic, examples of innovative changes abounded. For example, with placards and slogans like "May Day, ho, ho, billionaires have to go," it looked like a typical picket line protest. But it was very different. For one thing, the protesters followed safe distancing procedures prescribed for social interactions in the time of COVID-19. More interestingly, the new age labor coalitions like Gig Workers Collective and Rideshare Drivers United had reimagined collective action. They now used Facebook to create awareness, Telegram to communicate, and Slack to organize. They had ideated new forms of work stoppages, such as synchronized shutdowns of their work apps and refusals to accept gigs. In the pandemic times, when companies that did the right things with regard to social issues like employee welfare fared better in the stock markets, the Dreamer and Doer leaders of the new age labor collectives were onto something powerful.[6]

LIVING THE PHOENIX

The transformation of any enterprise is a Herculean task. Our experience suggests that one critical requirement for those leading a transformation is the ability to rally the rank and file around the Phoenix Breakthrough vision, so that everyone in the enterprise owns the change agenda. That transformation is aided by the personal leadership attributes mentioned in Chapter 4's Table 4.1:

* **Mindsets.** Decisive future-facing thinking and action across different leadership altitudes

* **Habits.** Prioritized renewal-seeking practices built on scanning, stakeholder centricity, and Completely Opposite Viewpoints Debate

* **Leadership Behaviors.** Future-embracing leadership development and capabilities with self-awareness and humility

The Phoenix leader makes certain that the organization has what it needs in terms of people who can (1) deliver sustained excellence at the core and (2) generate the options menu and nurture the Breakthrough innovations for organizational transformation. The Phoenix leader manages the Dreamers and Doers in ways that make sense, given their characteristics and context, while ensuring that each side supports and nurtures the other.

The right leadership attitude is a prerequisite to achieving the Phoenix Encounter's Breakthrough and embedding the Phoenix Attitude. This is supported by ongoing work by our INSEAD colleagues Phanish Puranam and Vibha Gaba and their coauthor, Julien Clement.[7] Using an agent-based simulation model, they have demonstrated that organizational change is a complex phenomenon involving beliefs, not just behaviors. Their work reinforces our conviction that organizational change happens when mindsets change. Rarely is it the outcome of process and project management.

The success of some legacy organization transformations, notably Microsoft, Disney, Unilever, Apple, and DBS, reminds us that it can be done, and very often it can be done by the people within the organization. There is no need for mass culling or wholesale hiring.[8] Leaders like Satya Nadella at Microsoft, Paul Polman at Unilever, Piyush Gupta at DBS, and Robert Iger at Disney, as well as such icons as Theodore Vail, the chairman of AT&T who created Bell Labs, and Steve Jobs in his second stint at Apple, model the kind of Phoenix Attitude characteristics that enable legacy firms to create their Phoenix Breakthrough.

MAKING THE PHOENIX STICK

Creating the Phoenix Attitude within the leader is essential, but it is just the beginning of essential actions. Long-term transformation requires leaders to adopt robust organizational change management strategies and actions over time. These are well known, if not always well applied. They include developing a shared sense of purpose and revitalized culture, effective change communication and engagement, fair process, fostering and empowering change champions, reinforcing and rewarding change behaviors, seeking early wins, and role-modeling leadership.[9]

Many activities can help embed change.[10] Two particularly important activities are nurturing the Phoenix Attitude by helping Dreamers and Doers break out of Altitude Sickness and the use of Phoenix Encounter exercises and tools (especially the Battlefield Attack and Defense and Proactive Scanning) discussed in Chapters 3 and 5. The benefits of those actions include:

- Building a wider appreciation of the individual and organizational challenges needed for dramatic transformation

- Instilling a recognition of the need for all parts of the organization to work together to think about radical moves and design and implement change

- Embedding the Breakthrough vision of change across the organization and building confidence that the organization can be as nimble and capable as any disruptor

Leaders can also help teams curate the list of possible strategic options generated from the Encounter's Extreme Attack, Horizon Defense, and Future-Facing Blueprint discussions, and they can articulate key tasks and actions critical to moving the strategic options forward. For example, they can ask what should be in the portfolio of pilot experiments for disruptive change. This leads to constructive debate about which projects should be on the shortlist of ideas that must be subjected to rigorous research and analysis. Note that these don't often correlate with the pet projects of the senior leadership team, but they are the projects that, if successful, will make the business stronger, create the Phoenix Breakthrough within the organization, and excite stakeholders about the future.

This debate often prompts further reflection on potential pilot projects that leadership have ignored. What have activists outside the company been saying? What are the real, on-the-ground customer viewpoints? Have good ideas been discarded because they didn't match the old business interests? Are current business projects wrongly prioritized, ordered, or timed?[11]

When we discuss this in encounter debriefs, we emphasize that the organization likely needs a broad portfolio of projects rather than a discrete set. This notion emerges in part from lessons from the venture capital (VC) world. Unlike the traditional bell curve of returns in a financial portfolio, pilot VC experience is more like a power-law distribution. Research shows that 65 percent of the pilots in a typical VC's portfolio lose money, 25 percent provide a modest return, and only about 10 percent are big hits. The solution calls for trying a lot of things, but trying them cheaply, and using the tools of discovery and validation to learn which bets will be successful, all of which must be done at speed. This means embracing the practice of "learning from failure," the ideas of "fail fast" and "celebrate failure." As Ram points out in his 2019 book on Amazon, that extremely successful company had at least 18 failures during 25 years—all abandoned, but all learning opportunities.[12]

There are obviously significant organizational issues for firms that let Dreamers flourish that leaders need to consider. For example, how might a leader convince Dreamers to stay in the firm, or share their ideas, rather than leaving for a startup? What might the reward, recognition, access to scalability, resources, customers, and partner approaches look like as incentives to stay? How is the culture evolving for learning from rather than punishing Dreamers' innovation failure?[13]

We also suggest that leaders consider some very practical issues, such as who should be involved in pilot projects and what leadership and resources they should have.

Pilot Project Leadership and Resources Checklist

1. People with an exploration focus who are attracted to ambiguity, are comfortable dealing with the unknown, love to experiment, and have a growth mindset. They demonstrate learning and growth activities outside of work as well (e.g., hobbies and passions). The pilot leader must role-model the Phoenix Attitude.

2. Talent who are different from traditionally assessed high-potential employees—those who have been profiled high potential because they have delivered results in a world of known risks.

3. Volunteers who can demonstrate their ability to make a difference for themselves and the organization. Ask for people; don't mandate participation in innovation teams.

4. Project sponsors who make it psychologically safe to try. Failure is the norm; the journey and learning velocity are what matters. Leaders should evaluate the project team outcomes and process, not the individuals. Let the team members, including their project team leader, evaluate one another and share this with the project sponsor. As Remo Ruffini, chair of the revamped luxury brand Moncler, said of his first leadership lesson: "While leading a team, it is crucial to generate energy around a project and persuade and engage without just imposing a decision."[14]

Leaders should resource this team as though it were a standalone entity, yet require the team to show evidence at each stage of development that validates the requests for the next stage of commitment. This must be data-driven.

ROLE MODELING

We are often asked to name organizations that organically discovered their Breakthrough because their leaders have the Phoenix Attitude. Two examples come immediately to mind. One is local to most of the authors—DBS (Development Bank of Singapore)—and another literally on the other side of the Earth—Disney.

DBS was way ahead of its peers in recognizing the disruptive force of technology and digitalization. It embarked on its Phoenix journey long before many of the larger and better-known banks in the world woke up to the same realization. Much has been written about this journey, largely because Euromoney awarded DBS, with its 20,000-plus employees and Singapore headquarters, the title of world's best digital bank in 2016.

Many of the points we highlighted earlier in the chapter can be seen in the transformational journey at DBS. The bank moved away from designing projects to giving employees the freedom to operate as a platform. It looked at what outcomes the platform could deliver to figure out how to fund it and then let it develop organically—this let DBS practice agility at scale. DBS took the time to understand the implications of pilot projects for organizational constructs, carefully considering how the different parts of the organization should work; how it should build the teams for these different parts; how those parts should interact; and how DBS should build and leverage technology to create systems that are scalable, elastic, and set for experimentation. Finally, it thought about how to automate everything from testing to deployment to accelerate the process of innovation across the length and breadth of the business. The company, for example, developed a powerful artificial intelligence–powered recruiting tool called JIM, for Jobs Intelligence Maestro.[15]

The results have been remarkable. In 2017, DBS launched Digibank in India, an entirely mobile-centric banking service with no branches that can be replicated across geographies. The CFO reported in the 2018 annual report highlights that "return on equity in 2018 is four percentage points better today than it was in 2007 when interest rates were twice the level today and capital requirements were less stringent." Perhaps most important, DBS recognized that its future competition may not come from its traditional banking sector competitors, but from firms like Alibaba and Amazon. DBS preempted this competition and created its own marketplace to handle transactions around property, automobiles, travel, and retail electricity.

Disney had a CEO who was one of the first Phoenix leaders to realize that the grounds were shifting under the media and entertainment industry. As Iger notes in his book *The Ride of a Lifetime*, the decision to disrupt businesses that are still working but whose future is in question requires courage. It also requires the leader to be present as routines and priorities shift, jobs change, and responsibilities are reallocated.[16]

Iger had recognized that Apple's "Rip. Mix. Burn." campaign was not just a threat to the music business; it could easily spread to the television and movie industry as well.[17] While the rest of the industry operated out of fear, Iger marched boldly down the less-traveled road. His pitch to the Disney board for appointment to the CEO position was made of three simple points: (1) devote most of Disney's time and capital to create the highest quality content, (2) foresee technology as an opportunity, not a threat, and leverage technology to enable creation of highest quality content and reach consumers in more modern and relevant ways, and (3) become a global company, with particular attention given to the world's most populous markets, such as China and India.[18]

One of Disney's most significant early moves was the acquisition of Pixar in 2006. With that deal, Disney acquired a lot more than just the standard bearer for inventive animated filmmaking. It also got John Lasseter, Pixar's chief creative officer, and Ed Catmull, its chief technical officer. The duo had helped create a culture at Pixar that seamlessly melded the creative with the technical, enabling the Dreamers and Doers.[19] In Iger's words: "This Yin and Yang was the soul of Pixar. Everything flowed from it."

The subsequent acquisition of Marvel and Star Wars consolidated the creative horsepower at Disney and set the stage for the next phase of transformation. Could Disney find the technology to deal with disruption created by new modes of content distribution exemplified by Netflix? Did it have the wherewithal to cannibalize its still-profitable traditional content distribution businesses to build the new model? Yes, it did.

Instead of building a whole new tech platform, in 2016 the company acquired BAMTech, which Major League Baseball had used to stream baseball games via an online service. In 2017, Disney announced plans to launch two streaming services, one for ESPN and the other for Disney. In November 2019, its launch of Disney+ at $6.99/month netted 10 million subscribers within 24 hours.[20]

Iger travelled constantly across the globe, communicating his thinking, responding to concerns, and demonstrating sensitivity to pressures felt across the organization. He created a new incentive structure to reward people for their work, one that did not penalize them for business erosion caused by self-inflicted disruption. Instead of letting the board award compensation based on existing business results, he determined compensation based on how much people contributed to the new strategy. Though this was necessarily subjective, as early results were not easily measured, it helped create a common shared agenda of driving transformation across the organization.

The success of Disney's business reinvention may be best seen in Rupert Murdoch's 2019 decision to sell 21st Century Fox to Disney for $71 billion. Murdoch believed the only way to respond to the disruption created by the new tech companies was to build scale, and he had concluded that Fox didn't have scale. Disney did. In the end, Disney acquired the three elements for success: content, technology, and global reach. Disney's Phoenix journey during the past 15 years led to its 2019 ranking as the world's largest media company.

The stories of DBS and Disney remind us that legacy firms can fight back if they have the will and Phoenix leadership. They must provide the will; the Phoenix Encounter method provides a way forward for any leader and any organization. Let's be clear. COVID-19 has affected both DBS and Disney, like everyone else. But thanks to their Phoenix thinking, they have done better than their peers in market performance and preparation for recovery.

CHAPTER **14** CHECKLIST

Summary Thoughts

1. The Phoenix leader is a Dreamer and a Doer, able to rise above the day-to-day and to think differently and debate differently about the future yet prioritize execution. Their Phoenix Attitude allows them to contemplate how they would kill their own business and give it rebirth—this is a leader who does not have Altitude Sickness.

2. Organizations need both Dreamers (explorers) and Doers (exploiters) working collaboratively to combine their contributions to achieve transformation and fortify the core. The environment must be psychologically safe and enable learning from failure.

3. Phoenix-like transformation is a Herculean task but is both imaginable and doable. The Encounter method systematizes this and enables everyone to engage—with a forward-facing view and Phoenix Attitude.

Reflection

1. Are you role-modeling the Phoenix leader—dreaming and doing? Where are you focusing in personal leadership development to strengthen this and hone your Phoenix Attitude?

2. Have you consciously worked to create an environment, structure, and systems where Doers and Dreamers can coexist and leverage one another's talents and complements?

3. What ways are you planning to stress-test, pilot, and implement your Phoenix Breakthrough ideas? What do you want these to secure immediately and in the short term, medium term, and long term? In light of seizing opportunities and confronting challenges in the post-COVID-19-crisis period, what should be your Phoenix Breakthrough moves?

XV CONCLUSION: the PHOENIX RISES

in HINDSIGHT   Switch your ATTITUDE

in FORESIGHT

Fly across ALTITUDES   in PERSON

STRATEGIC
OPERATIONAL
PERSONAL

1 ENCOUNTER GROUNDWORK   PHOENIX SEEKING

PHOENIX RISING

3 ENCOUNTER BREAKTHROUGH

2 ENCOUNTER BATTLEFIELD

○ EXTREME ATTACK

PHOENIX BURNING

○ HORIZON DEFENSE

PERCEIVING a THREAT   BRIDGE the GAP   DOING SOMETHING about it

LEAD like your BUSINESS is on FIRE!
...and PRACTICE REGULARLY!

CHAPTER 15

CONCLUSION: THE PHOENIX RISES

For once you have tasted flight, you will forever walk the earth with your eyes turned skyward, for there you have been, and there you will always long to return.
—Attributed to LEONARDO DA VINCI, Italian polymath of the Renaissance era

The Phoenix Encounter method starts with a question: How might someone destroy your business? The COVID-19 situation brought that from mere imagination to calamitous reality for many organizations.

The best person to think about the firestorm is you. It ends with a clarion call to arms: The time is now! This means leading like your business is on fire. An Encounter is not a one-time event. We recommend leadership teams do it at least once a year. The method's three phases are designed to move from preparation through Radical Ideation to transformative action. In the Encounter Groundwork, we switch attitudes, bust blinkered thinking, take stock of where we are, and prepare for battle. In the Encounter Battlefield, we scan for insights and firepower during the Completely Opposite Viewpoints Debates of the Extreme Attack and the Horizon Defense to generate a wider set of strategic options. This will combine contemporary firepower (digital, technology, and platforms) with the conventional arsenal (finance, optimization, and talent management). In the

Phoenix Breakthrough phase, we revise the Future-Facing Blueprint and set a forward direction with actions for the short term and break-throughs for the longer term.

Throughout it all, the Phoenix Attitude leader thinks and acts as both a Dreamer and a Doer. There is no Altitude Sickness whatsoever.

IN FORESIGHT, IN HINDSIGHT, AND IN PERSON

We close with three examples of the Phoenix Encounter's ability to switch attitude and generate breakthrough insights for any leader and across all the altitudes—50,000 feet, 50 feet, and 5 feet.

Phoenix Leader at the 50,000-Foot View

Joern Shuttleworth was the CEO of a public sector corporation in northern Europe, mandated to provide businesses with reinsurance services for extreme events. Established in the early 2000s, the mandate was reviewed and extended every three years. As it happened, just 18 months before Joern's Encounter exercise, his board had taken part in a planning exercise in which they considered the pros and cons of closing down the agency. They decided it was not a good idea.

> Joern's Encounter involved a diverse set of teammates (private sector companies and one nonprofit, coming from four other industries and countries). In the Extreme Attack, Joern realized that it was very possible for a very different Newco to completely eliminate his agency. Newco could be an industry-owned pool sustained by the market, not the government. Joern's team considered all the objections that the board had to closing the agency and envisioned ways for Newco to deal with them.
>
> As Joern recalls, "It was a surprise to be put in a position where you were told your mandate is to kill your organization. I wasn't prepared. The discussion was very uncomfortable, but it really helped with thinking differently. The process helped

me impartially think through the steps required to shut down my organization and put in place a much better solution."

In the three months following the Encounter, Joern engaged with the board, government, and treasury departments and got permission to conduct a commercial feasibility study for an open market industry pool. He determined that his solution would lower costs, better manage underwriting risks, and be much more efficient—all major gains for a business with around $10 billion in funding.

While that transformation is a work in progress, Joern is implementing other ideas from the Encounter's Horizon Defense to improve short- to medium-term business performance and increase market engagement.

Phoenix Leader at the 50-Foot View

We mentioned our colleague Dominique Lecossois earlier. He led the expansion of some of the biggest developed market retailers across Asia (e.g., Carrefour and Tesco). He is very familiar with the exercises and outcomes of Phoenix Encounters. We asked him how the growth trajectories for Carrefour and Tesco in Asia might have been different if he had initiated an Encounter. This is what he said:

> An Encounter would have helped me and the organizations I worked for—Carrefour and Tesco—in devising appropriate strategies, better appreciating cultural differences, zeroing in on apposite store formats, and, most important, bringing about a mindset shift.
>
> Strategically, I would have avoided a very expensive mistake in Thailand, where Carrefour negotiated building only a Bangkok presence with the government, and it took another eight years to expand elsewhere in Thailand. By agreeing to develop stores only in Bangkok, Carrefour gave the competition lead time to entrench itself outside Bangkok. This eventually prevented the group from becoming a market leader, despite its early entry into the market and skills in successfully managing retail chains.

An Encounter exercise would have helped me and the UK-based board of Tesco fully realize that land acquisition through the Taiwan-based subsidary, as opposed to the UK-based holding company, would have enabled the Taiwanese subsidiary to scale up operations faster.

Similarly, this exercise would have highlighted the benefits of operating with joint venture partners in Hong Kong and Singapore, both to me and to the French board of Carrefour. In retrospect, an Encounter would have helped me convince the parent board that exiting the Hong Kong joint venture was an erroneous decision.

While an expatriate board did help in skill transfer, it did not facilitate relationship building with local stakeholders, subscribing to country-specific industry best practices, and understanding cultural nuances. A multicultural, multiperspective board would have facilitated better relations with government officials.

As part of Encounter defense options, it would have helped me decide on an appropriate store format much earlier. I wasted almost 10 months of precious time figuring out that I would not be able to duplicate the French format (single-story big box) here in Asia, where multistory stores are the norm.

All of that illustrates that while expanding a business overseas, replicating strategies that are successful in the home market does not guarantee success. You need a wider set of different, even opposing views. Using an Encounter battle together would have enabled the board of directors and key personnel to anticipate challenges and customize management, strategy, product offering, and marketing to enable a single country– focused business to evolve with a global view.

Phoenix Leader at the 5-Foot View

When we met Archara Suttirat, she was the managing director of one of the leading decorative paint producers in Thailand. She had enjoyed a great run in this business for almost a decade but was looking for new ideas. Archara told us that her Phoenix Encounter exercise was a series of aha moments. It gave her a better understanding of self and what she could do very well. It also revealed what she could not do well—and what her current organization could not do at all. One question that arose was whether Archara was ambitious enough to follow a new dream.

> The Encounter focused attention on some important challenges and some new opportunities for Archara's company. The decorative paint industry in Thailand was far behind that of the developed markets in terms of offering products that were free of unwanted chemicals. Archara wondered if her company might move aggressively into the chemical-free space instead of waiting for the industry to change in response to external pressures. Her company had long focused on one set of paint applications and targeted markets in certain parts of the country where those applications were popular, but her Encounter led her to envision opportunities in developing new products for new applications. In the defense stage of the Phoenix Encounter exercise, Archara imagined a combinatorial innovation of new products, new markets, and new platform business models. It was brilliant and it was ambitious.
>
> After her Encounter, Archara didn't hesitate to answer the calling. Rather than return to the old company, she embarked on a new life path. She used the learnings and confidence she acquired to buy a large stake in an existing company, became CEO, and focused the company on a new line of solvent-free paints that targeted new applications in untapped market segments. Using new technologies and an asset-light business model, she turned erstwhile sales reps into entrepreneurs who built their own distribution businesses. In this way, Archara not only put her money where her dream was, she also built an ecosystem of people with the Phoenix Attitude.

We are not suggesting that readers do precisely what this book's examples did. What works for one organization will not necessarily work for another—solutions are never generic, and contexts are different. Instead, we have tried to show how each of the leaders and organizations throughout the book have followed the principles, processes, tools, and habits that encapsulate the Phoenix Encounter method.

The Phoenix Encounter stories and examples show how leaders with a Phoenix Attitude work to create and then embed transformations that enable organizations to achieve core growth and future success. Those leaders create better value outcomes, which in turn drives greater innovation and delivers competitive advantages that, with Phoenix renewal, can be sustainable.

We had never imagined that our method would be so important, so vital, to almost everyone and every organization. In responding to the COVID-19 pandemic, all organizations have attempted to survive and stabilize. Some have taken advantage of the dramatic shifts in circumstance and accelerated their positions—those with the platforms, technologies, or business-model agility to address the needs of stakeholders during lockdowns and restrictions. Others with flawed business models or inadequate leadership are closing their doors.

We believe the key is to focus on reimagining your Phoenix rebirth and surge towards the future. There is no choice. Quite simply, there has never been a more important time to be your own best (imaginary) enemy and to engage in a strategic dialogue that is a Completely Opposite Viewpoints Debate and gives Radical Ideation for a much wider set of options for the future. We hope that readers understand that for leaders with the Phoenix Attitude the phrase "own best enemy" implies a virtuous cycle of renewal and transformation. For leaders without the Phoenix Attitude, the phrase implies stagnation and, worse, destruction.

If your organization is in a firestorm near death, the time to reimagine is now—regroup and rebirth. In the COVID-19 era the firestorm is as real and as ferocious as it has ever been for most businesses. If you are doing well, ask yourself: Is this a passing moment of glory? Or have you built a sustainable future? If you're somewhere in between, the option set needs to be wide enough, and agile enough to encompass the myriad of possibilities beyond the crisis. Do not look in the rear-view mirror. It shows a dream, not a future reality.

A final note of encouragement: As we said in the introduction, the Phoenix Encounter method is designed to help leaders bridge the gap between perceiving a threat and doing something about it. Traversing that gap is a major accomplishment, and like many such accomplishments, it generates a surge of excitement, energy, and power. This will be a wonderful moment for leaders. It's the experience of the phoenix rising—an experience that galvanizes the Phoenix Attitude and engenders the courage and confidence needed for the leadership work of fortifying the organization and galvanizing it into something new. For many of those who join the Phoenix Encounter, it is a moment of profound joy.

FINAL REFLECTION

Your real battle is not with the outside world;
it is with an enemy that hides deep within you.
Find it, fight it and set yourself free.
The key to your freedom lies in your deepest fear.
—HENNA SOHAIL, Contemporary Internet commentator

Distinguished British composer Thea Musgrave composed a work for orchestra in 1997 titled "Phoenix Rising." She kindly gave us permission to share her description here: "The phenomenal image of the phoenix rising from the ashes of destruction has always given the world, and me personally, hope for our future. It defines a path of leadership and regeneration. One creates a work of art in exactly that way—out of chaos."

As we've described throughout this book, the Phoenix Encounter is an experience in leadership thinking, strategic debate, and option generation for a world of firestorm disruption.

By its nature, the method also forces leaders to examine themselves. We are deeply grateful to the distinguished British poet William Ayot, author of *Emails from the Soul*, for providing a final reflection for all of us on this personal matter through the unique lens of poetry.

Meeting the Phoenix

He was ready, but it still came as a shock.
Less of an encounter, more of an ambush,
Exploding unexpectedly around him
With questioning arcs of incoming tracer
That ripped into his self-assured positions,
Tearing his confident legacy apart,
Trashing his complacent ways of thinking.

More of a turkey-shoot than a battle,
Questions lobbed in from unexpected angles,
Un-seen scenarios war-gamed mercilessly—
Weaknesses exploited and savagely exposed.
The whole sad edifice of his careful conceit,
Outwitted, outflanked and shot to pieces,
Crumbling in a welter of gilded feathers

He hurts at this point—a mixture of anger,
The rush of adrenaline, age-old fears
And the sting of grief at the back of his throat.
The whole wrapped up in the cloak of shame;
His hopes exploded, his empire dismantled,
The once brightly feathered bird of his vision
Burning on the pyre of his second-hand dreams.

But now the team swings round to defend him,
Creative yet trusting, annealed by fire.
They push back strongly—to the perimeter,
Fleshing out the bones of regeneration,
Giving shape to a re-imagined whole;
The core of a dream and a way to grow it—
A blueprint, a beginning, a long-term plan.

And in the white heat of this great burning,
Something rare and new is ultimately forged.
A person that he had never imagined
Steps from the fire where he too was burned.
A doer and a dreamer, scanning horizons,
No longer naïve but fully prepared.
The gift then, of his meeting with the Phoenix,
Was that he too arose, entirely changed.

— William Ayot, 2019

Acknowledgments

We are very grateful for the assistance we have received from the time we decided to write this book until its publication. First and foremost, we acknowledge the support, deep engagement, and encouragement of hundreds of business executives who participated in our Encounter exercises, and we have anonymously shared many of their stories throughout the chapters.

A very big thank you to Art Jahnke and Nancy Zerbey of Boston, who worked as development editors throughout the entire project. In preparing the project we appreciate the work of Bethany Browne and her team at the Cadence Group in Chicago as well as the editorial assistance of Nandini Vijayaraghavan, Radha Sampath, and Lynn Wong and the graphic designs for the book's whiteboard notes from Benoit Picaud. Thanks also to Kiki Keating for the early publicity work. We also appreciate the research support from Aarti Gumaledar and www.mytechfrontier.com for the scans on technology firepower. Special thanks to our dear friend William Ayot for providing our reflective poem and to Thea Musgrave for her musical insights.

We sincerely thank Kevin Anderson, our agent; Mark Fortier, our publicist; and Jonas Forsslund and Daphne Ong, our website and project coordinators, for their continuing and ongoing work.

In bringing this book to publication in 2020 during the COVID-19 pandemic, we especially thank the commitment and support of Donya Dickerson, Associate Publisher at McGraw-Hill (MH), who championed our book as editor; designer Jeff Weeks; and other members of the MH team, including Joseph Kurtz, Maureen Harper, Nora Hennick, and Amanda Mueller. We acknowledge the work of

Steve Straus in supporting the book's editing, design, and production for MH.

We are lucky to have colleagues and friends like Shantanu Bhattacharya, Russell Boyce, Chris Howells, Vish Iyer, Chaitanya Kalipatnapu, Benjamin Kessler, Chan Kim, Wesley Koo, Christophe Le Caillec, Dominique Lecossois, Elizabeth A. Moore, Narayan Pant, Fred du Plessis, Phanish Puranam, Bala Vissa, and Michael Writer. Thanks to those who gave so generously of their time and scholarship, as well as to the countless other academic colleagues who engaged with us in Phoenix conversations.

We would like to highlight the encouragement and support that INSEAD provided to help us take *The Phoenix Encounter Method* from an idea conceived on a summer evening in the Biergarten in Fontainebleau, nurtured over many evenings at the Residence Bar in Singapore, to the book that you have in your hands now. Paddy also acknowledges the assistance Unilever provided through supporting his research work at INSEAD.

Finally, we thank some very special people. Deep appreciation to Cathryn and Amelia, who provided Ian with every ounce of emotional and academic energy to complete this work; whose constancy is a legend of both love and learning; and who completely live out the spirit of his mother, Peggy, who was "the great teacher for life." From Paddy, thanks to Geetha for giving breath to a second life; to Shreya, Samyuktha, Sanjeev, Prasad, and Amma, for making him look forward to tomorrow; and to Appa and Hyma for the memories. Thanks to Aarti for her love and support, and for being Sameer's intellectual sparring partner; Dia and Ansh for being Papa's cheerleaders throughout; and Mom, Dad, and Sonam for fostering his curiosity. In all Ram's writing and consulting, including this Encounter project, there are two people for whom he remains deeply grateful for their ongoing support: Cynthia Burr and Geraldine Willigan.

Notes

INTRODUCTION

1. Many leadership development scholars and practitioners describe behavioral characteristics of "alpha," or "type A," individuals and note that these personality depicters are common among senior executives (e.g., see Kate Ludeman and Eddie Erlandson, "Coaching the Alpha Male," *Harvard Business Review*, May 2004). While there is continuing debate in leadership psychology about the alpha construct, some of the most common characteristics include results, action, or goal orientation; drive; portrayed confidence; unemotional; demanding; and dominant. Although the military language used in the Encounter is alpha-like, we interpret the alpha here as action orientation with curiosity and as what might be called "positive alpha" behaviors—that is, outcome orientation combined with emotional intelligence for collaboration and engagement.

2. Some words about birds:

   In Greek mythology, a phoenix is a bird that cyclically regenerates itself by arising from the ashes of its predecessor. Across many different cultures, the mythical phoenix has been associated with immortality, rebirth, regeneration, or resurrection. This imagery is evident in works ranging from Dante's *Inferno* to Shakespeare's *Henry VIII* and Dumbledore's pet "Fawkes" in Harry Potter. In the United Nations Security Council chamber, there is a very large mural painted by the Norwegian artist Per Krogh in 1952, and the phoenix is central. It symbolizes the world being reborn after the Second World War, and its bright colors above symbolize the hope for a better future. Warsaw was likewise given the nickname "Phoenix" for its extensive post-war reconstruction. The city of Phoenix in Arizona uses the bird symbol central on its flag, as does San Francisco, California, which features a phoenix in the center of its flag, symbolizing rebuilding after the 1906 earthquake.

   The Phoenix appears in literature and in the arts. For example, the distinguished British composer Thea Musgrave wrote an orchestral work called "Phoenix Rising" in 1997—see: https://www.wisemusicclassical.com/work/8414/Phoenix-Rising--Thea-Musgrave/ and http://www.theamusgrave.com/, accessed February 2020.

   The dodo is an extinct flightless bird that inhabited the Indian Ocean island of Mauritius. Various sources suggest it was first seen by Portuguese and Dutch sailors in the sixteenth century, and it's thought to have become extinct less than a hundred years later. Its prominence as one of the best-known extinct animals, along with its appearance, contributed to its use in popular culture as a symbol of extinction or obsolescence.

As described in this book, crows are a widely spread group of birds of many different species in the *Corvus* genus. Nevertheless, many crow species are critically endangered (such as the Hawaiian 'Alalā, the Mariana crow of Guam, and the Indonesian Flores crow).

3. In the defense stage of the Encounter Battlefield exercise, after considering a wide range of future options, James Menta's company developed its new playbook. James's new plan for his company included a rapid buildup of digital capabilities to gain a first-mover advantage in his industry by shifting it toward a multisided platform with new partners. This was very different from the company's former business model, which prioritized shaving pennies from its procurement and supply chain processes.

4. INSEAD is one of the world's leading and largest graduate business schools, with campuses in Europe (France), Asia (Singapore), and the Middle East (Abu Dhabi) as well as a business innovation hub in North America (San Francisco). Its faculty body comprises more than 160 professorial scholars from more than 40 countries. Each year, INSEAD graduates more than 1,300 students in its master and doctoral degree programs, and more than 11,000 leaders and managers participate in its executive education programs.

5. Research and development work for the Phoenix Encounter included field trials with more than 1,500 executive leaders and the compilation and analysis of more than 5,000 articles, papers, reports, and books spanning academic research to business practice. Given the subject matter of the Encounter, we have deliberately used a very wide range of research articles across multiple disciplines (such as strategy, psychology, and business management) and diverse digital sources.

6. The Phoenix Encounter method is also consistent with the Socratic method, a type of constructive debate and dialogue based on asking questions to stimulate critical thinking and ideation, which is widely used in business schools across the world.

CHAPTER 1

1. Jens Lekman (b. 1981) is a Swedish pop musician and songwriter with a heavy emphasis on guitar use and sound sampling. In 2015, he released a new, freely available song every week on his website. His most recent album is *Life Will See You Now*, released on the Secretly Canadian label in 2017. He is considered a leader in the "indie pop" market.

2. We also note that there is the surprising behavior of players who are not associated with a particular sector but step in and change the landscape. Key moves include backward and forward integration, which changes the competitive landscape. It is often linked with new technologies and/or business models. For example: Amazon moving into cloud computing services; Grab Taxi moving into financial services; and IKEA moving into customized design services.

3. The FT View, "Sears's Towering Past and Its Diminished Future," *Financial Times*, March 24, 2017, https://www.ft.com/content/d46df090-0fda-11e7-a88c-50ba212dce4d, accessed October 2018.

Gary Silverman, Lindsay Whipp, and Joe Rennison, "Struggling Sears Signals Decline of US Malls," *Financial Times*, March 24, 2017, https://www.ft.com/content/599476e0-1071-11e7-a88c-50ba212dce4d, accessed October 2018.

The Editorial Board, "How Sears Was the Amazon of Its Day," *New York Times*, October 15, 2018, https://www.nytimes.com/2018/10/15/opinion/sears-bankruptcy-amazon-retail-disruption.html, accessed October 2018.

Michael Corkery, "Sears, the Original Everything Store, Files for Bankruptcy," *New York Times*, October 14, 2018, https://www.nytimes.com/2018/10/14/business/sears-bankruptcy-filing-chapter-11.html, accessed October 2018.

"Number of Retail Store closures in the United States in 2017, by Retail Chain," Statista, https://www.statista.com/statistics/385850/brick-and-mortar-retail-store-closings-in-the-us-by-retail-chain/, accessed October 2018.

Lucy Craymer, "The Last Place on Earth Where Everyone Still Loves Kmart," *Wall Street Journal*, January 16, 2018, https://www.wsj.com/articles/the-last-place-on-earth-where-everyone-still-loves-kmart-guam-1516118140, accessed October 2018. As an aside, the most popular Kmart store in the world happens to be in Guam. Not surprisingly, it is about 6,000 miles west of California and not on the list of locations eligible for free shipping by Amazon Prime!

4. Alan Livsey, "Dollar Shave Club Wins Market Share and Customers with Back-to-Basics approach," *Financial Times*, March 16, 2017, https://www.ft.com/content/9bb5cc54-d368-11e6-b06b-680c49b4b4c0#myft:list:page, accessed October 2018.

John M. Brown and Arash Massoudi, "Unilever Buys Dollar Shave Club for $1bn," *Financial Times*, July 20, 2016, https://www.ft.com/content/bd07237e-4e45-11e6-8172-e39ecd3b86fc#myft:list:page, accessed October 2018.

Lindsay Whipp, "P&G to Cut Gillette Razor Prices as It Tries to Lure Back Shavers," *Financial Times*, February 23, 2017, https://www.ft.com/content/21842808-d3d2-31b6-8ee9-181f5607f734#myft:list:page, accessed October 2018.

Sharon Terlep, "Rather Than Add More Blades to Its Razors, Gillette Trims Prices," *Wall Street Journal*, November 29, 2017, https://www.wsj.com/articles/rather-than-add-more-blades-to-its-razors-gillette-trims-prices-1511960400?mod=searchresults&page=1&pos=1, accessed October 2018.

5. Newley Purnell, "Two Years Ago, India Lacked Fast, Cheap Internet—One Billionaire Changed All That," *Wall Street Journal*, September 5, 2018, https://www.wsj.com/articles/two-years-ago-india-lacked-fast-cheap-internetone-billionaire-changed-all-that-1536159916, accessed December 2018.

"Reliance Industries 41st AGM: Full Text of Speech by Mukesh Ambani," Moneycontrol News, July 5, 2018, https://www.moneycontrol.com/news/business/companies/reliance-industries-41st-agm-full-text-of-speech-by-mukesh-ambani-2674391.html, accessed December 2018.

Naazneen Karmali, "Mukesh Ambani's $33 Billion Bet on India's Digital Revolution," *Forbes*, March 7, 2018, https://www.forbes.com/sites/naazneenkarmali/2018/03/07/mukesh-ambanis-33-billion-bet-on-indias-digital-revolution/#a5d8047a0c7f, accessed December 2018.

IANS, "After Jio, Mukesh Ambani Bets Big on Internet, Video Streaming Market," *Gulf News*, January 24, 2019, https://gulfnews.com/technology /after-jio-mukesh-ambani-bets-big-on-internet-video-streaming-market -1.1548306753853, accessed June 2019.

Suman Layak, "Why Mukesh Ambani-led RIL Needs to Be Viewed as a Tech and Consumer Player," *Economic Times*, October 28, 2018, https:// economictimes.indiatimes.com/industry/energy/oil-gas/why-mukesh-ambani -led-ril-needs-to-be-viewed-as-a-tech-and-consumer-player/printarticle /66395674.cms, accessed December 2018.

6. Clayton M. Christensen, *The Innovator's Dilemma: When New Technologies Cause Great Firms to Fail* (Boston, MA: Harvard Business School Press, 1997).

Rebecca Henderson and Kim Clark, "Architectural Innovation: The Reconfiguration of Existing Product Technologies and the Failure of Established Firms," *Administrative Science Quarterly* 35 (1990): 9–30.

Larry Downes and Paul Nunes, "Big-Bang Disruption," *Harvard Business Review*, March 2013, https://hbr.org/2013/03/big-bang-disruption, accessed June 2019.

W. Chan Kim and Renée Mauborgne, "Five Steps to Making a Blue Ocean Shift," https://www.blueoceanstrategy.com/blog/five-steps-making-blue-ocean-shift/, accessed December 2019.

Rita McGrath, *Seeing Around Corners: How to Spot Inflection Points in Business Before They Happen* (New York: Houghton Mifflin Harcourt Publishing Company, 2019).

7. Robert Armstrong, "Axa Boss Predicts Competitive Threat from Faangs," *Financial Times*, October 4, 2019, https://www.ft.com/content/f7f6d884 -e484-11e9-9743-db5a370481bc, accessed December 2019.

8. Rana Foroohar, "Meg Whitman: 'Businesses Need to Think, Who's Coming to Kill Me?'" *Financial Times*, January 18, 2019, https://www.ft.com/content /769d4144-18db-11e9-9e64-d150b3105d21, accessed December 2019.

9. Ram Charan and Julia Yang, *The Amazon Management System: The Ultimate Digital Business Engine That Creates Extraordinary Value for Both Customers and Shareholders* (United States: Ideapress Publishing, 2019).

10. For example, Scott Kirsner, the editor of *Innovation Leader*, reported on the largest obstacles to innovation in big companies being "politics, turf wars and no alignment" in a *Harvard Business Review* online article: https://hbr.org /2018/07/the-biggest-obstacles-to-innovation-in-large-companies, accessed December 2019.

11. Christopher Mims, "Wall Street to CEOs: Disrupt Your Industry, or Else," *Wall Street Journal*, May 26, 2017, https://www.wsj.com/articles/wall-street-to -ceos-the-future-is-now-1495791003, accessed June 2019.

12. We have found using the Encounter method as a complement to other strategic frames and models is very valuable. For example: we have had participants use the Encounter process to both encourage and then stress-test "Blue Ocean" ideas (Kim and Mauborgne, *Blue Ocean Strategy: How to Create Uncontested Market Space and Make the Competition Irrelevant*, Boston, MA: Harvard Business School Publishing, 2005). We have seen many startups use the Encounter method to rigorously test potential business models and plans. Many legacy firms use the Encounter as a counterpoint test to their existing

strategy development and product innovation work. We also have examples of corporates using the Encounter exercises as engaging and effective leadership training for high-potetial future leaders to accelerate development of their strategic thinking capacity.

CHAPTER 2

1. Edwin Land, quoted in Andrew Hill, "How to Keep Creative Geniuses in Check and in Profit," *Financial Times*, March 11, 2019, https://www.ft.com /content/907256a8-40d2-11e9-9bee-efab61506f44, accessed June 2019.

2. Ko Tin-yau, "Alibaba's Yuebao Posing Growing Challenge to Banks," EJ Insight, July 7, 2017, http://www.ejinsight.com/20170707-alibaba-s-yuebao -posing-growing-challenge-to-banks/, accessed June 2019.

3. Chanyaporn Chanjaroen and Joyce Koh, "Singapore's Biggest Bank Takes on China Giants in Fintech Battle," *Bloomberg Businessweek*, May 14, 2018, https://www.bloomberg.com/news/articles/2018-05-14/fintech-battle-pits -biggest-singapore-bank-against-china-giants, accessed June 2019.

4. For these and many other insights, we are grateful for the clear thinking of academics such as Chan Kim, Daniel Kahneman, Ronald Coase, Clayton Christensen, Rebecca Henderson, Kim Clark, Donald Hambrick, Anita Wolley, Adam Grant, Carol Dweck, Peter Salovey, Rita McGrath, and others. Their work has greatly influenced this book and our Encounter research and fieldwork.

5. Through work in directing and developing C-suite and leadership development programs between 2013 and 2019, Ian undertook an anonymized data analysis of more than 1,000 personal leadership development plans and related 360-degree feedback reports to categorize the proportion of participant leaders falling into each of the five types of strategic thinking leaders exemplified in the chapter. This research is part of an ongoing field research project on leadership development practices and approaches. For further details see endnote 3 of Chapter 4.

6. Andrew S. Grove, *Only the Paranoid Survive: How to Exploit the Crisis Points That Challenge Every Company* (New York: Bantam Doubleday Dell Publishing Group, Inc., 1996).

7. Alexander J. Rothman and Peter Salovey, "Shaping Perceptions to Motivate Healthy Behavior: The Role of Message Framing," *Psychological Bulletin* 121(1) (1997): 3–19.

8. Rebecca Henderson, "Underinvestment and Incompetence as Responses to Radical Innovation: Evidence from the Photolithographic Alignment Equipment Industry," *RAND Journal of Economics* 24(2) (1993): 248–270.

9. Ram Charan, *The Attacker's Advantage: Turning Uncertainty into Breakthrough Opportunities* (New York: PublicAffairs, 2015).

10. Rita McGrath, *Seeing Around Corners: How to Spot Inflection Points in Business Before They Happen* (New York: Houghton Mifflin Harcourt Publishing Company, 2019).

11. John D. Stoll, "CEO Tenure Is Getting Shorter. Maybe That's a Good Thing." *Wall Street Journal*, October 4, 2018, https://www.wsj.com/articles/ceo -tenure-is-getting-shorter-maybe-thats-a-good-thing-1538664764, accessed March 2019.

George Bradt, "Why HSBC CEO John Flint Got Fired: Poor Future Fit with His New Boss," *Forbes*, August 5, 2019, https://www.forbes.com/sites/georgebradt/2019/08/05/why-hsbc-ceo-john-flint-got-fired-poor-future-fit-with-his-new-boss/#56dab9ed7e11, accessed December 2019.

Christopher Mims, "Wall Street to CEOs: Disrupt Your Industry, or Else," *Wall Street Journal*, May 26, 2017, https://www.wsj.com/articles/wall-street-to-ceos-the-future-is-now-1495791003, accessed June 2019.

Rachel Sanderson, "Moncler Scraps Catwalk Shows for the Social Media Generation," *Financial Times*, November 13, 2017, https://www.ft.com/content/8f190394-c7af-11e7-ab18-7a9fb7d6163e, accessed June 2018.

Khadeeja Safdar, "J.Crew's Mickey Drexler Confesses: I Underestimated How Tech Would Upend Retail," *Wall Street Journal*, May 24, 2017, https://www.wsj.com/articles/j-crews-big-miss-how-technology-transformed-retail-1495636817, accessed June 2018.

12. See for example: Chris Isidore and Nathaniel Meyersohn, "J.Crew has filed for bankruptcy," *CNN Business,* https://edition.cnn.com/2020/05/04/business/j-crew-bankruptcy/index.html, accessed May 2020.

13. Dreamers and Doers:

Our depiction of leaders as Dreamers and Doers builds from our own research and also encompasses and extends the work of many other authors emphasizing characteristics of leaders who seek and promote innovation—for example, the characteristics of questioning and experimenting, highlighted by Jeff Dyer, Hal Gregersen, and Clayton M. Christensen in their book, *The Innovator's DNA* (Boston, MA: Harvard Business Review Press, 2011 and 2019). The thinking qualities of a Dreamer and Doer also incorporate the kind of dual-diametric and opposite thinking approaches discussed by Roger L. Martin in *The Opposable Mind: How Successful Leaders Win Through Integrative Thinking* (Boston, MA: Harvard Business Review Press, 2009).

14. For example, see: https://assets.kpmg/content/dam/kpmg/xx/pdf/2019/06/postal-services-in-the-internet-age.PDF, accessed December 2019.

15. Oliver Kmia, "Why Kodak Died and Fujifilm Thrived: A Tale of Two Film Companies," Petapixel, October 19, 2018, https://petapixel.com/2018/10/19/why-kodak-died-and-fujifilm-thrived-a-tale-of-two-film-companies/, accessed December 2019.

16. Joshua Gans, "The Other Disruption," *Harvard Business Review*, March 2016, https://hbr.org/2016/03/the-other-disruption, accessed June 2018.

17. Ushijima Bifue, "Fujifilm Finds New Life in Cosmetics," nippon.com, April 25, 2013, https://www.nippon.com/en/features/c00511/, accessed December 2019.

Wikipedia, "Fujifilm," https://en.wikipedia.org/wiki/Fujifilm, accessed October 2019.

Fujifilm Corporation, "Advanced Skincare Products That Only Fujifilm Could Create," https://www.fujifilm.com/innovation/achievements/skincare/, accessed December 2019.

Fujifilm Holdings Corporation, "Business Fields of Fujifilm Group," https://www.fujifilmholdings.com/en/investors/guidance/index.html, accessed December 2019.

For financial data, see: https://ir.fujifilm.com/en/investors/ir-materials /earnings-presentations.html, accessed December 2019.

18. Larry Downes and Paul Nunes, "Big-Bang Disruption," *Harvard Business Review*, March 2013, https://hbr.org/2013/03/big-bang-disruption, accessed June 2019.

19. Ronald H. Coase, "The Nature of the Firm," *Economica* 4(16) (1937): 386–405, https://doi.org/10.1111/j.1468-0335.1937.tb00002.x, accessed June 2018.

20. John McMillan, *Reinventing the Bazaar: A Natural History of Markets* (New York: W. W. Norton & Company, 2002).

21. TripAdvisor LLC, "BeingSattvaa," https://www.tripadvisor.com.sg /Hotel_Review-g297701-d7236782-Reviews-BeingSattvaa-Ubud_Gianyar _Regency_Bali.html, accessed December 2019.

Expedia, Inc., "BeingSattvaa Retreat Villa," https://www.expedia.com.sg /Ubud-Hotels-Beingsattvaa-Vegetarian-Retreat-Villa-Ubud.h9531011.Hotel -Information, accessed December 2019.

22. Casey Newton, "Slack Adds Action Buttons to Become a True Workplace Communication Hub," Verge, May 22, 2018, https://www.theverge.com /2018/5/22/17378228/slack-action-buttons-asana-jira-bitbucket-developer -conference, accessed June 2018.

Slack Technologies, Inc., "The Business Value of Slack," https://a.slack-edge .com/eaf4e/marketing/downloads/resources/IDC_The_Business_Value_of _Slack.pdf, accessed June 2018.

Chris O'Brien, "Slack IPO Starts Trading at $38.50 for $23 Billion Valuation," VentureBeat, June 20, 2019, https://venturebeat.com/2019/06/20/slack-ipo -starts-trading-at-38-50-for-23-billion-valuation/, accessed December 2019.

23. "Blockchain Platform Ujo Music Opening Up in Early 2017," Music Ally, September 2, 2016, https://musically.com/2016/09/02/blockchain-platform -ujo-music-opening-up-in-early-2017/, accessed June 2018.

Rethink Music, "Fair Music: Transparency and Payment Flows in the Music Industry," Rethink Music, July 14, 2015, http://www.rethink-music.com /research/fair-music-transparency-and-payment-flows-in-the-music-industry, accessed June 2018.

"Ujo Music on Blockchain: 'It's Such an Uphill Battle with Existing Companies,'" Music Ally, August 4, 2017, https://musically.com/2017/08/04/ujo -music-blockchain-uphill-battle-existing-companies/, accessed June 2018.

CHAPTER 3

1. Maya Angelou (1928–2014), the distinguished American poet, author, and civil rights activist, is best known for her autobiographical books such as *I Know Why the Caged Bird Sings* and extensive poetry collections including *And Still I Rise* (1978).

2. Peter C. Wason, "On the Failure to Eliminate Hypotheses in a Conceptual Task," *Quarterly Journal of Experimental Psychology* 12(3) (1960): 129–140.

Jesse M. Pines, "Profiles in Patient Safety: Confirmation Bias in Emergency Medicine," *Academic Emergency Medicine* 13(1) (2006): 90–94.

Gary Klein, "The Curious Case of Confirmation Bias," *Psychology Today*, May 5, 2019, https://www.psychologytoday.com/sg/blog/seeing-what-others-dont/201905/the-curious-case-confirmation-bias, accessed December 2019.

3. The Phoenix Encounter website (www.phoenixencountermethod.com) provides resource information on the differentiation of the Encounter method approach with war-gaming, scenario planning, and the use of competitive analysis tools. However, some other useful resources include:

Graham Longley-Brown, *Successful Professional Wargames: A Practitioner's Handbook* (United States: The History of Wargaming Project, 2019).

Daniel F. Oriesek and Jan Oliver Schwarz, *Business Wargaming: Securing Corporate Value* (New York: Routledge, 2016).

Mark Herman and Mark Frost, *Wargaming for Leaders: Strategic Decision Making from the Battlefield to the Boardroom* (United States: Booz Allen Hamilton, 2009).

Benjamin Gilad, *Business War Games: How Large, Small, and New Companies Can Vastly Improve Their Strategies and Outmaneuver the Competition* (New Jersey: The Career Press, Inc., 2009).

Bryce G. Hoffman, *Red Teaming: How Your Business Can Conquer the Competition by Challenging Everything* (New York: Crown Business, 2017).

4. The Phoenix Encounter method emphasizes the role of imagineering in Radical Ideation, as a leadership behavior to achieve breakthrough ideas, that can come into action to change the future trajectory of an organization. For example, see the 2018 article by Cyril Bouquet, Jean-Louis Barsoux, and Michael Wade, "Bring Your Breakthrough Ideas to Life," https://hbr.org/2018/11/bring-your-breakthrough-ideas-to-life, accessed December 2019.

5. Blue Ocean Strategy (BOS), developed by W. Chan Kim and Renée Mauborgne, focuses on creating and capturing uncontested market spaces through the simultaneous pursuit of differentiation and lower cost to open new markets and create new demand. "Blue Ocean" is distinguished as the opportunity for new value creation, as opposed to the intensely competitive incumbent "red ocean" of existing opportunities. The Phoenix Encounter method and BOS are extremely complementary, as the Encounter exercises can create mindsets to seek BOS initiatives. The Encounter processes can also be used by leadership teams to stress-test potential BOS initiatives.

Scenario analysis—as a widely used business tool—focuses on projecting a range of alternative possible outcomes or trajectories and then distilling their implications for current strategies and/or tactics. Red teaming is a process, originally developed for the military but adapted for business, designed to challenge specific plans and assumptions by invoking an external and separate adversarial group to pull apart a planned course of action. (For example, see: Bryce G. Hoffman, *Red Teaming: How Your Business Can Conquer the Competition by Challenging Everything.* New York: Crown Business, 2017).

CHAPTER 4

1. Psychology often describes an attitude as a set of emotions and beliefs toward a particular object, person, thing, or events that wields enormous influence over behavior. We believe that for leadership, the underpinning of attitudes is the mindsets that shape these emotions, beliefs, and actions. (For example, see

books or articles by Carol S. Dweck, Peter M. Gollwitzer, Alice Eagly, Shelly Chaiken, and many others).

2. Theodore Levitt, "Marketing Myopia," *Harvard Business Review* 38 (1960): 45–56.

3. Source: Ian's proprietary research analysis of leadership development program participant personal development plans and 360-degree feedback data from 2013–2019, using a sample of N=1,047, all C-suite and senior executive leaders (CEO to CEO minus three). This showed that 72.6 percent of executives reported some form of "Altitude Sickness"—of which, 72.9 percent were trapped at 50 feet, 18.8 percent were trapped at 50,000 feet, and 8.3 percent were trapped at 5 feet. This data is being collected and analyzed progressively, as part of a 10-year research study on various aspects of leadership development to be completed by 2023 (also discussed in endnote 5 of Chapter 2). This research also shows that of identified leadership development gaps, more than 90 percent of the C-suite executives had one or more gaps that could be described as challenges with (1) Strategic Thinking or Execution, (2) Emotional Intelligence Behaviors, (3) Effective Communication and Engagement. In terms of identified technical gaps, the most prominent gap in legacy industry C-suite leaders was described as "lacking in knowledge of new technology, digitization and algorithms"—64 percent.

4. Daniel Kahneman, *Thinking, Fast and Slow* (New York: Farrar, Straus and Giroux, 2011).

5. The attributes for this table were derived from proprietary research and analysis of the dataset described in the leadership development research referred to in endnote 5 in Chapter 2 and endnote 3 in this chapter.

6. The echo chamber is an environment in which a person encounters only beliefs or opinions that coincide with their own, so that their existing views are reinforced and alternative ideas are not considered.

7. Marshall Goldsmith, *What Got You Here Won't Get You There: How Successful People Become Even More Successful* (London: Profile Books Ltd, 2013).

8. For leadership altitudes, see:

   Ram Charan, *The Attacker's Advantage: Turning Uncertainty into Breakthrough Opportunities* (New York: PublicAffairs, 2015).

   Ram Charan, *Know-How: The 8 Skills That Separate People Who Perform from Those Who Don't* (New York: Crown Business, 2007).

   Ian C. Woodward, "The Three Altitudes of Leadership," *INSEAD Blog*, INSEAD Knowledge, October 27, 2017, https://knowledge.insead.edu /blog/insead-blog/the-three-altitudes-of-leadership-7541, accessed December 2019.

   Ian C. Woodward, "The Altitudes of Leadership," TEDx Talk, 2017, https:// www.youtube.com/watch?v=aU1mHzYYUrg&t=13s

   Harvard Business Review Staff, "You Can't Be a Wimp—Make the Tough Calls," *Harvard Business Review*, November 2013, https://hbr.org/2013/11 /you-cant-be-a-wimp-make-the-tough-calls, accessed June 2018.

9. Tim Bradshaw, "Apple Wins Race to Be First Trillion-Dollar Company," *Financial Times*, August 2, 2018, https://www.ft.com/content/aebad290-9644 -11e8-b67b-b8205561c3fe, accessed December 2019.

10. Larry Bossidy, Ram Charan, and Charles Burck, *Execution: The Discipline of Getting Things Done* (London: Random House Business Books, 2011).

11. Ian C. Woodward, Samah Shaffakat, and Vincent H. Dominé, *Exploring Leadership Drivers and Blockers* (Singapore: Palgrave Macmillan, 2019).

12. Chade-Meng Tan, Daniel Goleman, and Jon Kabat-Zinn, *Search Inside Yourself: The Unexpected Path to Achieving Success, Happiness (and World Peace)* (New York: HarperOne, 2014).

13. Sheryl Sandberg, *Lean In: Women, Work, and the Will to Lead* (New York: Alfred A. Knopf, 2013).

    Harris Collingwood, "Leadership's First Commandment: Know Thyself," *Harvard Business Review* 79 (2001): 8–14.

14. Drea Knufken, "The 25 Worst Business Failures in History," Business Pundit, January 14, 2009, http://www.businesspundit.com/the-25-worst-business-failures-in-history/, accessed December 2019.

    Sam Levin, "Squeezed Out: Widely Mocked Startup Juicero Is Shutting Down," *Guardian*, September 1, 2017, https://www.theguardian.com/technology/2017/sep/01/juicero-silicon-valley-shutting-down, accessed December 2019.

15. Richard Boyatzis and Annie McKee, "Inspiring Others Through Resonant Leadership," *Business Strategy Review* 17(2) (May 17, 2006): 15-19, https://doi.org/10.1111/j.0955-6419.2006.00394.x, accessed June 2018.

    Richard W. Woodman and Todd Dewett, "Organizationally Relevant Journeys in Individual Change," in *Handbook of Organizational Change and Innovation*, edited by Marshall S. Poole and Andrew H. Van de Ven (New York: Oxford University Press, 2004).

    Robert Kegan and Lisa L. Lahey, *How the Way We Talk Can Change the Way We Work: Seven Languages for Transformation* (San Francisco: Jossey-Bass, 2001).

    Ian C. Woodward, Samah Shaffakat, and Vincent H. Dominé, *Exploring Leadership Drivers and Blockers* (Singapore: Palgrave Macmillan, 2019).

    Ian C. Woodward, "Leadership Is a Journey, Not a Destination," *INSEAD Blog*, INSEAD Knowledge, November 2, 2017, https://knowledge.insead.edu/blog/insead-blog/leadership-is-a-journey-not-a-destination-7581, accessed June 2018.

16. See endnote 8 in this chapter.

17. For example, see:

    Ronald A. Heifetz, Alexander Grashow, and Marty Linsky, *The Practice of Adaptive Leadership: Tools and Tactics for Changing Your Organization and the World* (Boston, MA: Harvard Business Press, 2009).

    Robert Kegan and Lisa L. Lahey, *How the Way We Talk Can Change the Way We Work: Seven Languages for Transformation* (San Francisco: Jossey-Bass, 2001).

    Robert Kegan and Lisa L. Lahey, *Immunity to Change: How to Overcome It and Unlock the Potential in Yourself and Your Organization* (Boston, MA: Harvard Business Press, 2009).

    Otto Scharmer, "The Blind Spot of Institutional Leadership: How to Create Deep Innovation Through Moving from Egosystem to Ecosystem Awareness," paper presented at the World Economic Forum, Annual Meeting of the New Champions, Tianjin, People's Republic of China, September 2010.

C. Otto Scharmer, *Theory U: Leading from the Future as It Emerges* (San Francisco: Berrett-Koehler Publishers, Inc, 2008).

18. Carol S. Dweck, *Mindset: The New Psychology of Success* (New York: Ballantine Books, 2016).

19. Gary Klein, "Mindsets: What They Are and Why They Matter," *Psychology Today*, May 1, 2016, https://www.psychologytoday.com/intl/blog/seeing-what-others-dont/201605/mindsets, accessed June 2018.

Gary Klein, *Seeing What Others Don't: The Remarkable Ways We Gain Insights* (New York: PublicAffairs, 2013).

The Arbinger Institute, *The Outward Mindset: Seeing Beyond Ourselves* (Oakland, CA: Berrett-Koehler Publishers, Inc., 2016).

Max H. Bazerman and Michael Watkins, *Predictable Surprises: The Disasters You Should Have Seen Coming, and How to Prevent Them* (Boston, MA: Harvard Business School Press, 2004).

20. Daniel Kahneman, *Thinking, Fast and Slow* (New York: Farrar, Straus and Giroux, 2011).

21. Richard H. Thaler and Cass R. Sunstein, *Nudge: Improving Decisions About Health, Wealth, and Happiness* (New Haven. CT: Yale University Press, 2008).

Iris Bohnet, *What Works: Gender Equality by Design* (Cambridge, MA: The Belknap Press of Harvard University Press, 2016).

Jack B. Soll, Katherine L. Milkman, and John W. Payne, "Outsmart Your Own Biases," *Harvard Business Review*, May 2015, https://hbr.org/2015/05/outsmart-your-own-biases, accessed June 2018.

Rebecca K. Ratner, Dilip Soman, Gal Zauberman, Dan Ariely, Ziv Carmon, Punam A. Keller, B. Kyu Kim, Fern Lin, Selin Malkoc, Deborah A. Small and Klaus Wertenbroch, "How Behavior Decision Research Can Enhance Consumer Welfare: From Freedom of Choice to Paternalistic Intervention," *Marketing Letters* 19(3) (2008): 383–397.

Amos Tversky and Daniel Kahneman, "Judgment Under Uncertainty: Heuristics and Biases," *Science* 185(4157) (1974): 1124–1131.

22. Spyros Makridakis and Anil Gaba, "Judgment: Its Role and Value for Strategy," in *Forecasting with Judgment*, edited by George Wright and Paul Goodwin (Chichester, England: John Wiley & Sons, 1998), 1.

Ziv Carmon and Dan Ariely, "Focusing on the Forgone: How Value Can Appear So Different to Buyers and Sellers," *Journal of Consumer Research* 27(3) (2000): 360–370.

Klaus Wertenbroch, "Consumption Self-Control by Rationing Purchase Quantities of Virtue and Vice," *Marketing Science* 17(4) (1998): 317–337.

Dan Ariely and Klaus Wertenbroch, "Procrastination, Deadlines, and Performance: Self-Control by Precommitment," *Psychological Science* 13(3) (2002): 219–224.

23. Mark Bonchek, "Why the Problem with Learning Is Unlearning," *Harvard Business Review*, November 3, 2016, https://hbr.org/2016/11/why-the-problem-with-learning-is-unlearning, accessed June 2018.

24. For the wizardry metaphor, think of how the wizard Albus Dumbledore deals with his animal familiar, Fawkes, in the *Harry Potter* books of J. K. Rowling. Fawkes, of course, is a phoenix.

25. Chip Heath and Dan Heath, *Switch: How to Change Things When Change Is Hard* (New York: Broadway Books, 2010).

    Jonathan Haidt, *The Happiness Hypothesis: Finding Modern Truth in Ancient Wisdom* (New York: Basic Books, 2006).

    Ian C. Woodward, Samah Shaffakat, and Vincent H. Dominé, *Exploring Leadership Drivers and Blockers* (Singapore: Palgrave Macmillan, 2019).

CHAPTER 5

1. Miyamoto Musashi (1584–1645) was a famous seventeenth-century Japanese soldier, philosopher, strategist, and writer. He is credited with inventing *Niten Ichi-Ryu*, the style of fencing with two swords, and is referred to as *kensai* ("sword saint"). His most famous work is *Gorin no sho*, the Book Of Five Rings, on martial arts and their significance.

2. Carol S. Dweck, *Mindset: The New Psychology of Success* (New York: Ballantine Books, 2016).

3. Ram Charan, *Know-How: The 8 Skills That Separate People Who Perform from Those Who Don't* (New York: Crown Business, 2007).

4. Donald C. Hambrick, "Environment Scanning and Organizational Strategy," *Strategic Management Journal* 3(2) (1982): 159–174.

5. Chun Wei Choo, "The Art of Scanning the Environment," *Bulletin of the American Society for Information Science and Technology* 25(3) (1999): 21–24.

6. Yossi Sheffi, "Preparing for Disruptions Through Early Detection," *MIT Sloan Management Review*, September 15, 2015, https://sloanreview.mit.edu/article/preparing-for-disruptions-through-early-detection/, accessed June 2018.

7. Ram Charan, *The Attacker's Advantage: Turning Uncertainty into Breakthrough Opportunities* (New York: PublicAffairs, 2015).

    Ram Charan, "20/20 Foresight," *strategy+business*, August 3, 2015, https://www.strategy-business.com/article/00351?gko=01aa4, accessed June 2018.

    Harvard Business Review Staff, "You Can't Be a Wimp—Make the Tough Calls," *Harvard Business Review*, November 2013, https://hbr.org/2013/11/you-cant-be-a-wimp-make-the-tough-calls, accessed June 2018.

    Also see the reference material on various leadership tools from Ram Charan as part of our Phoenix Encounter online resources at www.phoenixencountermethod.com.

8. For example, see: https://www.zdnet.com/article/zillow-bets-new-normal-for-real-estate-is-virtual-tours-digital-processes-machine-learning/, accessed May 2020.

9. W. Chan Kim and Renée Mauborgne, "Nondisruptive Creation: Rethinking Innovation and Growth," *MIT Sloan Management Review*, February 21, 2019, https://sloanreview.mit.edu/article/nondisruptive-creation-rethinking-innovation-and-growth/.

10. In team-based activities, psychological safety exists when team members have a shared belief that the team and its members are safe for interpersonal risk

taking. Team members also feel respected, accepted, and included within psychologically safe environments. Psychological safety was defined as "being able to show and employ one's self without fear of negative consequences of self-image, status, or career." (See: William A. Kahn, "Psychological Conditions of Personal Engagement and Disengagement at Work," *Academy of Management Journal* 33(4) (1990): 692–724. Psychological safety is a core element for high-performance teams [e.g., Laura Delizonna, "High-Performing Teams Need Psychological Safety. Here's How to Create It," *Harvard Business Review*, August 24, 2017, https://hbr.org/2017/08/high-performing-teams-need -psychological-safety-heres-how-to-create-it.])

11. Ludo Van der Heyden, "Setting a Tone of Fairness at the Top," in *Business Compliance*, edited by Anthony Smith-Meyer (Amsterdam: Baltzer Science Publishers, 2013), 19, downloaded from Ludo Van der Heyden website, http://www.ludovanderheyden.com/blog/setting-a-tone-of-fairness-at-the-top -business-compliance, accessed June 2018.

Ian Woodward, Elizabeth More, and Ludo Van der Heyden, "'Involve': The Foundation for Fair Process Leadership Communication," INSEAD Working Paper No. 2016/17/OBH/TOM/EFE, https://papers.ssrn.com/sol3/papers .cfm?abstract_id=2747990, accessed June 2018.

Ian Woodward and Samah Shaffakat, "Innovation, Leadership, and Communication Intelligence," in *Strategy and Communication for Innovation*, edited by Nicole Pfeffermann and Julie Gould (Heidelberg: Springer International Publishing, 2017), 245–264.

Amy C. Edmondson, "Teamwork on the Fly," *Harvard Business Review*, April 2012, https://hbr.org/2012/04/teamwork-on-the-fly-2, accessed June 2018.

Jeanne Liedtka, "Why Design Thinking Works," https://hbr.org/2018/09/why -design-thinking-works, September–October 2018, accessed December 2019.

Rikke Friis Dam and Yu Siang Teo, "What Is Design Thinking and Why Is It So Popular?" Interaction Design Foundation, https://www.interaction-design .org/literature/article/what-is-design-thinking-and-why-is-it-so-popular, accessed January 2020.

IDEO Design Thinking, https://designthinking.ideo.com/, accessed December 2019.

Peggy Hollinger, "How Companies Draw on Science Fiction," *Financial Times*, October 2, 2017, https://www.ft.com/content/f603e438-a4ba-11e7 -9e4f-7f5e6a7c98a2, accessed June 2018.

12. A large number of ideation approaches can be practiced in business, including design thinking processes, Rapid Ideation, and brainstorming. Radical Ideation is a Phoenix Encounter tool designed to be an extreme form of structured yet rapid and unconstrained brainstorming, where the outcome is defined as options for a "devastating, destructive attack" on a firm or industry or the widest possible set of defensive ideas. Options arising from Radical Ideation are then stress-tested with other forms of analysis.

13. Hank Stuever, "Yes, 'The Day After' Really Was the Profound TV Moment 'The Americans' Makes It Out to Be," *Washington Post*, May 11, 2016, https:// www.washingtonpost.com/news/arts-and-entertainment/wp/2016/05/11/yes -the-day-after-really-was-the-profound-tv-moment-the-americans-makes-it -out-to-be/, accessed June 2018.

14. See the *Facilitation Guide for the Phoenix Encounter Method* (process manual) for further details, as well as the online resources (available at www .phoenixencountermethod.com) for using Radical Ideation in practice

15. The Phoenix Encounter concept of using the Separation Imperative is designed to discretely separate the steps of idea generation, synthesis, analysis, and decision-making. This is consistent with the principles of design thinking (see endnote 10 above). Combined with Radical Ideation, the Separation Imperative parallels approaches to lateral thinking by viewing problems and issues from very different perspectives, including the notion of thinking with different "hats" in sequence such as idea generation, evaluation of benefits, evaluation of detriments, and so forth. See: Edward De Bono, *Six Thinking Hats*, (Boston, MA: Back Bay Books, 1999).

16. Phrase adapted from a presentation to business executives on "Strategic Thinking" by Simon Henderson of Bain & Company, Sydney, March 2010.

17. The Phoenix Encounter online resources include materials to help you and your team develop and enforce the Separation Imperative, as well as information on how Proactive Scanning, Radical Ideation, and the Separation Imperative can work together in brainstorming to decision processes in business (www.phoenixencountermethod.com).

18. This is consistent with an agile approach relying on rapid experimentation in an iterative fashion in order to foster innovation and seek information on highly prospective ideas, as well as learning from those ideas that will fail. This is noted in relation to startups where early failures may occur and yet learning and adaption can be undertaken quickly. See: Eric Ries, *The Lean Startup: How Today's Entrepreneurs Use Continuous Innovation to Create Radically Successful Businesses* (New York: Crown Business, 2011).

19. Josh Horwitz, "Your Brilliant Kickstarter Idea Could Be on Sale in China Before You've Even Finished Funding It," *Quartz*, October 17, 2016, https://qz.com/771727/chinas-factories-in-shenzhen-can-copy-products -at-breakneck-speed-and-its-time-for-the-rest-of-the-world-to-get-over-it/, accessed June 2018.

CHAPTER 6

1. Rita McGrath, *Seeing Around Corners: How to Spot Inflection Points in Business Before They Happen* (New York: Houghton Mifflin Harcourt Publishing Company, 2019).

2. Livemint News Feed, Company News, "Satya Nadella: We saw 2 years of digital transformation in 2 months," https://www.livemint.com/companies /news/satya-nadella-we-saw-2-years-of-digital-transformation-in-2-months -11588219678520.html, accessed May 2020.

3. W. Chan Kim and Renée Mauborgne, "Five Steps to Making a Blue Ocean Shift," https://www.blueoceanstrategy.com/blog/five-steps-making-blue- ocean-shift/, accessed December 2019.

   W. Chan Kim and Renée Mauborgne, "Nondisruptive Creation: Rethinking Innovation and Growth," *MIT Sloan Management Review*, February 21, 2019, https://sloanreview.mit.edu/article/nondisruptive-creation-rethinking -innovation-and-growth/.

Joshua Gans, *The Disruption Dilemma* (Cambridge, MA: The MIT Press, 2016).

4. In addition to the firepower examples presented throughout this book, the online resources include additional links to assist in running the scanning sessions as part of Encounter exercises you undertake.

5. "Drinking the Kool-Aid" is an expression used to refer to a person who has extreme and often reckless dedication to a cause or purpose. It originates from the deaths in Guyana in 1978, where more than 900 fanatical followers of the Rev. Jim Jones drank (or were forced to drink) a flavored beverage laced with cyanide.

6. Vijay Govindarajan and Anup Srivastava, "No, WeWork Isn't a Tech Company. Here's Why That Matters," *Harvard Business Review*, August 21, 2019, https://hbr.org/2019/08/no-wework-isnt-a-tech-company-heres-why-that-matters, accessed December 2019.

   Maureen Farrell and Eliot Brown, "The Money Men Who Enabled Adam Neumann and the WeWork Debacle," *Wall Street Journal*, December 14, 2019, https://www.wsj.com/articles/the-money-men-who-enabled-adam-neumann-and-the-wework-debacle-11576299616, accessed December 2019.

7. Richard Waters, "Tech's Self-Declared Exceptionalism Is Coming to an End," *Financial Times*, September 19, 2019, https://www.ft.com/content/1cf9ac56-da5d-11e9-8f9b-77216ebe1f17, accessed December 2019.

   Richard Waters, "Tech's IPO Class of 2019 Gets Schooled by Wall St," *Financial Times*, September 12, 2019, https://www.ft.com/content/519f66e0-d56b-11e9-8367-807ebd53ab77, accessed January 2020.

8. Rachel Botsman, *Who Can You Trust? How Technology Is Transforming Human Relationships and What's Next* (London: Portfolio, 2018).

   Airbnb, "Airbnb Expands Beyond the Home with the Launch of Trips," November 17, 2016, https://news.airbnb.com/airbnb-expands-beyond-the-home-with-the-launch-of-trips/, accessed December 2019.

9. Eric J. Savitz, "Peloton Stock Skids as Analyst Questions the Size of the Market," *Barron's*, October 11, 2019, https://www.barrons.com/articles/peloton-stock-ipo-falls-size-of-market-51570825145, accessed December 2019.

   Richard Henderson, "Peloton Skids on Stock Market Debut," *Financial Times*, September 27, 2019, https://www.ft.com/content/60d378fe-dfde-11e9-9743-db5a370481bc, accessed December 2019.

   Anna Gross, "Peloton Punctured by Critical Reception to Viral Ad," *Financial Times*, December 6, 2019, https://www.ft.com/content/56480a16-1842-11ea-8d73-6303645ac406, accessed December 2019.

   "Peloton Exercise Bike Ad Mocked as Being 'Sexist' and 'Dystopian,'" BBC, December 4, 2019, https://www.bbc.com/news/business-50649826, accessed December 2019.

   Megan Graham, "Here's Why Some Peloton Users Love That Ad So Many Have Criticized," CNBC, December 5, 2019, https://www.cnbc.com/2019/12/05/peloton-users-defend-controversial-ad.html, accessed December 2019.

   DeAnna Janes, "What Is the Peloton Girl Meme? An Explanation of the Controversial Holiday Ad," *Oprah Magazine*, December 9, 2019, https://www.oprahmag.com/entertainment/a30172338/peloton-girl-commercial-meme-explanation/, accessed December 2019.

CHAPTER 7

1. Internet World Stats, "The Internet Big Picture: World Internet Users and 2019 Population Stats," https://www.internetworldstats.com/stats.htm, accessed January 27, 2019.

2. Ezra Greenberg, Martin Hirt, and Sven Smit, "The Global Forces Inspiring a New Narrative of Progress," *McKinsey Quarterly* 2 (2017): 32–52, https://www.mckinsey.com/business-functions/strategy-and-corporate-finance/our-insights/the-global-forces-inspiring-a-new-narrative-of-progress, accessed June 2018. We acknowledge the permission granted by McKinsey& Company to reprint Figure 7.1.

3. Steven A. Altman, Pankaj Ghemawat, and Phillip Bastian, *DHL Global Connectedness Index 2018: The State of Globalization in a Fragile World* (Germany: Deutsche Post DHL Group Headquarters, 2019), https://www.logistics.dhl/content/dam/dhl/global/core/documents/pdf/glo-core-gci-2018-full-study.pdf, accessed January 2019.

4. Robert Jensen provides compelling evidence on the impact of digital in reducing price dispersion across the wholesale markets using data collected in the state of Kerala over 1996–2001. See: "The Digital Provide: Information (Technology), Market Performance, and Welfare in the South Indian Fisheries Sector," *Quarterly Journal of Economics* 122(3) (2007): 879–924.

5. In fact, the fisherman was even picky about the telecom operator he preferred. He had chosen BSNL because he felt it had the best coverage for him offshore. While the fisherman had not even finished high school, he was probably among the most informed and sophisticated telecom consumers in India!

6. Bhaskar Chakravorti and Ravi S. Chaturvedi, *Digital Planet 2017: How Competitiveness and Trust in Digital Economies Vary Across the World* (Medford, MA: The Fletcher School, Tufts University, July 2017).

7. Digital penetration refers to the percentage of population in a country that has access to the Internet.

8. Eric Bellman, "The End of Typing: The Next Billion Mobile Users Will Rely on Video and Voice," *Wall Street Journal*, August 7, 2017, https://www.wsj.com/articles/the-end-of-typing-the-internets-next-billion-users-will-use-video-and-voice-1502116070, accessed September 2019.

9. Network externality refers to the effect that an additional user of a product/service has on the value of that product/service to others. So, positive externality implies that the benefits (i.e., marginal utility) of a product/service is an increasing function of the number of other users.

10. Wikipedia, "WhatsApp," https://en.wikipedia.org/wiki/WhatsApp, accessed October 2019.

    Farrell and Saloner (1985) and Katz and Shapiro (1986) are key references in the development of the theory of network effects: Joseph Farrell and Garth Saloner, "Standardization, Compatibility, and Innovation," *RAND Journal of Economics* 16(1) (1985): 70–83.

    Michael L. Katz and Carl Shapiro, "Technology Adoption in the Presence of Network Externalities," *Journal of Political Economy* 94(4) (1986): 822–841.

11. The year it was sold, WhatsApp had more than 700 million active monthly subscribers sending more than 30 billion messages a day. Global SMS traffic at

the time was only about 20 billion a day. The number of WhatsApp messages sent worldwide per day clocked in at 65 billion in May 2018.

Felix Richter, "WhatsApp Usage Shows No Signs of Slowing Down," *Statista*, May 7, 2018, https://www.statista.com/chart/13762/whatsapp-messages-sent -per-day/, accessed September 2019.

Parmy Olson, "Exclusive: The Rags-To-Riches Tale of How Jan Koum Built WhatsApp Into Facebook's New $19 Billion Baby," *Forbes*, February 19, 2014, https://www.forbes.com/sites/parmyolson/2014/02/19/exclusive-inside -story-how-jan-koum-built-whatsapp-into-facebooks-new-19-billion-baby/ #1d6083c62fa1, accessed September 2019.

12. Erik Heinrich, "Telecom Companies Count $386 Billion in Lost Revenue to Skype, WhatsApp, Others," *Fortune*, June 23, 2014, https://fortune.com /2014/06/23/telecom-companies-count-386-billion-in-lost-revenue-to-skype -whatsapp-others/, accessed September 2019.

13. Jon Hilsenrath and Jon Kamm, "How a Johns Hopkins Professor and Her Chinese Students Tracked Coronavirus," May 9, 2020, *Wall Street Journal* https://www.wsj.com/articles/how-a-johns-hopkins-professor-and-her -chinese-students-tracked-coronavirus-11589016603.

14. Philip Kotler and Kevin L. Keller, *Marketing Management*, 15th ed. (London: Pearson Education, Inc., 2016). We acknowledge the permission of these professors to present their framework in Figure 7.2.

James F. Engel, Roger D. Blackwell, and Paul W. Miniard, *Consumer Behavior*, 8th ed. (Chicago: Dryden Press, 1994).

15. Above-the-line (ALT) and below-the-line (BLT) are the two parts of a firm's overall marketing budget. ATL refers to all marketing expenditures that are targeted directly at the end-user/consumer (e.g., advertising expenditures on TV, print, and outdoor) and is commonly referred to as "pull" expenditures. BTL refers to all marketing expenditures targeted at the intermediaries (e.g., trade promotion expenditures) and is commonly referred to as "push" expenditures. See James M. Olver and Paul W. Farris, "Push and Pull: A One-Two Punch for Packaged Products," *Sloan Management Review* 53 (1989) and Cannondale Associates, *Trade Promotion Spending and Merchandising: 1999 Industry Study* (Wilton: Cannondale Associates, Inc., 1999) for compelling evidence of the growth of BTL in firms' marketing budgets over time.

16. David Court, Dave Elzinga, Bo Finneman, and Jesko Perrey, "The New Battleground for Marketing-Led Growth," *McKinsey Quarterly*, February 2017, https://www.mckinsey.com/business-functions/marketing-and-sales/our -insights/the-new-battleground-for-marketing-led-growth, accessed September 2019.

17. Kevin Roose, "Inside the Home of the Instant Pot, the Kitchen Gadget That Spawned a Religion," *New York Times*, December 17, 2017, https://www .nytimes.com/2017/12/17/business/instant-pot.html, accessed September 2019.

18. Amazon.com, https://www.amazon.com/Instant-Pot-Multi-Use -Programmable-Packaging/dp/B00FLYWNYQ/ref=sr_1_1_acs_twc_TWC1 1893_1?s=kitchen&ie=UTF8&qid=1515729432&sr=1-1-acs&keywords=ins tant+pot&tag=ospsearch-20&ascsubtag=TWC11893, accessed January 2018.

19. Pete Evans, "Owner of Pyrex, CorningWare Cooks Up Takeover of Instant Potmaker," *CBC News*, March 4, 2019, https://www.cbc.ca/news/business /instant-pot-merger-1.5041627, accessed September 2019.

    Michael J. de la Merced, "Instant Pot Maker Bought by Pyrex's Parent as Old Kitchen Meets New," *New York Times*, March 4, 2019, https://www.nytimes .com/2019/03/04/business/dealbook/instant-pot-corelle-pyrex.html, accessed September 2019.

20. Hau L. Lee, V. Padmanabhan, and Seungjin Whang, "The Bullwhip Effect in Supply Chains," *Sloan Management Review*, April 15, 1997, https:// sloanreview.mit.edu/article/the-bullwhip-effect-in-supply-chains/, accessed September 2019.

    Hau L. Lee, V. Padmanabhan, and Seungjin Whang, "Comments on Information Distortion in a Supply Chain: The Bullwhip Effect," *Management Science* 50(12) (2004): 1887–1893.

21. See for eample: https://www.economist.com/science-and-technology/2020 /05/07/scientific-research-on-the-coronavirus-is-being-released-in-a-torrent, accessed May 12, 2020.

22. Ben Potter, "Tesla Battery Boss: We Can Solve SA's Power Woes in 100 Days," *Financial Review*, March 9, 2017, https://www.afr.com/politics/tesla-battery -boss-we-can-solve-sas-power-woes-in-100-days-20170308-gut8xh, accessed September 2019.

    Australian Associated Press, "South Australia Turns on Tesla's 100MW Battery: 'History in the Making,'" *Guardian*, November 30, 2017, https://www .theguardian.com/australia-news/2017/dec/01/south-australia-turns-on-teslas -100mw-battery-history-in-the-making, accessed September 2019.

    Rob Taylor, "Tesla Delivers the World's Biggest Battery—and Wins a Bet," *Wall Street Journal*, November 23, 2017, https://www.wsj.com/articles /tesla-delivers-the-worlds-biggest-batteryand-wins-a-bet-1511439167?mod= searchresults&page=1&pos=5, accessed September 2019.

23. Richard Waters, "Why Wall Street Is Betting on Business Software," *Financial Times*, March 7, 2019, https://www.ft.com/content/2fea3c12-4071-11e9 -b896-fe36ec32aece, accessed December 2019.

24. Merchdope, "37 Mind Blowing YouTube Facts, Figures and Statistics—2019," September 29, 2019, https://merchdope.com/youtube-stats/, accessed September 2019.

25. Statista, "YouTube," 2019, https://www.statista.com/study/15475/youtube -statista-dossier/, accessed September 2019.

26. Andrew McAfee and Erik Brynjolfsson, in their *Machine, Platform, Crowd: Harnessing Our Digital Future* (New York: WW Norton & Co, 2017), have a very nice illustration of the power of knowledge creation in the UGC world— an estimated 130 million books have been published through the course of human history, and the Library of Congress (the biggest library in the world) has about 30 million books in its collections. In contrast, the portion of the World Wide Web visible to search engines in January 2018 is about 45 billion webpages.

27. James Surowiecki, *The Wisdom of Crowds* (United States: Anchor Books, 2004).

28. Inyoung Chae, David A. Schweidel, Theos Evgeniou, and V. Padmanabhan, "Does User Generated Content Help Publishers: Analyzing Content Consumption in a Hybrid Content Environment," INSEAD Working Paper, 2019.

29. Brett Hollenbeck, Sridhar Moorthy, and Davide Proserpio, "Advertising Strategy in the Presence of Reviews: An Empirical Analysis," *Marketing Science* 38(5) (2019): 793–811.

30. Wikipedia, "United Breaks Guitars," https://en.wikipedia.org/wiki/United _Breaks_Guitars, accessed October 2019.

31. Mark Tran, "Singer Gets His Revenge on United Airlines and Soars to Fame," *News blog, Guardian*, July 23, 2009, https://www.theguardian.com/news/blog /2009/jul/23/youtube-united-breaks-guitars-video, accessed September 2019.

"Did Dave Carol Lose United Airlines $180m?" July 24, 2009, https://www .economist.com/gulliver/2009/07/24/did-dave-carroll-lose-united-airlines -180m, accessed May 2020.

32. Oded Netzer, Ronen Feldman, Jacob Goldenberg, and Moshe Fresko,, "Mine Your Own Business: Market-Structure Surveillance Through Text Mining," *Marketing Science* 31(3) (2012): 521–543.

33. Brian Chesky (@bchesky), "If @Airbnb Could Launch Anything in 2017, What Would It Be?" Twitter, Dec 25, 2016, 7:08 PM, https://twitter.com /bchesky/status/813219932087390208?lang=en, accessed May 2020.

34. David Dubois and Katrina Bens, "Ombre, Tie-Dye, Splat Hair: Trends or Fads? 'Pull' and 'Push' Social Media Strategies at L'Oreal Paris," INSEAD No. 06/2014-6060 (Fontainebleau: INSEAD Case Publishing, 2014), https://cases .insead.edu/loreal-google/, accessed September 2019.

35. Eric Sylvers and Suzanne Kapner, "As Gucci Tripped on Social Media, Sales Fell," *Wall Street Journal*, September 15, 2019, https://www.wsj.com /articles/guccis-social-media-status-fell-and-its-north-american-sales-dropped -11568539802, accessed October 2019.

36. Richard Waters, "Tech's Self-Declared Exceptionalism Is Coming to an End," *Financial Times*, September 19, 2019, https://www.ft.com/content/1cf9ac56 -da5d-11e9-8f9b-77216ebe1f17, accessed October 2019.

Brooke Masters, "WeWork's Humbling Is a Cautionary Tale About Watching the Bottom Line," *Financial Times*, September 23, 2019, https://www.ft.com /content/99ee90b0-dde5-11e9-b112-9624ec9edc59, accessed October 2019.

37. Eline Chivot, "One Year On, GDPR Needs a Reality Check," *Financial Times*, June 30, 2019, https://www.ft.com/content/26ee4f7c-982d-11e9-98b9 -e38c177b152f, accessed October 2019.

Also see: Dina Srinivasan, "The Antitrust Case Against Facebook: A Monopolist's Journey Towards Pervasive Surveillance in Spite of Consumers' Preference for Privacy," *Berkeley Business Law Journal* 16(1) (2019): 39–101.

38. The terms "digitization," "digitalization," and "digital transformation" are often confused with each other. Digitization is conversion of information from a physical format to a digital format (e.g., converting a VHS videotape to a digital CD or DVD). Digitalization refers to the process of leveraging digitization to improve business processes (e.g., leveraging a CD collection to create an online rental service). Digital transformation refers to the transformation of business activities, processes, products, and models to fully leverage the power

of these new technologies (e.g., creating a new online streaming service that provides global coverage for entertainment along with recommendations and advertisements).

CHAPTER 8

1. The classical reference on platforms is Jean-Charles Rochet and Jean Tirole, "Platform Competition in Two-Sided Markets," *Journal of the European Economic Association* 1(4) (2003): 990–1029. For a nontechnical discussion, see: Richard Schmalensee, "An Instant Classic: Rochet & Tirole, Platform Competition in Two-Sided Markets," *Competition Policy International Journal* 10 (2014).

2. Fortune Media IP Limited, "Fortune 500," https://fortune.com/fortune500 /search/, accessed October 2019.

3. Hal R. Varian, "Innovation, Components and Complements," excerpt from the author's Mattoli Lectures on economics of information technology, delivered in Milano, Italy, 2003, https://pdfs.semanticscholar.org/c7a5/3d6b0f353 5085ee0c9654b1eb7eb092e8da2.pdf, accessed November 2019.

4. David A. Hounshell, *From the American System to Mass Production, 1800– 1932: The Development of Manufacturing Technology in the United States* (Baltimore, MD: Johns Hopkins University Press, 1984).

5. Crunchbase Inc., "List of Amazon's 86 Acquisitions," https://www.crunchbase .com/search/acquisitions/field/organizations/num_acquisitions/amazon, accessed November 2019.

6. By comaprison, platformatization emerged progressively at Apple. It is interesting to note that Steve Jobs initially resisted allowing outside developers to build apps for the iPhone. He later changed his mind—the iTunes store had 2.2 million apps for customers to choose from in March 2017. As McAfee and Brynjolfsson pointed out in 2017 (see endnote 28 in Chapter 7), the existence of free apps like Angry Birds and Shazam conveys additional benefits to the Apple platform. First, it allows Apple to leverage the wisdom of the crowds. It is unlikely that any company (even a company like Apple) can consistently come up with apps like Shazam and Angry Birds on their own. Second, the availability of a large portfolio of apps on the iTunes store increases the demand for iPhones. Clearly, quality control is extremely important, which is why Apple sets strict performance standards that app makers have to comply with before they get listed on the iTunes storefront. Andrew McAfee and Erik Brynjolfsson, *Machine, Platform, Crowd: Harnessing Our Digital Future* (New York: WW Norton & Co, 2017).

7. See David Streitfeld, "Whole Foods Deal Shows Amazon's Prodigious Tolerance for Risk," *New York Times*, June 17, 2017, https://www.nytimes.com /2017/06/17/technology/whole-foods-amazon.html for an interesting report on Amazon's philosophy as it relates to experimentation, long-term perspective, and success/failure.

8. Crunchbase Inc., "List of Alibaba Group's 29 Acquisitions," https://www .crunchbase.com/search/acquisitions/field/organizations/num_acquisitions /alibaba, accessed November 2019.

9. Alice Shen, "China Pulls Further Ahead of US in Mobile Payments with Record US\$12.8 Trillion in Transactions," *South China Morning Post*, February

20, 2018, https://www.scmp.com/tech/apps-gaming/article/2134011/china-pulls-further-ahead-us-mobile-payments-record-us128-trillion, accessed November 2019.

Zheping Huang, "All the Things You Can—and Can't—Do with Your WeChat Account in China," *Quartz*, December 28, 2017, https://qz.com/1167024/all-the-things-you-can-and-cant-do-with-your-wechat-account-in-china/, accessed November 2019.

10. Jason Kirby and Richard Henderson, "Shopify's swift ascent stirs talk to Canadian 'curse,'" *Financial Times*, May 9, 2020, https://www.ft.com/content/0f8f9591-1735-44cc-bd66-cb82abcac5c0, accessed May 2020.

Jeran Wittenstein, "Shopify Surges After CTO Touts 'Black Friday Level Traffic,'" Bloomberg, 17 April 2020, https://www.bloomberg.com/news/articles/2020-04-17/shopify-surges-after-cto-touts-black-friday-level-traffic-k94d2z4r, accessed May 2020.

11. Jean Tirole received the Nobel Prize in Economics in 2014 for a number of important accomplishments, including his contributions to the economics of multisided platforms. The interested reader is referred to David S. Evans and Richard Schmalensee, *Matchmakers: The New Economics of Multisided Platforms* (Boston, MA: Harvard Business Review Press, 2016) for nontechnical development of the key intuitions of this theory and its implications for business.

12. Kaifu Zhang, Theodoros Evgeniou, V. Padmanabhan, and Emile Richard, "Content Contributor Management and Network Effects in a UGC Environment," *Marketing Science* 31(3): 433–447.

13. It is unclear whether Amazon will try to get into this 30 percent, as it represents categories like automobiles, fuels, alcohol, and tobacco that are either heavily regulated or controversial.

14. Ram Charan and Julia Yang, *The Amazon Management System: The Ultimate Digital Business Engine That Creates Extraordinary Value for Both Customers and Shareholders* (United States: Ideapress Publishing, 2019).

15. See: https://www.indiatoday.in/business/story/e-conclave-brainstorm-paytm-oyo-and-byju-chiefs-on-how-start-ups-will-survive-covid-19-1675103-2020-05-06. accessed May 2020.

Amy Kazmin, "Byju's finds profitability in Indian consumers' hunger for education," *Financial Times,* March 30, 2020, https://www.ft.com/content/bb55de1c-6273-11ea-abcc-910c5b38d9ed, accessed May 2020.

16. Wikipedia, "Singles' Day," https://en.wikipedia.org/wiki/Singles%27_Day, accessed January 2020.

17. Agne Blazyte, "Alibaba: Singles' Day E-commerce Revenues 2011–2019," *Statista*, November 13, 2019, https://www.statista.com/statistics/364543/alibaba-singles-day-1111-gmv/, accessed January 2020.

18. In fact, Alibaba and Tencent's nonperforming loan ratios are even lower than that of the state-owned Chinese banks. For example see: Jianping Li, Yongjie Zhang, DengSheng Wu, and Wei Zhang, "Impacts of Big Data in the Chinese Financial Industry," *Bridge, National Academy of Engineering* 44(4) (Winter 2014): 20–27.

19. Ina Zhou, "Alibaba's Singles' Day Securities Find Admirers," *Reuters*, November 27, 2016, https://www.reuters.com/article/alibaba-debt-bonds-idUSL4N1DT17J, accessed November 2019.

20. Chin Yong Chang, "Use, Monetizing of Data Will Fuel Digital Revolution," *Business Times*, August 22, 2017, https://www.businesstimes.com.sg/technology/use-monetising-of-data-will-fuel-digital-revolution, accessed November 2019.

21. Henny Sender, "Piyush Gupta: Predicting Disruption," *Financial Times*, November 11, 2018, https://www.ft.com/content/00b7069c-d5ef-11e8-ab8e-6be0dcf18713, accessed November 2019.

22. Tanguy Catlin, Johannes-Tobias Lorenz, Jahnavi Nandan, Shirish Sharma, and Andreas Waschto, "Insurance Beyond Digital: The Rise of Ecosystems and Platforms," McKinsey & Company, Insurance Practice, January 2018, https://www.mckinsey.com/industries/financial-services/our-insights/insurance-beyond-digital-the-rise-of-ecosystems-and-platforms, accessed November 2019.

23. Clearly, there has been a lot of press coverage about the ill effects of platforms—for instance, the impact of platforms in creating the gig economy world and its impact on employment and wages. The J. P. Morgan Chase & Co Institute report "Paychecks, Paydays, and the Online Platform Economy," February 2016 (https://www.jpmorganchase.com/corporate/institute/document/jpmc-institute-volatility-2-report.pdf, accessed July 2018) showed platforms are largely a secondary source of income for their workers that they use to smooth volatility in their regular jobs' income. We will discuss these and other related concerns in the later chapters.

24. Alexandra Berzon, Shane Shifflett, and Justin Scheck, "Amazon Has Ceded Control of Its Site. The Result: Thousands of Banned, Unsafe or Mislabeled Products," *Wall Street Journal*, August 23, 2019, https://www.wsj.com/articles/amazon-has-ceded-control-of-its-site-the-result-thousands-of-banned-unsafe-or-mislabeled-products-11566564990, accessed November 2019.

25. Rolfe Winkler, "Uber and Lyft Get Creative with Numbers, but Investors Aren't Blind to the Losses," *Wall Street Journal*, May 14, 2019, https://www.wsj.com/articles/uber-and-lyft-get-creative-with-numbers-but-investors-arent-blind-to-the-losses-11557826202, accessed November 2019.

26. Charles Riley, "UK Proposes Another Huge Data Fine. This Time, Marriott Is the Target," CNN Business, July 9, 2019, https://edition.cnn.com/2019/07/09/tech/marriott-data-breach-fine/index.html, accessed January 2020.

27. Richard Waters, "Big Tech Veteran Scents Change in Rules of the Game," *Financial Times*, September 18, 2019, https://www.ft.com/content/1c0fb100-da17-11e9-8f9b-77216ebe1f17, accessed November 2019.

Dina Srinivasan, "The Antitrust Case Against Facebook: A Monopolist's Journey Towards Pervasive Surveillance in Spite of Consumers Preference for Privacy," *Berkeley Business Law Journal*, 2019, 16/1.

CHAPTER 9

1. Sapna Maheshwari, "This Thermometer Tells Your Temperature, Then Tells Firms Where to Advertise," *New York Times*, October 23, 2018, https://www.nytimes.com/2018/10/23/business/media/fever-advertisements-medicine-clorox.html, accessed September 2019.

2. Healthcare IT News, "Digital thermometer data may provide insight into COVID-19 surges," March 26, 2020, https://www.healthcareitnews.com /news/digital-thermometer-data-may-provide-insight-covid-19-surges.

3. Nanette Byrnes, "As Goldman Embraces Automation, Even the Masters of the Universe Are Threatened," *MIT Technology Review,* February 7, 2017, https:// www.technologyreview.com/s/603431/as-goldman-embraces-automation -even-the-masters-of-the-universe-are-threatened/, accessed September 2019.

4. Michelin North America Inc, "Fleet Solutions," https://www.michelintruck .com/services-and-programs/michelin-fleet-solutions/, accessed September 2019.

See also a case written on this by Chloe Renault, Frederic Dalsace, and Wolfgang Ulaga, "Michelin Fleet Solutions: From Selling Tires to Selling Kilometers," Reference No. 510-103-1, The Case Centre, 2010, https://www .thecasecentre.org/educators/products/view?id=96546, accessed September 2019.

5. We acknowledge the permission granted by mytechfrontier.com to reprint Figure 9.1.

6. Lauren Debter, "Amazon Surpasses Walmart as the World's Largest Retailer," May 15, 2019, https://www.forbes.com/sites/laurendebter/2019/05/15 /worlds-largest-retailers-2019-amazon-walmart-alibaba/#7729a5fa4171, accessed January 2020.

7. Definition adapted from Microsoft Primer on Cloud Computing. See: Microsoft, "What Is Cloud Computing?" https://azure.microsoft.com/en-in /overview/what-is-cloud-computing/, accessed September 2019.

8. Amazon Web Services, Inc., "Dow Jones Case Study," https://aws.amazon.com /solutions/case-studies/dow-jones/, accessed September 2019.

9. Amazon Web Services, Inc., "Announcing Amazon Elastic Compute Cloud (Amazon EC2)—beta," https://aws.amazon.com/about-aws/whats-new/2006 /08/24/announcing-amazon-elastic-compute-cloud-amazon-ec2---beta/, accessed September 2019.

10. Amazon, of course, is not alone in its cloud offerings. Microsoft, Google, IBM, and Alibaba are also deep into the cloud business. These big companies are leveraging their tech know-how and resources to develop cloud infrastructure and services that most individual enterprises cannot afford to develop on their own. The top players are reported to have invested nearly $120 billion (+43 percent YoY) in FY 2018 in capital expenditures in building, expanding, and upgrading large data centers. In fact, Amazon, Microsoft, and Google collectively invested $53 billion in capital expenditures in the first half of 2018 (up 70 percent YoY), according to company filings.

11. "Twilio CEO jumps back into billionaire ranks as demand for cloud computing services surges," *Forbes,* May 11, 2020, https://www.forbes.com /sites/jonathanponciano/2020/05/11/billionaire-twilio-stock-jeff-lawson/ #3a650e5e289c, accessed May 13, 2020.

"Will coronavirus compound the concentration of cloud computing champions?" Telecoms.com, May 10, 2020, https://telecoms.com/504201/will -coronavirus-compound-the-concentration-of-cloud-computing-champions/, accessed May 14, 2020.

12. Bala R. Iyer and John C. Henderson, "Preparing for the Future: Understanding the Seven Capabilities of Cloud Computing," *MIS Quarterly Executive* 9(2) (2010): 117–131. This article listed seven capabilities, in addition to cost savings, offered by cloud computing: *controlled interface, location independence, sourcing independence, ubiquitous access, virtual business environments, addressability and traceability*, and *rapid elasticity.*

    Also see: Will Venters, "The 7 Capabilities of Cloud Computing—A Review of a Recent MISQE Article on Cloud," Binary Blurring Blog, May 20, 2011, https://binaryblurring.com/2011/05/20/the-7-capabilities-of-cloud-computing-a-review-of-a-recent-misqe-article-on-cloud/, accessed October 2019.

13. RightScale Inc., *RightScale, 2019 State of the Cloud Report from Flexera*, 2019, https://resources.flexera.com/web/media/documents/rightscale-2019-state-of-the-cloud-report-from-flexera.pdf, accessed May 2020.

14. RightScale, Inc., *RightScale 2017 State of the Cloud Report*, 2017, https://assets.rightscale.com/uploads/pdfs/RightScale-2017-State-of-the-Cloud-Report.pdf, accessed October 2019.

    Arul Elumalai, James Kaplan, Mike Newborn, and Roger Roberts, "Making a Secure Transition to the Public Cloud," *McKinsey Insights*, January, 2018, https://www.mckinsey.com/business-functions/mckinsey-digital/our-insights/making-a-secure-transition-to-the-public-cloud#0, accessed September 2019.

    Tom Smith, "Public Cloud Adoption Grows as Private Cloud Wanes: 2017 State of the Cloud Report Executive Summary," DZone.com, February 15, 2017, https://dzone.com/articles/public-cloud-adoption-grows-as-private-cloud-wanes, accessed September 2019.

15. Cloud computing adoption has seen significant growth in the past few years as reflected in the revenue growth of top cloud services provider Amazon Web Services (AWS). AWS quarterly revenue has doubled in the past two years, generating $45 billion in revenue for the company in Q3 2017.

    Statista, "Quarterly Revenue of Amazon Web Services from 1st Quarter 2014 to 3rd Quarter 2019," 2019, https://www.statista.com/statistics/250520/forecast-of-amazon-web-services-revenue/, accessed October 2019.

16. Brian Caulfield, "What's the Difference Between a CPU and a GPU?" NVIDIA Blog, December 16, 2009, https://blogs.nvidia.com/blog/2009/12/16/whats-the-difference-between-a-cpu-and-a-gpu/, accessed January 2020.

    Steven Levy, "Inside Amazon's Artificial Intelligence Flywheel," *WIRED*, February 1, 2018, https://www.wired.com/story/amazon-artificial-intelligence-flywheel/, accessed September 2019.

17. Will Knight, "Meet the Chinese Finance Giant That's Secretly an AI Company," *MIT Technology Review*, June 16, 2017, https://www.technologyreview.com/s/608103/ant-financial-chinas-giant-of-mobile-payments-is-rethinking-finance-with-ai/, accessed September 2019.

18. NewVantage Partners LLC, "Big Data and AI Executive Survey 2019," http://newvantage.com/wp-content/uploads/2018/12/Big-Data-Executive-Survey-2019-Findings-Updated-010219-1.pdf, accessed October 2019.

19. Tom Groenfeldt, "Some Banks—Quietly—Use Big Data," *Forbes*, June 18, 2015, https://www.forbes.com/sites/tomgroenfeldt/2015/06/18/some-banks-quietly-use-big-data/#da09a8958cd2, accessed October 2019.

20. See: International Data Corporation (IDC) website: https://www.idc.com/.

21. Gartner, Inc., "Gartner Glossary," https://www.gartner.com/en/information-technology/glossary/advanced-analytics, accessed October 2019.

22. Kim S. Nash, "Phoenix Airport Upgrades Data Analytics to First Class," *Wall Street Journal*, March 14, 2017, https://blogs.wsj.com/cio/2017/03/14/phoenix-airport-upgrades-data-analytics-to-first-class/, accessed October 2019.

23. Rob Matheson, "Voice Analytics Software Helps Customer Service Reps Build Better Rapport with Customers," Phys.org, January 20, 2016, https://phys.org/news/2016-01-voice-analytics-software-customer-reps.html, accessed October 2019.

24. Arup Dasgupta, "Who's Buying All That Satellite Imagery?" Geospatialworld, July 30, 2018, https://www.geospatialworld.net/article/whos-buying-all-that-satellite-imagery/, accessed January 2020.

25. We acknowledge the permission granted by mytechfrontier.com to reprint Figure 9.2.

26. Hallie Cho, Sameer Hasija, and Manuel Sosa, "Reading Between the Stars: Understanding the Effects of Online Customer Reviews on Product Demand," INSEAD Working Paper No. 2018/36/TOM, https://papers.ssrn.com/sol3/papers.cfm?abstract_id=3240453, accessed October 2019.

27. Randy Bean and Thomas H. Davenport, "Companies Are Failing in Their Efforts to Become Data-Driven," *Harvard Business Review*, February 5, 2019, https://hbr.org/2019/02/companies-are-failing-in-their-efforts-to-become-data-driven, accessed October 2019.

28. Kaggle Inc., "2017 The State of Data Science & Machine Learning," https://www.kaggle.com/surveys/2017, accessed October 2019.

29. Gartner, Inc., "Gartner Says Worldwide Business Intelligence and Analytics Market to Reach $18.3 Billion in 2017," press release, February 17, 2017, Gartner website, https://www.gartner.com/en/newsroom/press-releases/2017-02-17-gartner-says-worldwide-business-intelligence-and-analytics-market-to-reach-18-billion-in-2017, accessed October 2019.

30. Sisense Inc., "Narrative Science and Sisense Unveil Strategic Partnership to Unleash Business Intelligence Insights," press release, February 28, 2017, https://www.sisense.com/press-release/narrative-science-sisense-unveil-strategic-partnership-unleash-business-intelligence-insights/, accessed January 2020.

Pedro Hernandez, "Microsoft Previews Conversational Q&A in Power BI Mobile," eWeek, June 13, 2017, https://www.eweek.com/mobile/microsoft-previews-conversational-q-a-in-power-bi-mobile, accessed October 2019.

31. Narrative Science, "Partner Network," https://narrativescience.com/partners/, accessed October 2019.

32. Patience Haggin, "Businesses Across the Board Scramble to Comply with California Data-Privacy Law," *Wall Street Journal*, September 8, 2019, https://www.wsj.com/articles/businesses-across-the-board-scramble-to-comply-with-california-data-privacy-law-11567947602, accessed October 2019.

33. Kris Holt, "Facebook's Latest Leak Includes Data on Millions of Users (Updated)," Engadget, September 4, 2019, https://www.engadget.com/2019/09/04/facebook-privacy-databases-phone-numbers/, accessed October 2019.

Chaim Gartenberg, "Apple Apologizes for Siri Audio Recordings, Announces Privacy Changes Going Forward," Verge, August 28, 2019, https://www.theverge.com/2019/8/28/20836760/apple-apology-siri-audio-recordings-privacy-changes-contractors, accessed October 2019.

34. Zack Whittaker, "FTC Slaps Equifax with a Fine of Up to $700M for 2017 Data Breach," TechCrunch, July 22, 2019, https://techcrunch.com/2019/07/22/equifax-fine-ftc/, accessed October 2019.

35. Peter Stone, et al, Stanford University Report of the Study Panel, 2015–2016, *Artificial Intelligence and Life in 2030,* https://ai100.stanford.edu/sites/g/files/sbiybj9861/f/ai_100_report_0831fnl.pdf, accessed October 2019.

36. Theodoros Evgeniou, "The Pivotal Management Challenge of the AI Era," INSEAD Blog, INSEAD Knowledge, April 8, 2019, https://knowledge.insead.edu/blog/insead-blog/the-pivotal-management-challenge-of-the-ai-era-11311, accessed January 2020.

37. Andrew McAfee and Erik Brynjolfsson, *Machine, Platform, Crowd: Harnessing Our Digital Future* (New York: WW Norton & Co, 2017).

38. Daniel Wroclawski, "Which Smart Appliances Work with Amazon Alexa, Google Home, and More," *Consumer Reports,* March 2, 2018, https://www.consumerreports.org/appliances/smart-appliances-that-work-with-amazon-alexa-google-home-and-more/, accessed October 2019.

39. Jordan Crook, "Amazon Is Putting Alexa in the Office," TechCrunch, November 29, 2017, https://techcrunch.com/2017/11/29/amazon-is-putting-alexa-in-the-office/, accessed October 2019.

   Amazon Web Services, Inc., "Alexa for Business," https://aws.amazon.com/alexaforbusiness/, accessed October 2019.

40. Digital twin refers to a digital replica of physical assets, processes, and systems that can be used for various purposes. The digital representation provides both the elements and the dynamics of how an Internet of Things device operates and lives throughout its life cycle.

   See: Wikipedia, "Digital Twin," https://en.wikipedia.org/wiki/Digital_twin, accessed January 2020.

   Sara Castellanos, "GE's Digital Replicas, Which Monitor Machines, Gain a Voice," *Wall Street Journal,* March 21, 2017, https://blogs.wsj.com/cio/2017/03/21/ges-digital-replicas-which-monitor-machines-gain-a-voice/, accessed October 2019.

41. Kelsey Gee, "In Unilever's Radical Hiring Experiment, Resumes Are Out, Algorithms Are In," *Wall Street Journal,* June 26, 2017, https://www.wsj.com/articles/in-unilevers-radical-hiring-experiment-resumes-are-out-algorithms-are-in-1498478400, accessed October 2019.

42. Philipp Gerbert, Martin Reeves, Sebastian Steinhäuser, and Patrick Ruwolt, "Is Your Business Ready for Artificial Intelligence?" BCG Henderson Institute, September 6, 2017, https://www.bcg.com/publications/2017/strategy-technology-digital-is-your-business-ready-artificial-intelligence.aspx, accessed October 2019.

43. Natasha Lomas, "Foxconn to Plug at Least $340M into AI R&D over Five Years," TechCrunch, February 3, 2018, https://techcrunch.com/2018/02/03/foxconn-to-plug-at-least-340m-into-ai-rd-over-five-years/, accessed October 2019.

44. "Why this myth and fake news buster app by IIIT Delhi profs is the coolest thing in this COVID-19 world," Edex Live, May 9, 2020, https://www .edexlive.com/happening/2020/may/09/why-this-myth-and-fake-news-buster -app-by-iiit-delhi-profs-is-the-coolest-thing-in-this-covid-19-wor-11890.html accessed May 13, 2020.

45. Jared Council, "Companies Bolster AI Governance Efforts," *WSJ Pro*, August 20, 2019, https://www.wsj.com/articles/companies-bolster-ai-governance -efforts-11566293400, accessed October 2019.

Ceri Parker, "Artificial Intelligence Could Be Our Saviour, According to the CEO of Google," World Economic Forum, January 24, 2018, https://www .weforum.org/agenda/2018/01/google-ceo-ai-will-be-bigger-than-electricity -or-fire/, accessed October 2019.

Sundar Pichai, "Why Google Thinks We Need to Regulate AI," Opinion Piece, January 20, 2020, https://www.ft.com/content/3467659a-386d-11ea -ac3c-f68c10993b04, accessed January 2020.

Brian Bergstein, "This Is Why AI Has Yet to Reshape Most Businesses," *MIT Technology Review*, February 13, 2019, https://www.technologyreview.com /s/612897/this-is-why-ai-has-yet-to-reshape-most-businesses/, accessed October 2019.

46. Stephen Hawking, Stuart Russell, Max Tegmark, and Frank Wilczek, "Stephen Hawking: 'Transcendence Looks at the Implications of Artificial Intelligence—But Are We Taking AI Seriously Enough?'" *Independent*, May 1, 2014, https://www.independent.co.uk/news/science/stephen-hawking -transcendence-looks-at-the-implications-of-artificial-intelligence-but-are-we -taking-9313474.html, accessed January 2020.

CHAPTER 10

1. Eric Lamarre and Brett May, "Making Sense of Internet of Things Platforms," *McKinsey Insights*, May 2017, https://www.mckinsey.com/business -functions/mckinsey-digital/our-insights/making-sense-of-internet-of-things -platforms#, accessed January 2020.

2. "Digital Twins: The Bridge Between Industrial Assets and the Digital World," GE Digital Blog, https://www.ge.com/digital/blog/digital-twins-bridge -between-industrial-assets-and-digital-world, accessed January 2020.

3. For a commentary from a senior researcher from Hirotec on the benefits the company derived from its IoT initiative, see PTC, "Hirotec Launches IoT Initiative," https://www.ptc.com/en/case-studies/hirotec, accessed January 2020.

4. Philippe Blaettchen, Sameer Hasija, and Niyazi Taneri, "Sharing of Heavy Equipment," INSEAD Working Paper No. 2019/50/TOM, https://papers .ssrn.com/sol3/papers.cfm?abstract_id=3254790, accessed January 2020.

Peter Newman, "Voice Assistant Integration Is the Top Smart-Home Trend at CES," *Business Insider*, January 9, 2018, https://www.businessinsider.com /voice-assistant-integration-top-smart-home-trend-ces-2018-1?IR=T, accessed January 2020.

Amazon.com, Inc., "Amazon Dash Replenishment," https://developer.amazon .com/en-US/alexa/dash-services, accessed January 2020.

Bryan Pearson, "The Internet of Things to Come: How Nespresso, Apple, Nest Grind Out Predictability," *Forbes*, March 30, 2016, https://www.forbes.com/sites/bryanpearson/2016/03/30/the-internet-of-things-to-come-how-nespresso-apple-nest-grind-out-predictability/#3a0d90fe7885, accessed January 2020.

5. Ryan Arsenault, "Stat of the Week: The (Rising!) Cost of Downtime," Aberdeen, April 21, 2016, https://www.aberdeen.com/techpro-essentials/stat-of-the-week-the-rising-cost-of-downtime/, accessed January 2020.

"What Is Predictive Maintenance?" IBM Services, January 21, 2019, https://www.ibm.com/services/technology-support/multivendor-it/predictive-maintenance, accessed January 2020.

6. HP Development Company, L.P., "HP Instant Ink—What Is HP Instant Ink?" https://support.hp.com/my-en/document/c03760650, accessed January 2020.

7. Michelin, "Services and Solutions," https://www.michelin.com/en/activities/related-services/services-and-solutions/, accessed January 2020.

Michelin, "EFFIFUEL™ from MICHELIN® Solutions Delivers Fuel Savings," September 23, 2014, https://www.michelin.com/en/documents/effifuel-from-michelin-solutions-delivers-fuel-savings/, accessed January 2020.

8. Mark Patel, Jason Shangkuan, and Christopher Thomas, "What's New with the Internet of Things?" *McKinsey Insights*, May 2017, https://www.mckinsey.com/industries/semiconductors/our-insights/whats-new-with-the-internet-of-things, accessed January 2020.

9. Elvia, "Internet of Things Security and Privacy Challenges," Reolink Blog, October 19, 2018, https://reolink.com/internet-of-things-security-privacy-challenges/, accessed January 2020.

10. "The Human Side of IoT: Digital Transformation Is About More than Technology," MIT Sloan Executive Education innovation@work Blog, September 30, 2017, https://executive.mit.edu/blog/the-human-side-of-iot-digital-transformation-is-about-more-than-technology, accessed January 2020.

11. Douglas MacMillan and Tim Higgins, "Waymo CEO Says Alphabet Unit Plans to Launch Driverless Car Service in Coming Months," *Wall Street Journal*, November 13, 2018, https://www.wsj.com/articles/waymo-ceo-says-alphabet-unit-plans-to-launch-driverless-car-service-in-coming-months-1542135341, accessed October 2019.

Phil LeBeau, "Waymo Starts Commercial Ride-Share Service," *CNBC*, December 5, 2018, https://www.cnbc.com/2018/12/05/waymo-starts-commercial-ride-share-service.html, accessed October 2019.

12. Wikipedia, "Self-Driving Car Liability," https://en.wikipedia.org/wiki/Self-driving_car_liability, accessed October 2019.

13. Marlene Cimons, "What Moral Code Should Your Self-Driving Car Follow?" *Popular Science*, July 5, 2017, https://www.popsci.com/conscience-self-driving-car/, accessed October 2019.

14. David Tuffley, "At Last! The World's First Ethical Guidelines for Driverless Cars," The Conversation, September 3, 2017, http://theconversation.com/at-last-the-worlds-first-ethical-guidelines-for-driverless-cars-83227, accessed October 2019.

KPMG International Cooperative, 2018 Autonomous Vehicles Readiness Index, https://assets.kpmg.com/content/dam/kpmg/nl/pdf/2018/sector/automotive/autonomous-vehicles-readiness-index.pdf, accessed October 2019.

15. The Brookings Institution study estimates $80 billion has been invested in Autonomous Vehicle Technology development so far. See: Cameron F. Kerry and Jack Karsten, "Gauging Investment in Self-Driving Cars," Brookings, October 16, 2017, https://www.brookings.edu/research/gauging-investment-in-self-driving-cars/, accessed October 2019.

Andrew J. Hawkins, "GM Will Make an Autonomous Car Without Steering Wheel or Pedals by 2019," Verge, January 12, 2018, https://www.theverge.com/2018/1/12/16880978/gm-autonomous-car-2019-detroit-auto-show-2018, accessed October 2019.

"Daimler, Bosch to Test Self-Driving Cars Soon: Automobilwoche," CNBC, February 4, 2018, https://www.cnbc.com/2018/02/04/daimler-bosch-to-test-self-driving-cars-soon.html, accessed October 2019.

"NAVYA Unveils First Fully Autonomous Taxi," Business Wire, November 7, 2017, https://www.businesswire.com/news/home/20171107006107/en/NAVYA-Unveils-Fully-Autonomous-Taxi, accessed October 2019.

Daimler AG, "Autonomous Driving," https://www.daimler.com/innovation/product-innovation/autonomous-driving/, accessed December 2019.

16. Gene Munster and Austin Bohlig, "Auto Outlook 2040: The Rise of Fully Autonomous Vehicles," Loup Ventures, September 6, 2017, https://loupventures.com/auto-outlook-2040-the-rise-of-fully-autonomous-vehicles/, accessed October 2019.

17. Roger Lanctot, "Accelerating the Future: The Economic Impact of the Emerging Passenger Economy," Strategy Analytics, June 2017, https://newsroom.intel.com/newsroom/wp-content/uploads/sites/11/2017/05/passenger-economy.pdf, accessed October 2019.

18. Wikipedia, "Microtransit," https://en.wikipedia.org/wiki/Microtransit, accessed October 2019.

19. "Inauguration of the Autonomous Shuttles Service at La Defense in Paris," Navya, July 3, 2017, https://navya.tech/en/inauguration-of-the-autonomous-shuttles-service-at-la-defense-in-paris-2/, accessed October 2019.

20. Zhaki Abdullah, "On-Demand Autonomous Shuttle Buses to Be Available on Sentosa from Aug 26," *Straits Times,* August 20, 2019, https://www.straitstimes.com/singapore/transport/on-demand-autonomous-shuttle-buses-to-be-available-on-sentosa-from-aug-26, accessed October 2019.

Matt Weinberger, "I Tried the First Self-Driving Mass Transit in the United States—and Now I'm Excited for the Future of Travel," *Business Insider,* January 14, 2018, https://www.businessinsider.sg/las-vegas-downtown-self-driving-shuttle-review-2018-1/?r=US&IR=T, accessed October 2019.

City of Helsinki, "Helsinki to Launch Self-Driving Bus in Regular Service on RoboBusLine," press release on GlobeNewswire website, June 14, 2017, https://www.globenewswire.com/news-release/2017/06/14/1301619/0/en/Helsinki-to-Launch-Self-Driving-Bus-in-Regular-Service-on-RoboBusLine.html, accessed December 2019.

21. Kyle Wiggers, "Udelv Partners with Walmart for Autonomous Deliveries, Reveals Next-Gen Van Design," Venture Beat, January 8, 2019, https://venturebeat.com/2019/01/08/udelv-partners-with-walmart-for-autonomous-deliveries-reveals-next-gen-van-design/, accessed December 2019.

    Andrew Moseman, "This Toyota Pod Is Tomorrow's Uber, Food Truck, and Amazon Delivery Van," *Popular Mechanics*, January 8, 2018, https://www.popularmechanics.com/cars/car-technology/a14783215/toyota-e-palette-ces-2018/, accessed December 2019.

    "Ford and Walmart Start Autonomous-Vehicle Partnership," *Automotive News*, November 14, 2018, https://www.autonews.com/article/20181114/MOBILITY/181119900/ford-and-walmart-start-autonomous-vehicle-partnership, accessed December 2019.

    Andrew J. Hawkins, "Thousands of Autonomous Delivery Robots Are About to Descend on US College Campuses," Verge, August 20, 2019, https://www.theverge.com/2019/8/20/20812184/starship-delivery-robot-expansion-college-campus, accessed December 2019.

22. "Drone Deliveries Become Reality as China Races to Take the Lead," *Business Times*, July 4, 2018, https://www.businesstimes.com.sg/technology/drone-deliveries-become-reality-as-china-races-to-take-the-lead, accessed December 2019.

23. Maulick Dave, "Autonomous Trucks: Your Next Wave of Savings in Road Freight," Spend Matters, November 16, 2016, https://spendmatters.com/2016/11/16/autonomous-trucks-next-wave-savings-road-freight/, accessed December 2019.

    For instance, the current transportation technology requires a decentralized distribution system for products with high demand variability. Autonomous technology could make centralized distribution feasible for these products. See: Winnesota, "How Blockchain Is Revolutionizing the World of Transportation and Logistics [Infographic]," https://www.winnesota.com/blockchain, accessed December 2019.

24. Sam Levin, "Amazon Patents Beehive-Like Structure to House Delivery Drones in Cities," *Guardian*, June 26, 2017, https://www.theguardian.com/technology/2017/jun/26/amazon-drones-delivery-beehive-patent, accessed December 2019.

    "United States Patent Application Publication: Multi-level Fulfillment Center For Unmanned Aerial Vehicles," Publication No. US 2017/0175413 A1, June 22, 2017, https://pdfaiw.uspto.gov/.aiw?PageNum=0&docid=20170175413&IDKey=6B4D0DADFC1F&HomeUrl=http%3A%2F%2Fappft.uspto.gov%2Fnetacgi%2Fnph-Parser%3FSect1%3DPTO1%2526Sect2%3DHITOFF%2526d%3DPG01%2526p%3D1%2526u%3D%2Fnetahtml%2FPTO%2Fsrchnum.html%2526r%3D1%2526f%3DG%2526l%3D50%2526s1%3D20170175413.PGNR.%2526OS%3D%2526RS%3D, accessed December 2019.

25. Nathan Vanderklippe, "Chinese Firm JD.com Pitches Trudeau on Drone Fleets to Deliver Seafood," *Globe and Mail*, December 5, 2017, https://www.theglobeandmail.com/news/world/chinas-jdcom-pitches-trudeau-on-drone-fleets-to-airlift-seafood/article37197583/, accessed December 2019.

26. Marco Margaritoff, "First Test Flight of Airbus Vahana Passenger Drone a Success," Drive, February 6, 2018, https://www.thedrive.com/aerial/18262/first-test-flight-of-airbus-vahana-passenger-drone-a-success, accessed December 2019.

Alex Davies, "Boeing's Experimental Cargo Drone Is a Heavy Lifter," Wired.com, January 14, 2018, https://www.wired.com/story/boeing-delivery-drone/, accessed December 2019.

Andrew J. Hawkins, "Uber's 'Flying Cars' Could Arrive in LA by 2020—and Here's What It'll Be Like to Ride One," Verge, November 8, 2017, https://www.theverge.com/2017/11/8/16613228/uber-flying-car-la-nasa-space-act, accessed December 2019.

27. Space Exploration Technologies Corp, "Hyperloop," https://www.spacex.com/hyperloop, accessed December 2019.

28. Hyperloop One, "Hyperloop Explained," https://hyperloop-one.com/hyperloop-explained, accessed December 2019.

29. Wikipedia, "Cargo Sous Terrain," https://en.wikipedia.org/wiki/Cargo_Sous_Terrain, accessed December 2019.

Cargo sous terrain AG, "Cargo Sous Terrain," https://www.cst.ch/en/, accessed December 2019.

30. "33 Industries Other Than Auto That Driverless Cars Could Turn Upside Down," CB Insights, September 20, 2018, https://www.cbinsights.com/research/13-industries-disrupted-driverless-cars/, accessed December 2019.

31. Dan Stanton, "Merck 'bio-inks' deal to use Organovo's 3D printed liver for preclinical studies." Outsourcing-Pharma,com, April 23, 2015, https://www.outsourcing-pharma.com/Article/2015/04/23/MSD-bio-inks-deal-to-use-3D-printed-liver-in-toxicology-studies, accessed December 2019.

Lizzie Plaugic, "L'Oreal Partners with Bioprinting Company to 3D Print Human Skin," Verge, May 18, 2015, https://www.theverge.com/2015/5/18/8621585/loreal-skin-printing-organovo, accessed December 2019.

Gareth Rubin, "How Do You Like Your Beef . . . Old-Style Cow or 3D-Printed?" *Guardian*, November 10, 2019, https://www.theguardian.com/technology/2019/nov/10/3d-printed-meat-european-restaurant-menus-environment, accessed December 2019.

Agnieszka de Sousa, "A Realistic Steak Is Fake Meat's Holy Grail," *Bloomberg Businessweek*, November 22, 2019, https://www.bloomberg.com/news/articles/2019-11-22/fake-meat-companies-are-racing-to-3d-print-steaks, accessed December 2019.

32. OLLI, "Autonomous for All of Us," https://localmotors.com/, accessed December 2019.

33. Richard Joy, "Maersk Plan 3D Printing Aboard Ships," Port Technology International, December 18, 2017, https://www.porttechnology.org/news/maersk_plan_3d_printing_aboard_ships/, accessed January 2020.

34. "3D Printers Start to Build Factories of the Future," *Economist*, June 29, 2017, https://www.economist.com/briefing/2017/06/29/3d-printers-start-to-build-factories-of-the-future, accessed January 2020.

35. For example of 3D printer marketplaces, see Xometry website, https://www .xometry.com/.

36. Angela Chen, "This 3D-Printed 'Living Ink' Could Someday Help with Skin Replacements," Verge, December 1, 2017, https://www.theverge.com/2017 /12/1/16723500/bacteria-cellulose-3d-printing-biotechnology-materials, accessed January 2020.

37. Wikipedia, "Robot," https://en.wikipedia.org/wiki/Robot, accessed December 2019.

38. Tom Nelson, "What Is a Robot?" Lifewire, September 23, 2019, https://www .lifewire.com/what-is-a-robot-4148364, accessed January 2020.

39. Wikipedia, "Industrial Robot," https://en.wikipedia.org/wiki/Industrial _robot, accessed January 2020.

40. Mytechfrontier, "Robotics Primer," https://mytechfrontier.com/openaccess /topic0.php, accessed January 2020.

41. Matt Simon, "Your Online Shopping Habit Is Fueling a Robotics Renaissance," Wired.com, December 6, 2017, https://www.wired.com/story/robotics -renaissance/, accessed January 2020.

   Kindred, Inc., "Products," https://www.kindred.ai/products/, accessed January 2020.

42. Keith Shaw, "Affectiva, SoftBank Robotics Team Up to Broaden Pepper's Emotional Intelligence," *Robotics Business Review*, August 28, 2018, https://www .roboticsbusinessreview.com/news/emotional-intelligence-affectiva-softbank -robotics-team-up/, accessed January 2020.

43. Many hotels are now using robots to deliver room service orders and egg preparations for breakfast (e.g., M Social hotel in Singapore). The post-COVID-19 situation will likely increase this kind of robotic service.

44. Fetch Robotics, Inc., "Wärtsilä and DHL Deploy Fetch Cloud Robotics Platform to Streamline Warehouse Operations," https://fetchrobotics.com/dhl -customer-success-story/, accessed January 2020.

45. Paul Sandle and Lisa Baertlein, "Kroger Inks Ocado Grocery Delivery Deal to Battle Amazon Threat," Reuters, May 17, 2018, https://www.reuters.com /article/us-ocado-group-contract-kroger/kroger-inks-ocado-grocery-delivery -deal-to-battle-amazon-threat-idUSKCN1II0L0, accessed January 2020.

46. "C2RO Cloud Robotics," *Robotics Business Review*, https://www .roboticsbusinessreview.com/robotic-company/directory/listings/c2ro -robotics/, accessed January 2020.

47. Bob Violino, "Robots in the Cloud: How Robotics-as-a-Service Can Help Your Business," ZDNet.com, May 1, 2017, https://www.zdnet.com/article /robots-in-the-cloud/, accessed January 2020.

48. We acknowledge the permission granted by mytechfrontier.com to reprint Figure 10.2.

49. Laura Shin, "Republic of Georgia to Pilot Land Titling on Blockchain with Economist Hernando De Soto, BitFury," *Forbes*, April 21, 2016, https:// www.forbes.com/sites/laurashin/2016/04/21/republic-of-georgia-to-pilot -land-titling-on-blockchain-with-economist-hernando-de-soto-bitfury/ #3dd977a44da3, accessed January 2020.

50. Qiuyun Shang and Allison Price, "A Blockchain-Based Land Titling Project in the Republic of Georgia: Rebuilding Public Trust and Lessons for Future Pilot Projects," *Innovations: Technology, Governance, Globalization* 12(3–4) (2019): 72–78, https://www.mitpressjournals.org/doi/pdf/10.1162/inov_a_00276, accessed January 2020.

51. Matt Higginson, Marie-Claude Nadeau, and Kausik Rajgopal, "Blockchain's Occam Problem," *McKinsey Insights*, January 2019, https://www.mckinsey.com/industries/financial-services/our-insights/blockchains-occam-problem, accessed January 2020.

52. Ian Allison, "World's Second-Largest Grocer Joins IBM Food Trust Blockchain," CoinDesk, April 11, 2019, https://www.coindesk.com/worlds-second-largest-grocer-joins-ibm-food-trust-blockchain, accessed January 2020.

53. At February 2020, research manuscript in preparation: Dmitry Sumkin, Sameer Hasija, and Serguei Netessine, "Blockchain and Responsible Sourcing in the Diamond Industry." Please contact these authors for access to latest draft.

54. "Robots help China manage the coronavirus pandemic," *Nikkei Asian Review*, April 6, 2020, https://asia.nikkei.com/Business/China-tech/Robots-help-China-manage-the-coronavirus-pandemic, accessed June 2020.

    "Autonomous Robots Are Helping Kill Coronavirus in Hospitals," IEEE Spectrum, March 11, 2020, https://spectrum.ieee.org/automaton/robotics/medical-robots/autonomous-robots-are-helping-kill-coronavirus-in-hospitals, accessed June 2020.

    "A robot named Little Peanut is delivering food to people in quarantine amid the Wuhan coronavirus outbreak," *Business Insider*, January 29, 2020, https://www.businessinsider.sg/wuhan-virus-robot-little-peanut-delivers-food-to-people-quarantine-2020-1, accessed June 2020.

    "Coronavirus: Robot dog enforces social distancing in Singapore park," BBC, May 11, 2020, https://www.bbc.com/news/av/technology-52619568/coronavirus-robot-dog-enforces-social-distancing-in-singapore-park, accessed June 2020.

    "3D Printing COVID-19 Rapid Response Initiative," World Economic Forum (Blog), May 12, 2020, https://cn.weforum.org/covid-action-platform/projects/3d-printing-covid-19-rapid-response-initiative, accessed June 2020.

    "Singapore demonstrates innovative IoT uses during COVID pandemic," Geospatial World, May 6, 2020, https://www.geospatialworld.net/blogs/singapore-demonstrates-innovative-iot-uses-during-covid-pandemic/, accessed June 2020.

    "Are robots overrated?" *Harvard Business Review*, April 30, 2020 https://hbr.org/2020/04/are-robots-overrated , accessed June 2020.

55. Devin Coldewey, "Quantum Computing's 'Hello World' Moment," TechCrunch, October 26, 2019, https://techcrunch.com/2019/10/26/quantum-computings-hello-world-moment/, accessed January 2020.

CHAPTER 11

1. The term "emerging markets" was originally coined by Antoine van Agtmael (an economist at IFC) to highlight a set of promising stock markets for global

investors. The most popular equity benchmark index for emerging markets, the MSCI EM index, started with 10 countries and now spans 24. It is important to recognize that the classification mixes together economies at very different stages of development (e.g., Qatar at one end to Pakistan at the other end)—in other words, there is considerable heterogeneity across countries classified as emerging markets.

2. For example, some of the most powerful innovations for elimination of poverty have come out of Bangladesh. Grameen Bank and its founder, Muhammad Yunus, who pioneered microfinance, were recognized for their work with the Nobel Peace Prize in 2006. See Bryan, Chowdhury, Mobarak (2014) and Akram, Chowdhury, Mobarak (2017) for more recent experiments focused on reducing the poverty trap in Bangladesh.

Gharad Bryan, Shyamal Chowdhury, and Ahmed Mushfiq Mobarak, "Under-investment in a Profitable Technology: the Case of Seasonal Migration in Bangladesh," *Econometrica* 82 (5) (2014): 1671–1748.

Agha Ali Akram, Shyamal Chowdhury, and Ahmed Mushfiq Mobarak, "Effects of Emigration on Rural Labor Markets," NBER Working Paper No. 23929, http://www.nber.org/papers/w23929.pdf, accessed January 2020.

An indicator of the dynamism of business in emerging markets can be seen in the fact that companies in Asia (excluding Japan) account for about 12.2 percent of the market capitalization of the MSCI ACWI (All Countries World Index) in 2017 but account for 25.9 percent of earnings of all companies in the index. Steve Johnson, "Emerging Asian Companies Post Dramatic Profit Surge," *Financial Times*, January 5, 2018, https://www.ft.com/content/eb492060-e418-11e7-97e2-916d4fbac0da, accessed, December 2019.

3. "4 ASEAN Infographics: Demography, Top Cities, Urbanization," ASEAN UP, March 26, 2018, https://aseanup.com/asean-infographics-demography-top-cities-urbanization/, accessed January 2020.

4. See https://www.ft.com/content/75fa6576-97c4-11e7-a652-cde3f882dd7b for illustrations of the bigger challenges faced by MNC in competing for market share in lower-tier cities relative to the top-tier cities, accessed September 2019

5. Danny Quah, "The Global Economy's Shifting Centre of Gravity," *Global Policy* 2(1) (2011): 3–9. We acknowledge the permission granted by Danny Quah to reprint Figure 11.3.

Rob Wile, "MAP: The World's Economic Center Of Gravity from AD 1 to AD 2010," *Business Insider*, June 29, 2012, https://www.businessinsider.com/mckinsey-worlds-economic-center-of-gravity-2012-6?IR=T, accessed January 2020.

6. UBS and PwC, "Billionaires Insights 2017: New Value Creators Gain Momentum," https://www.ubs.com/global/en/wealth-management/uhnw/billionaires-report/new-value.html, accessed January 2020.

7. Tariq Khokhar, "Where Are the Cheapest and Most Expensive Countries to Own a Mobile Phone?" World Bank Blogs, January 13, 2016, http://blogs.worldbank.org/opendata/where-are-cheapest-and-most-expensive-countries-own-mobile-phone, accessed January 2020.

The case of Africa is also very interesting. Mobile phones have actually stopped the development of physical landline infrastructure. For example, see:

Roxanne Bauer, "Can Developing Countries Skip the Landline?" World Economic Forum, April 7, 2015, https://www.weforum.org/agenda/2015/04/can -developing-countries-skip-the-landline/, accessed January 2020.

Jenny C. Aker and Isaac M. Mbiti, "Mobile Phones and Economic Development in Africa," *Journal of Economic Perspectives* 24(3) (June 2010): 207–232, https://www.researchgate.net/publication/279927521_Mobile_Phones_and _Economic_Development_in_Africa, accessed January 2020.

8. Hannah Ritchie and Max Roser, "Technology Adoption," Our World in Data, 2019, https://ourworldindata.org/technology-adoption, accessed January 2020.

9. Clay Chandler, "Grab vs. Go-Jek: Inside Asia's Battle of the 'Super Apps,'" *Fortune*, March 20, 2019, https://fortune.com/longform/grab-gojek-super-apps/, accessed January 2020.

Wikipedia, "Gojek," https://en.wikipedia.org/wiki/Gojek, accessed January 2020.

10. Eric Bellman, "The End of Typing: The Next Billion Mobile Users Will Rely on Video and Voice," *Wall Street Journal*, August 7, 2017, https:// www.wsj.com/articles/the-end-of-typing-the-internets-next-billion-users-will -use-video-and-voice-1502116070, accessed January 2020.

11. Michelle Toh, "This Startup Helps You Find Any Place on the Planet Without an Address," CNN Business, August 27, 2019, https://edition.cnn.com/2019 /08/27/tech/what3words-app-w3w-address-startup/index.html, accessed January 2020.

12. For example, see: https://www.economist.com/finance-and-economics/2020 /05/07/in-bleak-times-for-banks-indias-digital-payments-system-wins-praise, accessed June 2020.

13. Transsion, a Shenzhen-based handset manufacturer founded in 2006, focused laser-like on Africa starting in 2008 and showed it is possible to build a sustainable business in that continent. Not only did it sell in excess of 100 million handsets in 2018 (implying a market share in excess of Huawei and Samsung combined), it rounded that off with an IPO in September 2019 with an estimated market capitalization of around $6.5 billion.

Yomi Kazeem, "The Biggest Mobile Phone Maker in Africa Is Going Public in China," *Quartz Africa*, March 29, 2019, https://qz.com/africa/1583473 /chinas-transsion-of-african-tecno-phones-to-ipo-in-shanghai/, accessed January 2020.

Michael Moritz, "The Cloud Kitchen Brews a Storm for Local Restaurants," *Financial Times*, May 21, 2019, https://www.ft.com/content/5c104e5e-7aea -11e9-8b5c-33d0560f039c, accessed January 2020.

Discovery, a South African insurer, developed "Vitality"—a wellness-based insurance ecosystem that is among the fastest-growing and most global insurtech platforms today. Its power is evident in the insurers that have lined up to partner with it across the world (e.g., AIA across Asia, Generali across continental Europe, Manulife in Canada, Ping An in China, and Sumitomo in Japan).

For Rebel Foods, see: Saritha Rai, "Ex-McKinsey Consultant Turns Failed Restaurant into $535 Million Startup," *BloombergQuint*, August 1, 2019, https://www.bloombergquint.com/business/goldman-sachs-gojek-bet-on -india-s-rebel-foods, accessed January 2020.

14. Jonathan Woetzel, Anu Madgavkar, Jeongmin Seong, James Manyika, Kevin Sneader, Oliver Tonby, Andres Cadena, Rajat Gupta, Acha Leke, Hayoung Kim, and Shishir Gupta, "Outperformers: High-Growth Emerging Economies and the Companies That Propel Them," *McKinsey Global Institute*, September 2018, https://www.mckinsey.com/featured-insights/innovation-and-growth /outperformers-high-growth-emerging-economies-and-the-companies-that -propel-them, accessed January 2020.

15. For example, see: John Storey, Dave Ulrich, and Patrick M. Wright, *Strategic Human Resource Management: A Research Overview* (London: Routledge, 2019).

16. Schon Beechler and Ian C. Woodward, "The Global 'War for Talent,'" *Journal of International Management* 15(3) (2009): 273–285.

17. International Monetary Fund Regional Economic Outlook, "Asia and Pacific: Building on Asia's Strengths During Turbulent Times," May 2016, https:// www.imf.org/en/Publications/REO/APAC/Issues/2017/03/06/Building -on-Asia-s-Strengths-during-Turbulent-Times, accessed January 2020. We acknowledge the permission granted by the IMF to reprint Figure 11.4. Permission granted by RightsLink, Copyright Clearance Center, Order No: 4678491304535, September 29, 2019.

18. PwC, "How Will Automation Impact Jobs?" https://www.pwc.co.uk/services /economics-policy/insights/the-impact-of-automation-on-jobs.html, accessed January 2020.

19. Generational cohorts are a group of people or an aged cohort sharing some common attributes such as educational, cultural, and technological experiences. While there is debate about the date ranges of generations, commonly accepted groupings for birth dates are traditionalists or veterans (pre-WWII), baby boomers (1945–1965), Generation X (1965–1980), and Generation Y or millennials (1980–1995). For more details see: Ian C. Woodward and Pisitta Vongswasdi, "More that unites than divides: intergenerational communication preferences in the workplace," *Communication Research and Practice* 3(4) (2017): 358–385.

20. The current youngest workforce generation is variously called Generation Z or Generation V and was born between 1996 and 2010. This represents the current school-age population taking its first steps into tertiary studies and the workforce. The term "Gen Z" (or "centennials") is the most commonly used term for this post–Gen Y cohort. See for example: https://www.businessinsider .com/generation-z?IR=T, accessed June 2020.

21. Ian C. Woodward and Pisitta Vongswasdi, "More That Unites Than Divides: Intergenerational Communication Preferences in the Workplace," *Communication Research and Practice* 3(4) (2017): 358–385.

22. For a comprehensive review of academic research on international matters, see: Ian Woodward, Pisitta Vongswasdi, and Elizabeth More, "Generational Diversity at Work: A Systematic Review of the Research," INSEAD Working Paper No. 2015/48/OB, July 2015, https://papers.ssrn.com/sol3/papers.cfm ?abstract_id=2630650, accessed January 2020.

Sean T. Lyons, Linda Duxbury, and Christopher Higgins, "An Empirical Assessment of Generational Differences in Basic Human Values," *Psychological Reports* 101(2)(2007): 339–352.

Jean M. Twenge and Stacy M. Campbell, "Generational Differences in Psychological Traits and Their Impact on the Workplace," *Journal of Managerial Psychology* 23(8)(November 7, 2008): 862–877.

Jean M. Twenge, Stacy M. Campbell, Brian J. Hoffman, Charles E. Lance., "Generational Differences in Work Values: Leisure and Extrinsic Values Increasing, Social and Intrinsic Values Decreasing," *Journal of Management* 36(5) (March 1, 2010): 1117–1142.

23. Maddie Shepherd, "11 Surprising Working from Home Statistics," Fundera, July 23, 2019, https://www.fundera.com/resources/working-from-home-statistics, accessed January 2020.

Richard Hartung, "Finding Meaningful Work at a Social Enterprise or Non-Profit," *Today*, March 2, 2019, https://www.todayonline.com/singapore/finding-meaningful-work-social-enterprise-or-non-profit, accessed January 2020.

Judith Evans, "Shared Offices Gain Popularity as Companies Value the Flexibility," *Financial Times*, August 29, 2017, https://www.ft.com/content/84a8f010-7eb0-11e7-ab01-a13271d1ee9c, accessed January 2020.

Adam Hickman, and Lydia Saad, "Reviewing Remote Work in the U.S. Under COVID-19," https://news.gallup.com/poll/311375/reviewing-remote-work-covid.aspx, accessed June 2020.

24. Kevin Roose, "Executive Mentors Wanted. Only Millennials Need Apply," *New York Times*, October 15, 2017, https://www.nytimes.com/2017/10/15/technology/millennial-mentors-executives.html, accessed January 2020.

Jennifer Jordan and Michael Sorell, "Why Reverse Mentoring Works and How to Do It Right," *Harvard Business Review*, October 3, 2019, https://hbr.org/2019/10/why-reverse-mentoring-works-and-how-to-do-it-right, accessed January 2020.

25. Meghan M. Biro, "The Real Millennial Challenge: The Skills Gap," Future of Work, January 11, 2016, https://fowmedia.com/the-real-millennial-challenge-the-skills-gap/, accessed January 2020.

See also: McKinsey Quarterly (2020), "Soft Skills for a Hard World" https://www.mckinsey.com/featured-insights/future-of-work/five-fifty-soft-skills-for-a-hard-world, accessed February 2020.

26. Schon Beechler and Ian C. Woodward, "The Global 'War for Talent,'" *Journal of International Management* 15(3) (2009): 273–285.

27. James Manyika, "Technology, Jobs, and the Future of Work," *McKinsey Global Institute*, May 2017, https://www.mckinsey.com/featured-insights/employment-and-growth/technology-jobs-and-the-future-of-work, accessed January 2020.

28. World Economic Forum, Centre for the New Economy and Society, "Insight Report: The Future of Jobs Report 2018," http://www3.weforum.org/docs/WEF_Future_of_Jobs_2018.pdf, accessed January 2020.

James Manyika, Susan Lund, Kelsey Robinson, John Valentino, and Richard Dobbs, "Connecting Talent with Opportunity in the Digital Age," *McKinsey*

Global Institute, June 2015, https://www.mckinsey.com/featured-insights /employment-and-growth/connecting-talent-with-opportunity-in-the-digital -age, accessed January 2020.

Stephane Kasriel, "Here's How Freelancers Are Changing the World of Work," World Economic Forum, November 5, 2018, https://www.weforum.org /agenda/2018/11/we-studied-freelancing-for-five-years-here-s-how-work-is -changing/, accessed January 2020.

29. Gwen Moran, "Why You Need to Pay Attention to Gen X Leaders," Fast Company, April 19, 2018, https://www.fastcompany.com/40558008/why-you -need-to-pay-attention-to-gen-x-leaders, accessed January 2020.

    Lisa Rabasca Roepe, "Are Gen X Women Being Squeezed Out of the Workplace?" FastCompany, December 14, 2015, https://www.fastcompany.com /3054410/are-gen-x-women-being-squeezed-out-of-the-workplace, accessed January 2020.

30. Ryan Jenkins, "How Generation Z Will Transform the Future Workplace," *Inc.,* January 15, 2019, https://www.inc.com/ryan-jenkins/the-2019 -workplace-7-ways-generation-z-will-shape-it.html, accessed January 2020.

31. David A. Garvin, "Building a Learning Organization," *Harvard Business Review*, July–August 1993, https://hbr.org/1993/07/building-a-learning -organization, accessed January 2020.

32. David A. Garvin, Amy C. Edmondson, and Francesca Gino, "Is Yours a Learning Organization?" *Harvard Business Review*, March 2008, https://hbr .org/2008/03/is-yours-a-learning-organization, accessed January 2020. They have also developed an online tool, "The Learning Organization Survey." See: https://hbs.qualtrics.com/jfe/form/SV_b7rYZGRxuMEyHRz.

33. Much coverage relating to talent, workforce and future of work occurred during the COVID-19 pandemic lockdown periods of early 2020. For example:

    https://blogs.cisco.com/collaboration/the-future-of-work-is-here

    https://www.businesstoday.in/current/corporate/post-coronavirus-75-percent -of-3-5-lakh-tcs-employees-permanently-work-from-home-up-from-20 -percent/story/401981.html

    https://www.cnbc.com/2020/05/01/major-companies-talking-about -permanent-work-from-home-positions.html

    https://www.crn.com/news/running-your-business/some-may-work-from -home-permanently-after-covid-19-gartner

    https://www.zdnet.com/article/majority-of-workers-are-more-productive-and -communicative-at-home/

CHAPTER 12

1. "Who's Afraid of Disruption?" *Economist*, September 30, 2017, https://www .economist.com/business/2017/09/30/whos-afraid-of-disruption, accessed January 2020.

2. "2018 Will Be the Year That Big, Incumbent Companies Take on Big Tech," *Economist*, January 3, 2018, https://www.economist.com/business/2018/01 /03/2018-will-be-the-year-that-big-incumbent-companies-take-on-big-tech, accessed January 2020.

3. The construct of combinatorial innovation, which we have highlighted earlier, is closely related to the concept of dynamic capabilities advanced by the following management scholars among others:

Kathleen M. Eisenhardt and Jeffrey A. Martin, "Dynamic Capabilities: What Are They?" *Strategic Management Journal*, 21(10–11) (2000): 1105–1121.

Constance Helfat, Sydney Finkelstein, Will Mitchell, Margaret Peteraf, Harbir Singh, David Teece, and Sidney G. Winter, *Dynamic Capabilities: Understanding Strategic Change in Organization* (Oxford: Blackwell Publishing, 2007).

4. Saabira Chaudhuri and Eliot Brown, "IKEA Jumps Into 'Gig Economy' with Deal for TaskRabbit," *Wall Street Journal*, September 29, 2017, https://www.wsj.com/articles/ikea-to-acquire-online-freelancer-marketplace-taskrabbit-1506618421, accessed January 2020.

Richard Milne, "Ikea Assembles Deal for TaskRabbit's Odd-Jobs Service," *Financial Times*, September 28, 2017, https://www.ft.com/content/f17fb18c-a468-11e7-9e4f-7f5e6a7c98a2, accessed January 2020.

5. Tim McKeough, "Putting a Designer's Polish on Ikea Products," *New York Times*, October 2, 2017, https://www.nytimes.com/2017/10/02/style/ikea-cabinet-hack-refacing.html, accessed January 2020.

Anna Ringstrom, "IKEA Reports Record Sales as Online Revenue Surges," *Reuters*, September 25, 2019, https://www.reuters.com/article/us-ikea-sales/ikea-reports-record-sales-as-online-revenue-surges-idUSKBN1WA161, accessed January 2020.

6. See Michael Gort and Steven Klepper, "Time Paths in the Diffusion of Product Innovations," *Economic Journal* 92 (367)(1982): 630–653, which reviews a series of major innovations and reports the average time from first patentability to first commercialization was 29 years.

See James Bessen, *Learning by Doing: The Real Connection Between Innovation, Wages, and Wealth* (New Haven and London: Yale University Press, 2015) for additional perspectives on the relationships between innovation and outcomes (e.g., individual, firm, and society).

7. "Nearly 70 Percent of Indian Farms Are Very Small, Census Shows," *Business Standard*, December 9, 2015, https://www.business-standard.com/article/news-ians/nearly-70-percent-of-indian-farms-are-very-small-census-shows-115120901080_1.html, accessed January 2020.

8. Wikipedia, "Uber," https://en.wikipedia.org/wiki/Uber, accessed January 2020.

9. Wikipedia, "TransferWise," https://en.wikipedia.org/wiki/TransferWise, accessed January 2020. See also: https://transferwise.com/sg.

10. Wikipedia, "Net metering," https://en.wikipedia.org/wiki/Net_metering, accessed January 2020.

11. "Attack of the Bean-Counters," *Economist*, March 19, 2015, https://www.economist.com/business/2015/03/19/attack-of-the-bean-counters, accessed January 2020.

12. Greg Ip, "The Antitrust Case Against Facebook, Google and Amazon," *Wall Street Journal*, January 16, 2018, https://www.wsj.com/articles/the-antitrust-case-against-facebook-google-amazon-and-apple-1516121561, accessed January 2020.

Rochelle Toplensky and Madhumita Murgia, "EU Fines Facebook €110m Over WhatsApp Merger," *Financial Times*, May 18, 2017, https://www.ft.com /content/28efe3ed-6ab5-3993-8e16-f0d787aba8b3, accessed January 2020.

David J. Lynch, "Big Tech and Amazon: Too Powerful to Break Up?" *Financial Times*, October 29, 2017, https://www.ft.com/content/e5bf87b4-b3e5-11e7 -aa26-bb002965bce8, accessed January 2020.

13. Jeremy Grant, "Exchanges Race to Become One-Stop Shop," *Financial Times*, February 11, 2011, https://www.ft.com/content/63c3248e-3541-11e0-aa6c -00144feabdc0, accessed January 2020.

14. Patrick McGee, "Airbus Signs Deal to 3D-Print Drones and Self-Driving Cars," *Financial Times*, October 11, 2019, https://www.ft.com/content /3e07394a-ec00-11e9-a240-3b065ef5fc55, accessed January 2020.

15. Laura Kusisto, "Airbnb Enlists San Francisco's Biggest Landlord," *Wall Street Journal*, November 5, 2017, https://www.wsj.com/articles/airbnb-enlists-san -franciscos-biggest-landlord-1509890405, accessed January 2020.

16. Wikipedia, "Sriracha sauce (Huy Fong Foods)," https://en.wikipedia.org/wiki/ Sriracha_sauce_(Huy_Fong_Foods), accessed January 2020.

17. Roberto A. Ferdman, "The Highly Unusual Company Behind Sriracha, the World's Coolest Hot Sauce," *Quartz,* October 21, 2013, https://qz.com /132738/the-highly-unusual-company-behind-siracha-the-worlds-coolest-hot -sauce/, accessed January 2020.

18. Amy Watson, "Number of Music Streaming Subscribers Worldwide from 2015 to 2018," *Statista*, August 30, 2019, https://www.statista.com/statistics /669113/number-music-streaming-subscribers/, accessed January 2020.

Anna Nicolaou, "Taylor Swift's 'Reputation' Album Sales Defy Streaming Trend," *Financial Times*, November 21, 2017, https://www.ft.com/content /e9458168-ce7a-11e7-b781-794ce08b24dc, accessed January 2020.

Fiona Symon, "Adele Finds Path to Success without Streaming," *Financial Times*, November 26, 2015, https://www.ft.com/content/0accc65f-90a5-489a -b492-be1e93072a9b, accessed January 2020.

Matthew Garrahan and Robert Cookson, "Streaming Services Dance to Adele's Tune," *Financial Times*, November 1, 2015, https://www.ft.com /content/85e53b16-7f55-11e5-ae43-f6d4a22c5a1a, accessed January 2020.

19. Helena Asprou, "Vinyl Records to Outsell CDs in 2019 for the First Time in 40 Years," ClassicFM.com, October 22, 2019, https://www.classicfm.com /discover-music/millennials-are-going-nuts-for-vinyl-revival/, accessed January 2020.

Paul Glynn, "The Beatles' Abbey Road Returns to Number One 50 Years On," *BBC News*, October 4, 2019, https://www.bbc.com/news/entertainment-arts -49931789, accessed January 2020.

Keith Caulfield, "U.S. Vinyl Album Sales Hit Nielsen Music-Era Record High in 2017," Billboard.com, January 3, 2018, https://www.billboard.com/articles /columns/chart-beat/8085951/us-vinyl-album-sales-nielsen-music-record -high-2017, accessed January 2020.

20. Nathan R. Furr and Daniel C. Snow, "Intergenerational Hybrids: Spillbacks, Spillforwards, and Adapting to Technology Discontinuities," *Organization Science* 26(2) (April 2015): 475–493.

21. Benjamin Mullin, "CNN Plans to Offer Subscriptions for Digital News Next Year," *Wall Street Journal*, November 3, 2017, https://www.wsj.com/articles /cnn-plans-to-offer-subscriptions-for-digital-news-next-year-1509701401, accessed January 2020.

22. Costas Paris, "The Panama Canal's Big Bet Is Paying Off," *Wall Street Journal*, October 8, 2017, https://www.wsj.com/articles/the-panama-canals-big-bet-is -paying-off-1507464000, accessed January 2020.

   Joseph Bonney, "Panama Canal Expansion Will Affect Shipping—But How?" JOC.com, June 25, 2016, https://www.joc.com/port-news/panama-canal -news/panama-canal-expansion-will-affect-shipping-how_20160625.html, accessed January 2020.

23. See: BIMA website, http://www.bimamobile.com/, accessed December 2019.

24. See for example: John Hagel, John Seely Brown, Maggie Wooll, and Andrew de Maar, *Deloitte Insights*, 2016, "Unbundle Products and Services: Giving You Just What You Want, Nothing More," https://www2.deloitte.com/us/en /insights/focus/disruptive-strategy-patterns-case-studies/disruptive-strategy -unbundling-strategy-stand-alone-products.html, accessed December 2019.

25. Matthew Garrahan and Shannon Bond, "Disney Takes on Netflix with Streaming Services," *Financial Times*, August 9, 2017, https://www.ft.com /content/2a2eac78-7c95-11e7-ab01-a13271d1ee9c, accessed January 2020.

26. Kenneth Tsang, "To Cover China, There's No Substitute for WeChat," *New York Times*, January 9, 2019, https://www.nytimes.com/2019/01/09 /technology/personaltech/china-wechat.html, accessed January 2020.

27. Geeta Anand, "The Henry Ford of Heart Surgery," *Wall Street Journal*, November 25, 2009, https://www.wsj.com/articles/SB125875892887958111, accessed January 2020.

28. Karan Girotra, "The Henry Ford of Cardiac Surgery," *INSEAD* Blog, INSEAD Knowledge, February 15, 2012, https://knowledge.insead.edu/blog/insead -blog/the-henry-ford-of-cardiac-surgery-2806, accessed January 2020.

29. Marc Levinson, "How a Box Transformed the World," *Financial Times*, April 24, 2006, https://www.ft.com/content/4bdb14b2-d3b7-11da-b2f3 -0000779e2340, accessed January 2020.

   See Anthony J. Mayo and Nitin Nohria, "The Truck Driver Who Reinvented Shipping," *Harvard Business School, Working Knowledge,* October 3, 2005, https://hbswk.hbs.edu/archive/the-truck-driver-who-reinvented-shipping, accessed January 2020, for the hurdles place by the Interstate Commerce Commission against McLean.

   See Wikipedia, "Malcom McLean," https://en.wikipedia.org/wiki/Malcom _McLean, accessed January 2020, for the reaction of the top official of the International Longshormen's Association: "I would like to sink that son of a bitch."

30. Robin Harding, " 'Prince of Taxis' Plots Uber's Defeat in Japan," *Financial Times*, January 9, 2018, https://www.ft.com/content/882c88f8-f42d-11e7 -88f7-5465a6ce1a00, accessed January 2020.

   Kana Inagaki, "Japan Taxi Industry Seeks to Navigate New Roads," *Financial Times*, August 15, 2016, https://www.ft.com/content/402c455a-6038-11e6 -b38c-7b39cbb1138a, accessed January 2020.

31. Sarah O'Connor and Aliya Ram, "Uber Loses Appeal in UK Employment Case," *Financial Times*, November 10, 2017, https://www.ft.com/content /84de88bc-c5ee-11e7-a1d2-6786f39ef675, accessed January 2020.

CHAPTER 13

1. Six months before he was assassinated, Martin Luther King Jr. spoke to a group of students at Barratt Junior High School in Philadelphia on October 26, 1967. He opened his speech: "I want to ask you a question, and that is: What is your life's blueprint? Whenever a building is constructed, you usually have an architect who draws a blueprint, and that blueprint serves as the pattern, as the guide, and a building is not well erected without a good, solid blueprint. Now each of you is in the process of building the structure of your lives, and the question is whether you have a proper, a solid, and a sound blueprint."

2. W. Chan Kim and Renée Mauborgne, "Five Steps to Making a Blue Ocean Shift," Blue Ocean, https://www.blueoceanstrategy.com/blog/five-steps -making-blue-ocean-shift/, accessed December 2019.

   W. Chan Kim and Renée Mauborgne, *Blue Ocean Strategy: How to Create Uncontested Market Space and Make the Competition Irrelevant* (Boston, MA: Harvard Business School Publishing, 2005).

   "Bottom of the pyramid" is an idea popularized by C. K. Prahalad, *The Fortune at the Bottom of the Pyramid* (Upper Saddle River, NJ: Prentice Hall, 2005). It refers to the poorest socioeconomic group in a country.

3. Deloitte Development LLC, "Can CEOs Be Un-Disruptable?" *Deloitte Insights,* 2017, https://www2.deloitte.com/content/dam/insights/us/articles /3411_undisruptable-CEO/DeloitteInsights_Undisruptable-CEO.pdf, accessed January 2020.

4. Karan Girotra and Serguei Netessine, "How Xiaomi Beats Apple at Product Launches," *Harvard Business Review*, June 2, 2014, https://hbr.org/2014/06 /how-xiaomi-beats-apple-at-product-launches, accessed January 2020.

5. We use the term "disruptive innovation" in a slightly different way from Clayton M. Christensen in *The Innovator's Dilemma: When New Technologies Cause Great Firms to Fail* (Boston, MA: Harvard Business School Press, 1997). Please see Chapters 1 and 2.

6. W. Chan Kim and Renée Mauborgne, "Nondisruptive Creation: Rethinking Innovation and Growth," *MIT Sloan Management Review*, February 21, 2019, https://sloanreview.mit.edu/article/nondisruptive-creation-rethinking -innovation-and-growth/, accessed January 2020.

7. Gary Hamel, "The Why, What, and How of Management Innovation," *Harvard Business Review*, February 2006, https://hbr.org/2006/02/the-why-what -and-how-of-management-innovation, accessed January 2020.

8. "How GE Does Reverse Innovation," *Harvard Business Review*, October 2009, https://hbr.org/2009/10/how-ge-does-reverse-innovation, accessed January 2020.

   Chip Heath and Dan Heath, *Switch: How to Change Things When Change Is Hard* (New York: Broadway Books, 2010).

9. Scott D. Anthony, "Three Steps to Innovating in Struggling Industries," *Harvard Business Review*, September 10, 2008, https://hbr.org/2008/09/three -steps-to-innovating-in-s, accessed January 2020.

CHAPTER 14

1. See: "Disney Brainstorming Method: Dreamer, Realist, and Spoiler," Idea Sandbox Blog, https://idea-sandbox.com/blog/disney-brainstorming-method-dreamer-realist-and-spoiler/, accessed January 2020.

   Disney also used a team of people whose job it was to tear a movie idea to shreds, absolutely destroy it as spoilers, so they could then build a watertight plot structure—but only once the vision or dream was created.

2. John D. Stoll, "Every Company Wants to Become a Tech Company—Even If It Kills Them," *Wall Street Journal*, March 8, 2019, https://www.wsj.com/articles/how-to-nail-or-fail-the-pivot-to-tech-11552057210, accessed January 2020.

   David Epstein, *Range: Why Generalists Triumph in a Specialized World* (New York: Riverhead Books, 2019).

   Our Dreamer and Doer distinction is also very similar to Freeman Dyson's description of "Visionary Birds and Focused Frogs" ("Birds and Frogs," *Notices of the American Mathematical Society*, 56/2).

3. James G. March, "Exploration and Exploitation in Organizational Learning," *Organization Science* 2(1) (1991): 71–87.

4. Safi Bahcall, *Loonshots: How to Nurture the Crazy Ideas That Win Wars, Cure Diseases, and Transform Industries* (Nw York: St. Martin's Press, 2019).

5. Walter Isaacson, *Steve Jobs* (New York: Simon & Schuster, 2011).

6. "Could the Pandemic Give America's Labor Movement a Boost?" *Economist*, May 9, 2020 https://www.economist.com/finance-and-economics/2020/05/09/could-the-pandemic-give-americas-labour-movement-a-boost, accessed June 2020.

   Wenzhi Deng, Ross Levine, Chen Lin, and Wensi Xie, "Corporate Immunity to the COVID-19 Pandemic," NBER Working Paper Series, 27055, April 2020.

7. Based on a direct discussion with academics Julien Clement, Vibha Gaba, and Phanish Puranam in 2018 following a seminar on their ongoing research "When Change Agents Change Their Minds: Network Diffusion and the Failure of Organization Change Efforts."

8. Matt Murray, "Microsoft's Resurgence Under Satya Nadella," *Wall Street Journal*, February 1, 2019, https://www.wsj.com/articles/microsofts-resurgence-under-satya-nadella-11549022422, accessed January 2020.

   Michael Skapinker, "Unilever's Paul Polman Was a Standout CEO of the Past Decade," *Financial Times*, December 10, 2018, https://www.ft.com/content/e7040df4-fa19-11e8-8b7c-6fa24bd5409c, accessed December 2019.

   Jason Bloomberg, "How DBS Bank Became the Best Digital Bank in the World by Becoming Invisible," *Forbes*, December 23, 2016, https://www.forbes.com/sites/jasonbloomberg/2016/12/23/how-dbs-bank-became-the-best-digital-bank-in-the-world-by-becoming-invisible/#6a6114d23061, accessed January 2020.

9. Many scholars have worked in the field of organizational change research, for example:

   Kim S. Cameron and Robert E. Quinn, *Diagnosing and Changing Organizational Culture.* (Reading, PA: Addison-Wesley, 1999).

John P. Kotter, "Leading Change: Why Transformation Efforts Fail," *Harvard Business Review*, May–June 1995, https://hbr.org/1995/05/leading-change-why-transformation-efforts-fail-2, accessed January 2020.

John P. Kotter and Dan S. Cohen, *The Heart of Change: Real-Life Stories of How People Change Their Organizations* (Boston: Harvard Business School Publishing, 2002).

Kurt Lewin, *Field Theory in Social Science*, (New York: Harper & Row, 1947). Psychologist Lewin was an early pioneer in change research.

10. They also echo many of the important points made in David Kidder and Christina Wallace's book *New to Big: How Companies Can Create Like Entrepreneurs, Invest Like VCs, and Install a Permanent Operating System for Growth* (New York: Currency, 2019). We would also like to acknowledge valuable inputs from our colleagues Bala Vissa and Peter Goodson on these matters.

11. David Clarke, "A Manual for Self-Disruption," Strategy+Business, September 6, 2017, https://www.strategy-business.com/blog/A-Manual-for-Self-Disruption?gko=80308, accessed January 2020.

Tim Harford, "Why Big Companies Squander Good Ideas," *Financial Times*, September 6, 2018, https://www.ft.com/content/3c1ab748-b09b-11e8-8d14-6f049d06439c, accessed November 2019.

One very interesting enterprise working directly with legacy firms on corporate entrepreneurship and innovation is *Mach49*, whose CEO and founder is Linda A. Yates. *Mach49* has been working with more than a thousand global companies as they develop a pipeline or portfolio of new ventures. *Mach49* uses a number of methodologies for this, including "Disrupting InsideOut™" for creating, building and launching new ventures generated from within the organization and "Disrupting OutsideIn™" to help design and manage corporate venture groups. See: www.mach49.com.

12. Based on direct discussions by this book's authors with academic Professor Phanish Puranam regarding his ongoing research on celebrating and learning from failures.

Ram Charan and Julia Yang, *The Amazon Management System: The Ultimate Digital Business Engine That Creates Extraordinary Value for Both Customers and Shareholders* (United States: Ideapress Publishing, 2019).

13. These key questions on entrepreneurial and intrapreneurial activities arose during research discussions by the book's authors with entrepreneurship Professor Bala Vissa during 2019.

14. Rachel Sanderson, "Moncler's Remo Ruffini: Knowing When to Change Course," *Financial* Times, April 13, 2019, https://www.ft.com/content/c4ee350c-5b74-11e9-939a-341f5ada9d40, accessed January 2020.

15. DBS Bank Ltd, "DBS Named World's Best Digital Bank," July 11, 2016, https://www.dbs.com/newsroom/DBS_named_Worlds_Best_Digital_Bank_hk, accessed January 2020.

"Transforming a Bank by Becoming Digital to the Core," *McKinsey Insights*, April 2018, https://www.mckinsey.com/industries/financial-services/our-insights/transforming-a-bank-by-becoming-digital-to-the-core, accessed January 2020.

Jason Bloomberg, "How DBS Bank Became the Best Digital Bank in the World by Becoming Invisible," *Forbes*, December 23, 2016, https://www .forbes.com/sites/jasonbloomberg/2016/12/23/how-dbs-bank-became-the -best-digital-bank-in-the-world-by-becoming-invisible/#6a6114d23061, accessed January 2020.

"How Transformation Is Infinitely Ongoing at DBS Bank," HRM Asia, April 30, 2019, https://hrmasia.com/how-transformation-infinite-dbs-bank/, accessed January 2020.

In the words of Paul Cobban, COO at DBS, "I told our innovation team: don't innovate. Instead, teach the rest of the organization to innovate."

"How a New AI-Recruiter Is Impacting Business at DBS," People Matters, September 5, 2019, https://www.peoplemattersglobal.com/article /hr-technology/how-a-new-ai-recruiter-is-impacting-business-at-dbs-22984, accessed January 2020.

16. Robert Iger, *The Ride of a Lifetime: Lessons Learned from 15 Years as CEO of the Walt Disney Company* (New York: Random House, 2019).

17. " 'Rip. Mix. Burn." Apple iTunes Advertisement from 2001.

18. Robert Iger, *The Ride of a Lifetime: Lessons Learned from 15 Years as CEO of the Walt Disney Company* (New York: Random House, 2019).

19. Steve Jobs learned the ability to meld the Dreamers and Doers within an organization at Pixar first. He then replicated this with Jony Ive and Tim Cook at Apple.

20. Maria Vultaggio, "Disney+ Hits 10 Million Subscribers within 24 Hours," Statista, November 15, 2019, https://www.statista.com/chart/19970/disney -10-million-subscribers-24-hours/, accessed January 2020.

Index

ABB, 186
Above-the-line (ATL), 131, 301n15
Access, ownership vs., 222–223
Acquisitions, 116, 144–145, 225–226
Activism, 214
Acton, Brian, 126
Adele, 228
Aeropostale, 219
Air Asia, 231
Airbnb, 118, 139, 144, 149, 164, 191
Airbus, 183, 227
'Alalā crows, 5
Alibaba:
  boundary-busting by, 32
  cloud business of, 307n10
  data assets of, 167
  drone shipping by, 182
  in mobile banking, 146
  monetization of big data by, 151–152
  nonperforming loan ratio of, 305n18
  platform business model of, 145
  retail technology stack of, 116
AliExpress, 105
Alpha individuals, 4, 285n1
Altitude Sickness, 82–84, 250, 257, 262, 268, 272, 293n3
Altitudes (*see* Leadership altitudes)
Amazon:
  adoption of, 144
  AI used by, 171
  automation of warehouses by, 115–116
  and cloud computing, 164–165
  competitive edge for, 106
  Dash Replenishment Service of, 179
  data assets of, 167
  disruption by, 38
  failures of, 263
  fulfillment centers of, 182–183
  growth of, 149
  Instant Pot page on, 132–133
  mirroring growth of, 117–118
  platform business model of, 144–145, 154
Amazon Kindle, 19
Amazon Web Services (AWS), 106, 164–165, 308n15
Ambani, Mukesh, 73
Angelou, Maya, 47, 291n1
Ant Financial, 32
Apple:
  AI used by, 171

as competitor of tomorrow, 19
and COVID-19 pandemic, 162
disruption by, 39
ecosystem of, 232–233
Jobs' mindset at, 260
music business threat from, 266
personal thermometer from, 159–160
platformization at, 304n6
success of, 261
Apple Music, 228
"Are Robots Overrated?" (Hasija), 193
Arrogant leaders, 34, 38
Artificial intelligence (AI), 170–173
  applications of, 115
  as central for future survival, 177
  defined, 170
  Hawking on, 173–174
  infrastructure for, 166
  investments in, 167
ASEAN, 199
Asset optimization, 233–234
Atari, 19
Atlassian, 135–136
The Attacker's Advantage (Charan), 96
Attitudes, 292–293n1
  flawed, 72
  in Phase One (Phoenix Groundwork), 50
  switching, 91
Audible, 144
Automation, 207–208
Autonomous vehicles and mobility, 181–184, 314n23
AXA, 18–19
Ayot, William, 279–281

Bahcall, Safi, 258–259
BAMTech, 232, 266
Bank for International Settlements, 202
Barclays, 213
Battlefield exercise, 21, 48, 54–55
  embedding of, 63
  example in DFC leaders, 241–245
  Extreme Attack stage in (*see* Extreme Attack stage)
  firepower examples for, 119–121
  future vision emerging from, 65
  Horizon Defense stage in (*see* Horizon Defense stage)
  involving Dreamers and Doers in, 257
  need for, 48

About The Authors

The Phoenix Encounter Method captures the knowledge of four globally recognized experts, each of whom brings expertise from a different area of business research and practice. Together they see thousands of senior business executives from around the globe in their classrooms and consulting work each year.

Ian C. Woodward (www.iancwoodward.com) is a Professor of Management Practice at INSEAD, where he specializes in strategic thinking, leadership, and communication, as well as personal leadership transformation. He is the Director of both its flagship Advanced Management Program and its online Leadership Communication with Impact course. Dr. Woodward has extensive experience in financial services, energy utilities, and the government sector, including working for the US government. He is the lead author of the academic monograph *Exploring Leadership Drivers and Blockers* (Palgrave Macmillan, May 2019).

V. Paddy Padmanabhan (www.professorpaddy.com) is the Unilever Chaired Professor of Marketing at INSEAD, where he is also the Academic Director of the Emerging Markets Institute. Dr. Padmanabhan has been recognized for writing some of the most influential academic research papers in management, and he frequently consults for multinationals, leading regional businesses and startups across the world.

Sameer Hasija (www.sameerhasija.com) is a Professor of Technology and Operations Management at INSEAD. He is the Shell Fellow in Business and the Environment and Chair of INSEAD's Technology and Operations Management area. Dr. Hasija's latest research studies the economics of business models in the wake of new technologies such as blockchain, artificial intelligence, and the Internet of Things.

Ram Charan (www.ram-charan.com) is a world-renowned business advisor and the author of more than 25 major business books, including bestsellers such as *Execution: The Discipline of Getting Things Done* and *Confronting Reality: Doing What Matters to Get Things Right*. He has spent the past 35 years working with world-leading companies such as GE, MeadWestvaco, Bank of America, DuPont, Novartis, EMC, 3M, Verizon, Aditya Birla Group, Tata Group, GMR, Max Group, Yildiz Holdings, and Grupo RBS.